EXPERIMENTS IN BUDDHIST-CHRISTIAN ENCOUNTER

EXPERIMENTS IN BUDDHIST-CHRISTIAN ENCOUNTER

From Buddha-Nature to the Divine Nature

By

Peter Feldmeier

ORBIS BOOKS
Maryknoll, New York 10545

ORBIS BOOKS
Maryknoll, New York 10545

Fathers and Brothers MARYKNOLL

Founded in 1970, Orbis Books endeavors to publish works that enlighten the mind, nourish the spirit, and challenge the conscience. The publishing arm of the Maryknoll Fathers and Brothers, Orbis seeks to explore the global dimensions of the Christian faith and mission, to invite dialogue with diverse cultures and religious traditions, and to serve the cause of reconciliation and peace. The books published reflect the views of their authors and do not represent the official position of the Maryknoll Society. To learn more about Maryknoll and Orbis Books, please visit our website at www.maryknollsociety.org.

Published by Orbis Books, Maryknoll, New York 10545-0302.

Manufactured in the United States of America

Library of Congress Cataloging-in-Publication Data

Names: Feldmeier, Peter, author.
Title: Experiments in Buddhist-Christian encounter : from Buddha-nature to the divine nature / by Peter Feldmeier.
Description: Maryknoll, NY : Orbis Books, [2018] | Includes bibliographical references and index.
Identifiers: LCCN 2018034642 (print) | LCCN 2018041085 (ebook) | ISBN 9781608337613 (e-book) | ISBN 9781626983069 | ISBN 9781626983069 (paperback)
Subjects: LCSH: Christianity and other religions—Buddhism. | Buddhism—Relations—Christianity. | Spirituality—Comparative studies.
Classification: LCC BR128.B8 (ebook) | LCC BR128.B8 F45 2018 (print) | DDC 261.2/43—dc23
LC record available at https://lccn.loc.gov/2018034642

Contents

Acknowledgments

I want to acknowledge with gratitude those responsible for this book. First and foremost, I am grateful for the support of the University of Toledo, which granted me a sabbatical to see this project through. I'd particularly like to thank Dr. John Sarnecki, my friend and department chair, for his complete support and encouragement. I am also grateful to Orbis Books for taking on its publication—particularly Jill Brennan O'Brien, whose attention and care throughout the publication process were nothing short of excellent. I'd also like to recognize and thank Francis X. Clooney, who has inspired and mentored a whole generation of scholars doing comparative theology. The whole field owes massive gratitude to Frank. Finally, I'd like to thank my partner and spouse Angie Gerdeman, who inspires everything that I do and am. I dedicate this book to her.

Chapter 1

The Importance of the Religious Other

From Modernity to Postmodernity

Modernity can mean a number of things. To be "modern" is to be up to date or even fashionable. In philosophical discourse, however, it is hardly de rigueur. Here modernity refers to the cultural shift after the beginning of the Enlightenment that sought, among other things, a kind of comprehensive perspective. While humans always continue to learn, this progressive knowledge operates to create a better, more inclusive, fuller framework so as to make universal claims. Modernity reflects a kind of *epistemic confidence*. In religion, such confidence could be considered variously. Even in the context of recognizing the religious plurality in the world, one could stand by the exclusive claims of one's own religious tradition. In doing so, one would have to account for other religious claims that either had to be dismissed a priori or had to be reframed so as to look like the same kind of claims one's home religion makes. The latter move makes other religions at best unwitting and partial versions of one's own religion, although smacking of inaccuracies and superstitions that one's own avoids.

Another possibility is to let go of one's absolute, provincial claims and recognize that all (or most) religions are doing the same thing in different ways. Narratives that understand a given religion to speak for the entire universe here are eschewed as arrogant and imperialistic. On this view, exclusively framed religions seem to forget that God necessarily transcends concepts and language. Doctrine cannot speak for God *as* God, but can offer a valuable path to God.

In theologies of religion, the first way of considering the religious other is either fundamental dismissal, known as *exclusivism*, or a kind of respect that the religious other has something of value, known as *inclusivism*. In both cases the universal claims in one's religion ought to be taken as literal and factual. Certainly, in inclusivism other religions have philosophical, theological, and spiritual depth. Their deep insights are understood, however, as fragmentary, and they are imagined as ultimately able to be assumed under one's own religious rubrics. Take, for example, Roman Catholicism's Second Vatican Council. After assuring the possibility for salvation of non-Christians, the Council fathers pronounced, "Whatever good or truth is found amongst them is considered by the Church to be a preparation for the Gospel and given by him who enlightens all men that they may at length have life."[1] Further, "The Catholic Church rejects nothing of what is true and holy in these religions. . . . Yet she proclaims and is in duty bound to proclaim without fail, Christ who is the way, the truth and the life. In him, in whom God reconciled all things to himself, men find the fullness of their religious life."[2] And finally, "Missionary activity is nothing else, and nothing less, than the manifestation of God's plan, its epiphany and realization in the world and in history. . . . So, whatever goodness is found in the minds and hearts of men, or in the particular customs and cultures of peoples, far from being lost is purified, is raised to a higher level and reaches its perfection, for the glory of God."[3]

That final possibility in the modernist perspective, letting go of one's universal claims, takes on the agenda of *pluralism*. Here all or most religions are imagined to be about the same project. Typically, religions simply represent different expressions of the same Divine Ultimate. Philosopher of religion John Hick has argued that the ineffable God spoken of by Christian theologians is the same as the *Ein Sof* of Jewish Kabbalah, the *al Haq* of Islamic Sufism, the *Dharmakaya* of Mahayana Buddhism, and *Brahman* of Hinduism, and that their various descriptions and appropriations of their mystery are limited by human subjectivity.[4] Hick writes, "The great post-axial faiths constitute different ways of experiencing, conceiving and living in relation to an ultimate divine Reality which transcends all our varied visions of it."[5] Other pluralistic projects see various religions *doing* the same thing. The renowned scholar of religion Wilfred Cantwell Smith declares, "Faith differs in form, but not in kind. This applies both within communi-

---

[1] *Lumen Gentium*, no. 16. All citations of Vatican II documents are from Austin Flannery, ed., *Vatican Council II*, vol. 1 (rev.) (Northport: NY: Costelo, 1975).

[2] *Nostra Aetate*, no. 2.

[3] *Ad Gentes*, no. 9.

[4] John Hick, "The Next Step beyond Dialogue," in *The Myth of Religious Superiority*, ed. Paul Knitter (Maryknoll: NY: Orbis Books, 2005), 9.

[5] John Hick, *An Interpretation of Religion: Human Responses to the Transcendent*, 2nd ed. (New Haven, CT: Yale University Press, 2004), 235–36.

ties and from one community to another."[6] For Smith, all true religions save. In them we are "saved from nihilism, from alienation, anomie, despair; from the bleak despondency of meaninglessness. Saved from unfreedom; from being the victim of one's own whims within, or of pressures without; saved from being merely an organism reacting to its environment."[7] Religions differ, of course, and their adherents participate in their specific "patterns" of faith.[8] Still, when skillfully embraced, they all achieve the same fundamental outcomes.

Modernity, as I have just framed it, is slowly but surely becoming a museum piece. It is being replaced by *postmodernity*, a recognition that the epistemic confidence the Enlightenment assured is misplaced.[9] More and more, we are living in an age of heightened historical consciousness. We are now particularly sensitive to the fact that all conceptualizations and expressions are rooted in unique places and times. No articulation of truth, therefore, is exempt from historical or philosophical critique. The postmodern perspective is particularly suspicious of a *classicist* notion of knowing or of having privileged access to truth. Particularly challenged is the Enlightenment assumption that truth can be extricated from cultural assumptions, especially when the Enlightenment itself is a dominating Western European interpretation of culture. What were previously understood as objective expressions of truth in the West are now widely suspected as being assumptions of Western culture. Postmodernity argues that we must take the religious other as potentially expressing a very different version of reality. In essence, we have come to a greater appreciation of the relativity of our own perspectives.[10] Roger Haight says it well: "The sheer age and size of reality compounds our sense of relativity."[11] While both Hick and Smith might agree with the claim that every religious framing is relative, their critics have pointed out that they have only rejected a given religion's metanarrative in order to provide their own: all religions are fundamentally the same. Mark Heim declares, "These hypotheses themselves seem to run afoul of the same problem [as the inclusivists they criticize], however, since they

[6] Wilfred Cantwell Smith, *Towards a World Theology: Faith and the Comparative History of Religion* (Philadelphia: Westminster Press, 1981), 168.

[7] Ibid.

[8] Ibid.

[9] Much of the following description I also provided in Feldmeier, "Is the Theology of Religions and Exhausted Project?" *Horizons* 25, no. 2 (2008): 253–70, see 263.

[10] See, for example, Paul Lakeland's *Postmodernity* (Minneapolis: Augsburg Fortress, 1997).

[11] Roger Haight, *Jesus, Symbol of God* (Maryknoll, NY: Orbis Books, 1999), 396.

must involve a claim to understand the character of this religious referent more adequately than any religious tradition does."[12]

Could different religions have different ends and different modes of transformation unique unto them? Heim argues for the possibility of different religious ends as a more fruitful endeavor, as it "directs us unavoidably toward the religious traditions themselves and their accounts of their own religious aims . . . not a generic construct imposed on them . . . Such perspectives indicate the intrinsic value of study and dialogue that deals with the 'thick' descriptive natures of religions."[13]

Roman Catholic understanding of the religious other has grown since the Second Vatican Council (1962–1965). In 1984, the Vatican's Pontifical Council for Interreligious Dialogue published a document titled *The Attitude of the Church toward Followers of Other Religions*.[14] This document describes several kinds of dialogue: (1) dialogue of life, focusing on common humanity; (2) dialogue of collaboration, focusing on humanitarian issues; (3) theological dialogue, seeking greater mutual understanding; and (4) dialogue of religious experience, including sharing one's spiritual life and even sharing religious practices. Dialogue is here described as "not only discussion, but also includes all positive and constructive relations with individuals and communities of other faiths which are directed at mutual understanding and enrichment" (no. 3). Here *mutual understanding and enrichment* represents the key. It presumes that the religious other has spiritual truths or insights that the Church can learn from.

> The Church opens itself to dialogue toward fidelity to man. . . . This is the case whether one regards the need to receive or, even more, when one is conscious of possessing something which is to be communicated. As the human sciences have emphasized, in interpersonal dialogue one experiences one's own limitations as well as the possibility of overcoming them. A person discovers that he does not possess the truth in a perfect and total way but can walk together with others toward that goal. Mutual affirmation, reciprocal correction, and fraternal exchange lead the partners

---

[12] S. Mark Heim, *Salvations: Truth and Difference in Religion* (Maryknoll, NY: Orbis Books, 1995), 118.

[13] S. Mark Heim, *The Depth of Riches: A Trinitarian Theology of Religious Ends* (Grand Rapids: Eerdmans, 2001), 30.

[14] Vatican Pontifical Council for Interreligious Dialogue, *The Attitude of the Church toward Followers of Other Religions: Reflections and Orientations on Dialogue and Mission*, May 10, 1984.

> in dialogue to a greater maturity which in turn generates interpersonal communion. Religious experiences and outlooks can themselves be purified and enriched in this process of encounter. The dynamic of human encounter should lead us Christians to listen to and strive to understand that which other believers communicate to us in order to profit from the gifts which God bestows so generously. (no. 21)

Note that the document allows for "mutual affirmation" and "reciprocal correction"; such radical concepts in interfaith dialogue were perhaps foreshadowed in the documents of Vatican II but not explicitly contained in them.

In the past thirty years, some Roman Catholic scholars have engaged other religions along the lines of the Vatican's document on interreligious dialogue. This document argues that both non-Christian traditions *and* the Christian tradition can be reciprocally corrected, that non-Christian insights can lead the Christian toward a greater maturity, and that both can be mutually enriched by the encounter. Thus, non-Christian traditions presumably have religious goods the church does not have and could use.

These scholars have also appealed to postmodern insights eschewing metanarratives and opened themselves up to whole other expressions of truth different from the Christian paradigm.[15] Postmodern theologian Steven Kaplan writes, "It is philosophically and religiously plausible to assert that there can be multiple, different, and even contradictory models of ultimate reality. Reality is multidimensional and so there is neither need nor possibility to correct all models of reality and reduce them to a single, dominant one."[16] Others have appealed to theological principles that expand beyond the bounds of Christianity. Jacques Dupuis, for example, has tried to bridge inclusivism and pluralism for a kind of *regno-centric* theology. Here the "kingdom of God" is taken as the absolute framing and one that extends beyond the borders of Christian doctrine. Dupuis, who strives to highlight the universality of the Christian faith, also describes the necessary "asymmetrical complementarity" of other religions that demands a Christian priority, but also allows for mutual learning and possibly mutual belonging.[17] Others have attempted a *pneuma-centric* theology that extends

---

[15] See, for example, Haight's *Jesus, Symbol of God* and "Pluralist Christology as Orthodox," in *The Myth of Religious Superiority*; and Lakeland, *Postmodernity*.

[16] Steven Kaplan, *Different Paths, Different Summits: A Model for Religious Pluralism* (Lanham, MD: Rowman and Littlefield, 2002), 321. Kaplan, while not a Christian, articulates what pluralist and mutualist Christian scholars believe to be true.

[17] See Jacques Dupuis, *Toward a Theology of Religious Pluralism* (Maryknoll, NY:

the presence and revelatory expression of the Holy Spirit beyond the boundaries of Christianity. Peter Phan writes, "What the Holy Spirit says and does may be truly different from, though not contradictory to, what the Logos says and does, and what the Logos and the Spirit do and say in non-Christian religions may be truly different from, though not contradictory to, what Jesus said and did."[18]

This book is not about a theology of religions, nor does it take a stand on the values and problems found in inclusivism and pluralism. It is not looking for the hidden Christian message in Buddhism, and it is not looking for some kind of larger vision of the spiritual world that both Christianity and Buddhism might witness to. On the one hand, it recognizes that religions can be different, really different. And it does not serve any religion to flatten those differences. Postmodern scholar George Lindbeck rightly argues, "Adherents of different religions do not diversely thematize the same experience, rather they have different experiences. Buddhist compassion, Christian love and . . . French revolutionary *fraternité* are not diverse modifications of a single human awareness, emotion, attitude, or sentiment, but are radically (i.e., from the root) distinct ways of experiencing and being oriented toward self, neighbor, and cosmos."[19]

On the other hand, I presume that different religions, and in this case Buddhism and Christianity, are not so different, so incommensurable, that they cannot understand each other or learn from each other. In fact, sometimes the very fact that they are diverse brings new insights to the fore that otherwise would remain unknown. Nirvana is not simply another version of the kingdom of God. Still, Nirvana, if taken as a serious religious goal, says something about reality that is either unknown in Christianity or known only partially. Francis Clooney observes,

> Our time and place therefore urge upon us a necessary interreligious learning. Diversity becomes a primary context for a tradition's inquiry and self-understanding; particular traditions in

---

Orbis Books, 2001), and *Christianity and the Religions: From Confrontation to Dialogue*, trans. Philip Berryman (Maryknoll, NY: Orbis Books, 2003).

[18] Peter Phan, *Being Religious Interreligiously: Asian Perspectives on Interfaith Dialogue* (Maryknoll, NY: Orbis Books, 2004), 65.

[19] George Lindbeck, *The Nature of Doctrine: Religion and Theology in a Postliberal Age* (Philadelphia: Westminster, 1984), 77, as cited in Marianne Moyaert, "Absorption or Hospitality: Two Approaches to the Tension between Identity and Alterity," in *Interreligious Hermeneutics*, eds. Catherine Cornille and Christopher Conway (Eugene, OR: Cascade Books, 2010), 66.

their concreteness become the place where the religious meaning of diversity is disclosed. By such learning, intelligently evaluated and extended, we make deeper sense of ourselves intellectually and spiritually, in light of what we find in the world around us. We can respond to diversity with a distinctive set of sensitivities and insights that balances respect for tradition and community with the wider play of what is possible in our era, such as none of our traditions has been able to anticipate.[20]

Interpretation Theory and Comparative Theology

In *Truth and Method* Hans-Georg Gadamer argued that theological hermeneutics carried an essential tension between text and the sense arrived at by its application in the particular moment of interpretation.[21] Religious proclamation is not simply there to be understood as some dataset, but exists for us at every moment in a new and different way. While not recommending a slavish solicitude to the text, and recognizing the historical biases of any texts, Gadamer still insisted on a kind of subordination to a classical text's claim on our consciousness.[22]

Aristotle's influence on Gadamer's argument is of notable importance. Aristotle accepted the idea of an absolutely unchangeable law, but he limited this to the realm of the gods and did not think it applicable in the phenomenal world. Thus, absolute truth and absolute morality have a critical function, for they condition the possibility for the existence of truth and morality. Even so, these cannot be instantiated by inviolable principles or laws on earth. Every situation calls for a new application to truth and morality. For Gadamer, Aristotle's analysis provides an insight to the issue of hermeneutics. Here, too, application is not that of conforming to some pregiven universal to the particular situation, but it requires ongoing, fresh engagement. A classic text, for example, does not represent absolute, dogmatic, propositional claims that simply now need to be applied. Rather, understanding is determined by every new interpretive situation.[23]

---

[20] Francis X. Clooney, *Comparative Theology: Deep Learning across Religious Borders* (Malden, MA: Wiley-Blackwell, 2010), 5.

[21] The following description is taken from my "Christian Transformation and the Encounter with the World's Holy Canons," *Horizons* 40, no. 2 (2013): 178–98.

[22] Hans-Georg Gadamer, *Truth and Method*, trans. Garrett Barden and John Cummings (New York: Seabury Press, 1975), 274–75.

[23] Ibid., 278–89.

Allow me to provide a shorthand sketch of Gadamer's hermeneutical framework. First, you attend to your own preunderstanding. We come to the text with ideas, values, and judgments about meaning. Indeed, if the text is a classic, it has probably already affected one's preunderstanding, since it has affected one's culture. Every interpreter enters into the act of interpretation bearing the history of the effects, conscious and unconscious, of the classics that participated in forming one's preunderstanding. Second, you engage the text itself. The actual experience of any classic text provokes and elicits a claim to serious attention. Here you have to recognize the level of authority your preunderstanding gives to the text. Third, you engage what Gadamer calls "the game of conversation." Interpreters allow the text to provoke their questioning. Then you enter into the logic of question and response, that is, the text provokes a new way of considering things. This creates the condition not only to rethink your prior understanding, but also to come back to the text seeing differently, and thus posing new questions. Hermeneutically, therefore, the primary meaning of the text does not lie behind it in the mind of the author or even in the text itself. Rather, meaning lies in front of the text, in the dynamic of conversation.

Let me provide an additional gloss of the contributions by Paul Ricoeur insofar as it applies to my approach to engaging world religions.[24] Ricoeur considered what happens when a text goes beyond its original audience. He argued that the shift to a new audience renders the text somewhat autonomous from the author. Of course, the text is not an authorless entity, and authorial intention remains an important dimension of the text. Still, that is just one dimension. Once the text passes from the intended audience with its own religious and cultural horizons and to a new audience and situation, the text's meaning can no longer coincide with what the author originally intended.

Ricoeur calls this dynamic *distanciation*, and distanciation frees the reader from the misguided and impossible task of getting inside the mind of the author. Like Gadamer, Ricoeur believed that interpretation is not a search for the psychological intentions of the author concealed behind the text. Rather, interpretation involves entering into a proposed world unfolded by the text. To interpret is to explicate the type of being-in-the-world provided by the text. What must be interpreted then is a proposed world, which one could inhabit and wherein one could project one's own possibilities. The text is a medium through which we understand ourselves

[24] Here I am broadly relying on Paul Ricoeur, *Interpretation Theory: Discourse and Surplus of Meaning* (Fort Worth: Texas Christian University Press, 1976), and *Hermeneutics and the Human Sciences: Essays on Language, Action, and Interpretation*, trans. and ed. John B. Thompson (Cambridge: Cambridge University Press, 1981).

anew. Interpreting a text and appropriating insights from it is not a response to the author; it is a response to the proposed world provided therein. For Ricoeur, to understand is not to project oneself into the text; it is to receive an enlarged self from the appropriation of the text's proposed world. This is how religious texts become revelatory: they occasion an event of encounter with things transcendental, both outside of us in its proposed world and within us by our experience of that world.

More recently, there has been a great advance in taking these hermeneutical insights and applying them to encounters with other religious traditions. Some, such as David Tracy in his *Plurality and Ambiguity*, argue that any good theological thinking ought to be done in light of religious plurality, taking in larger frameworks than the assumptions of one's own tradition.[25] James Fredericks points out, "Christians now live in a time when looking on the plurality of faiths as a subsidiary problem for their theology and practice is no longer possible."[26] This is the work of comparative theology, which is an approach to doctrine and spirituality that takes seriously the religious plurality in which we live. Here one passes over into the texts and religious imagination of other faiths and returns to one's own, asking new questions or bringing new insights into one's theological horizon. This is not merely a comparison of religions but rather taking the message of Gadamer, Ricoeur, and others seriously and now globally.[27] One ought not to think that comparative theology is merely a Christian begrudging adjustment to the fact of the religious others' proximity due to the fact of our ongoing globalization. As Fredericks wisely remarks, "Christians need to open themselves to other religious believers in such a way that the other religion comes to be seen as a genuine spiritual resource for living more faithfully the path of Christ."[28] The point of comparative theology is not to create new theological truths, and certainly not to suggest a new religious metanarrative by merging insights from other religious traditions. Rather, this procedure "can make possible fresh insights into familiar and revered truths, and new ways of receiving these truths."[29]

---

[25] David Tracy, *Plurality and Ambiguity: Hermeneutics, Religion, Hope* (Chicago: University of Chicago Press, 1987).

[26] James Fredericks, "Introduction," in *The New Comparative Theology: Interreligious Insights from the Next Generation*, ed. Francis X. Clooney (New York: T & T Clark, 2010), xix.

[27] See also David Tracy's essay "Comparative Theology," in the *Encyclopedia of Religion*, vol. 13, 2nd ed., ed. Lindsay Jones (Detroit: Macmillan Reference USA, 2005), 9125–34.

[28] James Fredericks, *Buddhists and Christians: Through Comparative Theology to Solidarity* (Maryknoll: NY: Orbis Books, 2004), 112.

[29] Clooney, *Comparative Theology*, 112.

Method in comparative theology is hardly exact. Francis Clooney, one of the foremost leaders in the field, describes the practice as somewhat "arbitrary and intuitive . . . It is a back-and-forth learning, confident about the possibility of being intelligently faithful to tradition even while seeking fresh understanding outside that tradition."[30] Even the choice of which texts to draw upon requires something more of a cultivated instinct that a given comparison will be fruitful than an already-decided-upon agenda. Clooney writes, "There is no overarching narrative that explains, already in advance, how we are to make our own multiple religious insights and experiences of the human race."[31] Typically, one would compare small, discrete texts. Such a comparison facilitates a deep understanding of the religious other. Depth lends itself to breadth here. But this approach is not entirely necessary. It wouldn't be unusual to address larger themes or insights by means of comparing greater swaths of religious material.[32] In this book I follow this latter approach.

The Aim of This Book

This book offers a dialogue between various forms and specific expressions of Buddhism and Christianity. In doing so, it also offers possibilities of rethinking Christian faith in light of this dialogue. This book also makes demands on the reader. It challenges the reader to consider the religious other, particularly Buddhism, as an expression of truths either framed differently or not actually found in Christianity. Where framed differently, we have the opportunity to rethink and so enrich our Christian tradition, even along its own lines. Where not actually found in Christianity, we have the opportunity to consider whether Buddhism enlarges our very sense of the sacred, of the cosmos, of ultimate things.

This book is not merely a comparison of doctrines or metaphysics, though we will certainly be doing that. It is also not merely an invitation to learn about various different religious paths, though again this will be provided. More than just these ends, this book seeks to help the reader

---

[30] Ibid., 11.

[31] Ibid., 105.

[32] Clooney is again a good example. Of the former approach, see Francis X. Clooney, *The Truth, The Way, The Life: Christian Commentary on the Three Holy Mantras of the Srivaisnavas* (Leuven: Peeters, 2008). Here this Hindu text involves just three mantras, collectively just twenty words. Of the latter approach, see Francis X. Clooney, *Hindu Wisdom for All God's Children* (Maryknoll: NY: Orbis Books, 1998).

enlarge her own soul. Clooney again: "A comparative theologian must do more than listen to others explain their faith; she must be willing to study their traditions deeply alongside her own, taking both to heart. In the process, she will begin to theologize as it were from both sides of the table, reflecting personally on old and new truths in an interior dialogue."[33]

I have been studying other religions since my college religious studies program at Purdue University. In the early 1980s I was intrigued by one of my professors, Donald Mitchell. He had been deeply involved in Zen Buddhism but later converted to Christianity. Mitchell witnessed a profound respect for other religious traditions, and a particular one for Zen. There in the classroom, he commended the value of appropriating a Mahayana Buddhist understanding of *shunyata* (emptiness). Why, I wondered, would a Christian think this religiously foreign concept true or even valuable? How could it be true and even potentially essential if it had little to do with our own shared religion where Christ is "the way, the truth, and the life" (Jn 14:6)?

Somewhere midway through my college studies I began to see that wider religious horizons enhanced my soul, rather than undermining my Christian faith. After college I continued to read deeply in Jewish theology, Daoist sources, and Zen. Finally in graduate school I robustly engaged Theravada Buddhism. There I saw an extraordinarily different religious framework that, when practiced, seemed to assist my own Christian faith. And practice I did! I did *vipassana* (insight) meditation two hours a day. I went on deeply meditative silent retreats that ranged from one to three weeks and even one that went three months. What I discovered was that Buddhist meditation was certainly not like Christian contemplation and yet it was extraordinarily powerful. This discovery did not undermine my Christian life, and I continued to go to daily Mass and meditate daily on the Scriptures. In Christian prayer, I experienced the personal love of a personal God. In Buddhist meditation, I experienced a kind of inner deconstruction where it was quite impossible to locate any self. Over the years, I have plunged deeper into other religious traditions and various other forms of Buddhism. I am certainly not a Buddhist-Christian; I am a Christian. But I am now a Christian whose inner life is enriched by Buddhist insights, Hindu insights, Daoist insights, and Jewish and Muslim insights. I draw on their wisdom to see things differently, to form various interpretations of a given situation before me. I am not alone. My friend and colleague Paul Knitter notes,

---

[33] Clooney, *Comparative Theology*, 13.

> Like many of my theological colleagues, I have come to realize that I have to look *beyond* the traditional borderlines of Christianity to find something that is vitally, maybe even essentially, important for the job of understanding and living the Christian Faith: *other religions*. . . . It was only after I began to take seriously and to explore other religious Scriptures and traditions that I was able to more adequately understand my own. Stated more personally: my engagement with other ways of being religious—that is, with what I have studied, discovered, been excited about, or perplexed by in other religious—has turned out to be an unexpected but immense help in my job of trying to figure out what the message of Jesus means to our contemporary world.[34]

The following chapters are experiments in Buddhist-Christian encounter. Each chapter looks to a seminal expression of Buddhism and creates a kind of Christian dialogue with it. What does the text or path mean in itself and how might it fruitfully be engaged with a Christian correlate? We consider Buddhist and Christian teachings, ultimate paths to liberation, spiritual experiences, and modes of transformation. Ultimately, each comparison operates as a way to expand both Christian and Buddhist sensibilities. I am not seeking a unity of perspectives between the two, but rather an expanded and more creative appropriation of them by their being in dialogue with each other.

Brief note on transliterations: We have decided to withhold diacritical marks for Sanskrit and Pali words, as they would be distracting to virtually all readers not familiar with these original languages. Further, unless a technical term is reserved only to the Theravada tradition, which uses Pali, we have decided to only provide the Sanskrit term. This slightly affects quotes from the Theravada canon where we substitute the Pali rendering with the Sanskrit term with which more readers are acquainted.

---

[34] Paul Knitter, *Without the Buddha, I Could Not Be a Christian* (Oxford: Oneworld, 2009), xi–xii.

Chapter 2

The Buddha and His Teaching

The Buddha (c. 563–483 BCE) and His Biographies

Like all religions, Buddhism is a polymorphous set of traditions. There are, and historically always have been, various conceptualizations about what the Buddha taught. And living the Buddha Dharma has taken significantly different shapes in the cultures in which it has planted itself over the past twenty-five hundred years. Even beliefs of who the Buddha was historically and how he was enlightened dramatically differ among Buddhist schools. In the Theravada tradition, for example, we find the ascetic Siddhartha Gautama earnestly struggling for enlightenment for six years until he finally attained Nirvana while meditating under the Bodhi tree. According to the famous Mahayana text, the Lotus Sutra, all this was show, since he had actually attained it incalculable lifetimes ago. Here the Buddha is supreme and essentially always has been. He represents a cosmic figure, now only experienced on the human plain of existence.

> In all the worlds the heavenly and human beings and asuras [titans] all believe that the present Shakyamuni Buddha, after leaving the palace of the Shakyas, seated himself in the place of practice not far from the city of Gaya and there attained *anuttara-samyak-sambodhi* [perfect-supreme-enlightenment]. But good men, it has been immeasurable, boundless hundreds, thousands, ten thousands, millions of nayutas of kalpas [world cycles] since I in fact attained Buddhahood. . . . Suppose all these worlds, whether they received a particle of dust or not, are once more reduced to dust. Let one particle represent one kalpa. The time that has passed since I attained Buddhahood surpasses this by a hundred, a thousand, ten thousand, a million nayuta asambkhya kalpas. . . . Constantly I have

> preached the law, teaching, converting countless millions of living beings, causing them to enter the Buddha way, all this for immeasurable kalpas.[1]

For the Theravadin, the Buddha, having taught for forty-five years after his enlightenment, died at eighty years old, having eaten spoiled meat, and thereupon entered Final-Nirvana. There would be no more access to him historically. But again, the Lotus Sutra would have none of this: "In order to save living beings, as an expedient means I appear to enter nirvana but in truth I do not pass into extinction. I am always here, preaching the Law. I am always here, but through my transcendental powers I make it so that living beings in their befuddlement do not see me when close by. . . . I tell all living beings that I am always here."[2]

Which, if either, of these stories tells the truth about the Buddha? And what do we even mean by truth in this case? How ought the universe be conceived in Buddhism? Could it be that both renderings point to something potentially quite true? Could Siddhartha Gautama have really been a man who lived and died around the fifth century BCE, and could he also legitimately represent an instantiation of something more universal or absolute? For Mahayana traditions, *Buddha* is a transcendental term depicting various *bodies* of Buddha-reality. These traditions envision an earthly body that represents a physical instantiation of universal Buddha-reality. Consider the historical Buddha as a personification of Buddha-reality as this earthly body. In addition, there is a bliss-body or heavenly realm of celestial Buddhas interacting through the various universes of time and space. And, finally, there is the truth-body of absolute Buddha-reality that transcends all forms.

Even the more modest interpretation of the historical Buddha's life in the Theravada tradition is difficult to pin down. The massive Pali canon contributes a good deal of information about the Buddha's life, but the material is not arranged with any real historical interest, and one essentially stumbles across a teaching where the Buddha references a period of his life mostly as an aside. Piecing together his life from this source is also fraught in that the material itself does not always appear consistent. Consider it something like comparing the birth narratives of Matthew and Luke; specifics do not always align. Further, the canon itself was not preserved in writing until around the first century BCE, some three hundred to four hundred years after the Buddha's death. In the first century of the common era, the monk

---

[1] Burton Watson, trans., *The Lotus Sutra* (New York: Columbia University Press, 1993), 225.

[2] Ibid., 229–30.

and poet Ashvagosha wrote a complete story of the Buddha, from his birth to his attaining Final-Nirvana. This *Buddhacarita* (Acts of the Buddha) was originally composed of twenty-eight songs, of which only thirteen are extant in Sanskrit. This work follows the classical Indian style of heroic poetry. The *Buddhacarita* represents episodes of the Buddha-narrative common to most schools of Buddhism.[3] The following story of the Buddha utilizes this rather universal source along with various accounts from the Pali canon.

Prehistory of the Buddha

The story of the Buddha did not begin in the sixth century BCE. There was a complicated prehistory that led up to his enlightenment. The part of the canon that details his past lives, the Jataka tales, recounts over five hundred previous life stories. Many of the stories are used to describe his numerous heroic examples of striving to attain a superlative degree of the *ten perfections*.[4] Others explain the karmic consequences of his current life. His cousin Devadatta, for example, was an extraordinarily problematic monk in the Buddha's ministry. We discover that his past lives and those of the future Gautama were regularly linked and contesting. Beyond the Jataka we also learn how someone like the Buddha could have a headache (he was a fisherman's son in a past life who took a little pleasure in a fish killed with a blow to the head) or how the Buddha could have a backache (he was a wrestler in a past life).[5] One also discovers that his career was marked by great intentionality. In the Buddha-Chronicle of the Pali canon, we discover his aim to become a Buddha by encountering past Buddhas. The canon references twenty-four past Buddhas whom the future Buddha met.[6] The first story is paradigmatic, and the rest follow the same pattern in various ways. In this first encounter, four incalculable ages and one hundred thousand eons ago,[7] the future Buddha was a brahmin ascetic named Sumedha.

---

[3] I will be utilizing Edward B. Cowell's translation as found in https://www.ancient-buddhist-texts.net/Texts-and-Translations/Buddhacarita/index.htm.

[4] The ten perfections (*paramita*) are generosity (*dana*), morality (*shila*), renunciation (*nekkhamma*), wisdom (*panna*), energy/exertion (*viriya*), patience (*khanti*), determination/resolution (*adhitthana*), truthfulness (*sacca*), lovingkindness (*metta*), and equanimity (*upekkha*).

[5] See *Apadana* 39.10; https://www.ancient-buddhist-texts.net/English-Texts/Why-the-Buddha-Suffered/Why-the-Buddha-Suffered.pdf.

[6] One fourteenth-century Sinhalese vernacular life of the Buddha claims that there were 125,000 past Buddhas. See John Strong, *The Buddha* (Oxford: Oneworld, 2009), 31.

[7] An incalculable age is often left unspecified, but sometimes said to be 10 to the

Seeing the Buddha Dipamkara approaching a muddy section of the road he was walking on, Sumedha throws himself down on the ground and spreads his matted hair out so that Dipamkara can walk over him rather than in the mud. At that moment, Sumedha makes a firm resolve to become a Buddha himself with the further intention to pursue the ten perfections to the utmost. Hearing this resolution, Dipamkara publicly makes the prediction that Sumedha will indeed become a Buddha. He even specifies his name, Gautama, his lineage, and the names of his most important disciples. This is the start of the bodhisattva's[8] quest that will only realize itself innumerable lifetimes later.

Here is the pattern: the bodhisattva makes a public physical act of devotion, then resolves to become a Buddha, and this resolution is affirmed by a Buddha who predicts that it will happen.[9] In most of these stories, the future Buddha is a male human being, though two of them render him as a serpent-king, and eighteen hundred eons ago he was the god Indra. One can imagine the values being expressed here. Every story highlights the importance of devotion to a Buddha. This is a central value in Buddhism. Further, each story highlights the karmic consequences of such resolve. Each expression of resolve is not simply a redundancy. Rather, each reinforces and reinvigorates the eons-long struggle for Buddhahood. Finally, the stories themselves describe just how difficult it is to become a Buddha. In the Buddha's day, teems of adherents became arhats by attaining Nirvana; this of course was affected by their own past good karma. Still, it appears not so hard. But to become a Buddha! This requires a feat of endurance that only exaggerated tales can assist the imagination to consider.

The Birth and Early Life of the Bodhisattva

Like all future Buddhas, the bodhisattva's birth was one of timing. He existed in the heavenly realm of *tushita*, also known as the realm of "contended devas" (a *deva* is a being that exists in a kind of celestial paradise) awaiting the most auspicious time to be reborn in the human realm and teach the Dharma. Ashvagosha depicts his father, Shuddhodana, as a king, though Pali texts render him as a leading aristocrat in Kapilavastu,

140th power of years, and an eon (*kalpa*) is often said to be 4,320 million years, the time it takes for the universe to form, evolve, and then dissolve again.

[8] A bodhisattva is a highly spiritually developed being who vows to continue to perfect himself so as to become a Buddha himself. This aspiration far outshines that of someone who aspires only to attain Nirvana (an arhat).

[9] Strong, *Buddha*, 30.

a city that would today border India and Nepal. According to Ashvagosha, his mother, Maya, conceived him when she dreamed that a white elephant entered her body through her side. When it came time to give birth, she stood with her outstretched hand on a tree and gave birth to the bodhisattva, this without blood or any other contaminants discharged. "When the bodhisattva came forth from his mother's womb, he did not touch the earth. The young gods received him and set him before his mother saying: 'Rejoice, O Queen, a son of great power has been born to you.'" Then "two jets of water appeared to pour from the sky, one cool and one warm, for bathing the bodhisattva and his mother. As soon as the bodhisattva was born, he stood firmly with his feet on the ground; then he took seven steps to the north. . . . [He declared] 'I am the highest in the world, I am the best in the world, I am the foremost in the world; this is the last birth; now there is no more renewal of being for me.'"[10] Both his inception and his birth shook and illuminated the entire universe:

> When the bodhisattva passed away from the Tushita heaven and descended into his mother's womb . . . [and again] when the bodhisattva came forth from his mother's womb, then a great immeasurable light surpassing the splendor of the gods appeared in the world with its gods, its Maras, and its Brahmas, in this generation with its recluses and brahmins, with its princes and its people. And even in those abysmal world interspaces of vacancy, gloom, and utter darkness, where the moon and the sun, mighty and powerful as they are, cannot make their light prevail—there too a great immeasurable light surpassing the splendor of the gods appeared. . . . And this ten-thousandfold world system shook and quaked and trembled, and there too a great immeasurable light surpassing the splendor of the gods appeared.[11]

When this young soon-to-be Buddha was presented to the temple, the statues of all the gods fell at his feet and sang a hymn in his honor. He received the name Siddhartha, which means "goal attained." At that time, temple priests recognized thirty-two fundamental and eighty secondary

---

[10] *Accariya-abbhuta Sutra* (*Majjhima Nikaya* 123). Unless otherwise stated, all citations from the *Majjhima Nikaya* come from *The Middle Length Discourses of the Buddha: A New Translation of the Majjhima Nikaya*, trans. Bhikkhu Nanamoli and Bhikkhu Bodhi (Boston: Wisdom Publications, 1995).

[11] *Accariya-abbhuta Sutra* (*Majjhima Nikaya* 123) and *Bakkula Sutra* (*Majjhima Nikaya* 124).

signs of a great man and declared that Siddhartha would become either a universal sovereign or an extraordinary spiritual liberator.[12] His father committed himself to assuring that he would be the former. As Ashvagosha writes, "But he let his heart be influenced by the thought, 'he will travel by the noble path,'—he was not in truth averse to religion, yet still he saw alarm at the prospect of losing his child."[13]

Seven days after giving birth, his mother, Maya, died. Shuddhodana married her sister, Mahaprajapati, who raised him. Coming of age, he married the daughter of an elite family in a nearby town, Yashodhara, who bore him a son, Rahula, a term meaning "fetter" or "impediment," something of an indication that he found the householder life problematic. As the Buddha himself reflected, "Before my enlightenment, while I was still only an unenlightened bodhisattva, I thought: 'Household life is crowded and dusty; life gone forth is wide open.'"[14]

According to Ashvagosha, Siddhartha lived a life of extreme luxury, with three separate mansions to live in during the three seasons of northern India. Shuddhodana strove to indulge him in sensual pleasures so as not to awaken any desire to become religiously serious. Not only had he arranged a marriage for his son in late adolescence, he also surrounded Siddhartha with women and distractions. Despite these precautions, on four separate occasions he left the palace and witnessed three disturbing sights and one intriguing one: he saw an old man, a sick man, a corpse, and finally a holy man, a *shramana* (literally, "striver") seeking liberation. Thus, he saw the ravages of the human condition as well as an example of someone striving to escape. So it was that one night he stealthily left the palace forever, determined to confront these three ravages and find liberation for himself. He was twenty-nine years old at the time.

The Buddha's story surely on many fronts stretches the imagination and certainly historical credibility. Still, we may glean some insight from Ashvagosha's depiction: "When he thus gained insight into the fact that the blemishes of disease, old age, and death vitiate the very core of this world, he lost at the same moment all self-intoxication, which normally arises from

---

[12] These signs include such things as the soles of his feet marked with a thousand-spoked-wheel sign; his skin is the color of gold; his body hairs grow straight up, are bluish-black, and curl to the right; he has blue eyes; and his tongue is particularly long. See *Lakkana Sutra* (*Majjhima Nikaya* 30.1.2).

[13] *Buddhacarita* 1.84. Here I am relying on Edward Conze, trans. and ed., *Buddhist Scriptures* (New York: Penguin, 1959).

[14] *Mahasaccaka Sutra* (*Majjhima Nikaya* 36).

pride in one's own strength, youth, and vitality."[15] While it is impossible to imagine that aging, sickness, and death were unknown to the twenty-nine-year-old Siddhartha, Ashvagosha's depiction is apt: these realities vitiate the depth of existence. Now appraising them with absolute seriousness, one's sense of self-importance becomes utterly deflated. People live knowing about such realities, of course, but they rarely live *as though* they are one's reality. We are *self-intoxicated*, but the bodhisattva no longer was.

As I once earlier reflected,

> Coming to terms with one's mortality is a critical moment in the spiritual life. Doing so is not merely conceding that people age and die. What is at stake is seeing the truth of one's mortality for what it is and incorporating that truth into one's life, living now in the context of this truth. To see aging, sickness, and death in this case is to realize fully their implications. To see a holy man seeking liberation is to recognize someone who has taken the issue of mortality seriously, a spiritual seeker who has placed himself in the very heart of life's truth and unflinchingly committed himself to stop living in delusion.[16]

Going Forth to Enlightenment

Having shaved his head and taken on the quest of a *shramana*, Siddhartha became a disciple of two famous masters of meditation. The first was Alara Kalama, who taught him to attain the "base of nothingness." Soon Siddhartha equaled his teacher in this attainment: "Thus Alara Kalama, my teacher, placed me, his pupil, on an equal footing with himself and awarded me the highest honor. But it occurred to me: 'This Dharma does not lead to disenchantment, to dispassion, to cessation, to peace, to direct knowledge, to enlightenment, to Nirvana, but only to the reappearance in the base of nothingness.' Not being satisfied with that Dharma, I left it and went away."[17] He then went to the master Uddaka Ramaputta. This master taught him to attain the meditative state of neither-perception-nor-non-perception.

---

[15] *Buddhacarita* 5.14. Cowell's translation renders it: "As he thus considered thoroughly, these faults of sickness, old, age, and death which belong to all living things, all the joy which he had felt in the activity of his vigor, his youth, and is life, vanished in a moment."

[16] Peter Feldmeier, *Encounters in Faith: Christianity in Interreligious Dialogue* (Winona, MN: Anselm Academic, 2011), 147.

[17] *Ariyapariyesana Sutra* (*Majjhima Nikaya* 26.15).

Again, he attained proficiency and was awarded the title "teacher" by his master. And again, "But it occurred to me: 'This Dharma does not lead to disenchantment, to dispassion, to cessation, to peace, to direct knowledge, to enlightenment, to Nirvana, but only to the reappearance in the base of neither-perception-nor-non-perception.' Not being satisfied with that Dharma, I left it and went away."[18]

Siddhartha decided to go the path that required something else. Following the advice of the Jain monk Saccka, Siddhartha tried a concentrated form of breath control and then blocking his ears, though it is difficult to know what this actually consisted of. Neither of these practices gave him anything but intense pain.[19] Joining the company of five other ascetics, he practiced severe fasting. His own description in the Pali canon expresses something of his state:

> I thought: "Suppose I take very little food, a handful each time . . ." So I took very little food. . . . While I did so, my body reached a state of extreme emaciation. Because of eating so little my limbs became like the jointed segments of vine stems . . . my backside became like a camel's hoof . . . my scalp shriveled and withered . . . my belly skin adhered to my backbone. [Siddhartha then realized the fruitlessness of these austerities]: I thought: "Whatever recluses or brahmins in the past have experienced painful, racking, piercing feelings due to exertion, this is the utmost, there is none beyond this. . . . But by this racking practice of austerities I have not attained any superhuman states, any distinction in knowledge and vision worthy of the noble ones. Could there be another path to enlightenment?"[20] [And then]: I ate some solid food—some boiled rice and bread. Now at that time five bhikkhus [monks] were waiting upon me, thinking: "If our recluse Gautama achieves some higher state, he will inform us." But when I ate the rice and bread, the five bhikkhus were disgusted and left me thinking: "The recluse Gautama now lives luxuriously; he has given up his striving and reverted to luxury."[21]

In other parts of the Pali tradition, the offering of food—here rice and bread—for the Buddha was made by a young maiden named Sujata who believed him to be a tree-deity who had manifested himself as a human to

---

[18] *Majjhima Nikaya* 26.16.

[19] See *Mahasaccaka Sutra* (*Majjhima Nikaya* 36.21–25).

[20] *Majjhima Nikaya* 36.30.

[21] *Majjhima Nikaya* 36.33.

receive the offering. This would be theoretically enough to sustain him for the next forty-nine days. He divided the offering into forty-nine rice-balls (*pinda*) before eating it (*pinda* both refers to offerings made to Buddhist monks during their daily begging rounds and also to lumps of rice offered to spirits). This particular tradition is fascinating because forty-nine days (seven weeks) was also believed to be the length of time between the death of a sentient being and its rebirth.

So, Siddhartha, whether consuming food all at once and being enlightened shortly after or taking seven weeks to become enlightened, sat under a peepal tree (kind of fig tree) and resolved not to move until he became liberated. The Sutra Nipata of the Pali canon briefly describes the being Mara, who is something of a tempter god, as alarmed by Siddhartha's soon-to-be attainment of Nirvana.[22] Siddhartha is not moved by his temptations, whose armies he names, such as Desire and Craving.[23] In the Samyutta Nikaya, he also describes Mara's daughters, Tanha (Craving), Arati (Aversion), and Raga (Attachment). Collectively, they manifest themselves as women intending to seduce him, but to no avail. "Fools!" Mara exclaims. "You tried to batter a mountain with the stalks of lotus flowers." The Sutra concludes with, "They had come to him glittering with beauty—Tanha, Arati, and Raga—but the Teacher swept them away right there as the wind, a fallen cotton tuft."[24]

Siddhartha's night of enlightenment is most clearly described in the *Mahasaccaka Sutra*. Here we find that he entered into the four levels of meditative concentration,[25] and from the fourth level he saw the nature of reality in three phases corresponding to the three watches in the night:

> When my concentrated mind was thus purified, bright, unblemished, rid of imperfection, malleable, wieldy, steady, and attained

---

[22] Mara can be understood variously as death itself (*mrtyu-Mara*), which corresponds to its etymology, as an expression of conditioned existence (*skandha-Mara*), as unskillful emotions (*klesha-Mara*), or as a deva of the sensuous realm—typically the lord of the sensuous realm (*devaputra-Mara*). See Robert Buswell and Donald Lopez, eds., *Princeton Dictionary of Buddhism* (Princeton, NJ: Princeton University Press, 2013), 530–31, 550, 829.

[23] Specifically, they are Desire, Dislike, Hunger-Thirst, Craving, Lethargy-Laziness, Doubt, Obstinacy-Restlessness, and then a minor list of material gain, honor and fame obtained by wrongful means, thinking highly of oneself, and disparaging others. See *Sutra Nipata* 3.2.

[24] *Samyutta Nikaya* 1.4.4. Unless otherwise noted, all citations from the *Samyutta Nikaya* come from *The Connected Discourses of the Buddha: A Translation of the Samyutta Nikaya*, trans. Bhikkhu Bodhi (Boston: Wisdom Publications, 2000).

[25] We address these levels of meditative attainment as well as those Siddhartha attained from his early masters in the following chapter.

> to imperturbability, I directed it to knowledge of the recollection of past lives. I recollected my manifold past lives. [In the second watch of the night], I directed it to knowledge of the passing away and reappearance of beings. . . . Thus with the divine eye, which is purified and surpasses the human, I saw beings passing away and reappearing . . . and I understood how beings pass on according to their actions. [In the third watch of the night], I directed it to knowledge of the destruction of the taints. I directly knew as it actually is: "This is suffering. . . . This is the origin of suffering. . . . This is the cessation of suffering. . . . This is the way leading to the cessation of suffering. . . . Three are the taints. . . . This is the origin of the taints. . . . This is cessation of the taints. . . . This is the way leading to cessation of the taints." When I know and say thus, my mind was liberated from the taint of sensual desire, from the taint of being, and from the taint of ignorance. When it was liberated there came the knowledge: "It is liberated." I directly knew: "Birth is destroyed, the holy life has been lived, what had to be done has been done, there is no more coming to any state of being."[26]

The Buddha's Dharma

Setting in Motion the Wheel of Dharma

According to the *Ariyapariyesana Sutra*, the newly become Buddha hesitated to teach because he believed the Dharma simply too difficult to successfully transmit:

> I considered: "This Dharma that I have attained is profound, hard to see and hard to understand . . . But this generation delights in worldliness. . . . It is hard for such a generation to see this truth, namely, the stilling of all formations, the relinquishing of all attachments, the destruction of craving, dispassion, cessation, Nirvana. If I were to teach the Dharma, others would not understand me, and that would be wearying and troublesome for me." . . . Considering thus, my mind inclined to inaction rather than to teaching the Dharma.[27]

---

[26] *Majjhima Nikaya* 36.35–43.

[27] *Majjhima Nikaya*, 26.19.

At that point, a Brahma deity named Sahampati, reading his mind, entered his presence and pleaded with him. Dressing him in what would become a standard monastic robe, he urged the Buddha to teach, assuring him that some would understand and attain awakening. Then the Buddha surveyed the world with his supranormal powers and realized that indeed there were ripe candidates for Nirvana. He then set out to find his five earlier companions at the Deer Park near Benares and issued his first sermon, "Setting in Motion the Wheel of the Dharma." Here the Buddha proclaimed the *middle way*, that is neither one of self-mortification nor sensual pleasures.

> And what bhikkhus [monks] is that middle way awakened by the Tathagata,[28] which gives rise to vision . . . which leads to Nirvana? It is the Noble Eightfold Path; that is right view, right intention, right speech, right action, right livelihood, right effort, right mindfulness, right concentration. . . . Now this, bhikkhus, is the noble truth of suffering: birth is suffering, aging is suffering, illness is suffering, death is suffering, union with what is displeasing is suffering; separation from what is pleasing is suffering; not to get what one wants is suffering; in brief, the five aggregates subject to clinging is suffering. Now this, bhikkhus, is the noble truth of the origin of suffering: it is this craving which leads to renewed existence, accompanied by delight and lust, seeking delight here and there; that is, craving for sensual pleasures, craving for existence, craving for extermination. Now this, bhikkhus, is the noble truth of the cessation of suffering: it is the remainderless fading away and cessation of that same craving, the giving up and relinquishing of it, freedom from it, nonreliance on it. Now this, bhikkhus, is the noble truth of the way leading to the cessation of suffering: it is this Noble Eightfold Path.[29]

In his second sermon the Buddha taught the five ascetics his understanding of the constitution of the human being. Sentient beings are nothing more or less than five interrelated aggregates or "bundles." The Sanskrit word for them is *skandha*, and they are form, sensation, perception, mental formations, and consciousness. Upon examination, he taught, they are all empty of any essential self: "Form is nonself. . . . Feeling is nonself. . . . Perception is nonself. . . . Volitional formations are nonself. . . . Consciousness is nonself." Further, they are impermanent, always changing, and filled with suffering (*duhkha*).

---

[28] Tathagata means "Thus Gone" and was a regular reference to the Buddha, both as a self-reference and by his disciples.

[29] *Samyutta Nikaya* 56.11.

> Seeing thus, bhikkhus, the instructed noble disciple experiences revulsion towards form, revulsion towards feeling, revulsion towards perception, revulsion towards volitional formations, revulsion towards consciousness. Experiencing revulsion, he becomes dispassionate. Through dispassion [the mind] is liberated. When it is liberated there comes the knowledge: "It is liberated." He understands: "Destroyed is birth, the holy life has been lived. . . . There is no more for this state of being."[30]

These two seminal sermons certainly need to be unpacked. The goal, realized by developing the Fourth Noble Truth, can be understood as the *Three Trainings*: discernment (right view and resolve), virtue (right speech, action, and livelihood), and concentration (right effort, mindfulness, and concentration). They are mutually dependent. Some of the sutras portray a kind of linear progression, whereby one begins with virtue as a necessary prelude to concentration practices. These eventually allow for the possibility of discerning the conditions of suffering and their resolution by direct experience. More typically, the sutras favor the Three Trainings as a mutually informing spiral, whereby one progressively appropriates deeper and subtler forms of them all as they collectively support each other. *Right view* involves recognizing skillful and unskillful acts and their karmic fruit. *Right resolve* involves the determined intention to refrain from unskillful acts and to engage the path wholeheartedly. *Right speech* abstains from lying, divisive, harsh, or idle speech. *Right action* abstains from unskillful bodily deeds. *Right livelihood* abstains from occupations that harm sentient beings. *Right effort* persists in avoiding and eliminating unskillful mental qualities and nurturing skillful ones. *Right mindfulness* focuses on learning how to recognize physical, mental, and emotional states—their qualities and causes, and their arising and dissipation. *Right concentration* is both learning deep levels of mental absorption as well as a deep, direct experience of the Four Noble Truths.

What did the Buddha actually mean by characterizing all things and every experience as suffering, characteristics toward which one should practice revulsion? Often he made it clear that many things are indeed pleasurable. In several sermons, he assures his disciples of this: "Bhikkhus, if there were no gratification in the earth element, beings would not become enamored with it; but because there is gratification in the earth element, beings

---

[30] *Samyutta Nikaya* 22.59.

become enamored with it" (and so on with water, fire, and air).[31] And again, "If . . . this form were exclusively suffering, immersed in suffering, steeped in suffering, and if it were not [also] steeped in pleasure, beings would not become enamored with it. But because form is pleasurable, immersed in pleasure, steeped in pleasure, and is not steeped [only] in suffering, beings become enamored with it. By being enamored with it, they are captivated by it, and by being captivated by it they are defiled" (and so on with the other aggregates).[32]

Not all *duhkha* (suffering) is the same. Experiences that are actually physically, mentally, or emotionally painful are *duhkha-duhkha*. Many experiences are simply not that. Another form of duhkha is *viparinama-duhkha*, which is the dissatisfaction one experiences when pleasant experiences change. Quickly, when our pleasurable experiences lose their intensity, we experience loss and we want to cling to the original pleasure. This clinging is painful, even if subtly so. Finally, there is *samskhara-duhkha*. Nothing we experience, including ourselves, is fully satisfying. Because all things change, nothing can act as a secure refuge; everything except Nirvana is a conditioned state. Thus, the revulsion the Buddha insisted on is not yet another reactivity, itself an experience of *duhkha-duhkha*. Rather, it represents a rejection that oneself or anything else is worthy of clinging. Any craving becomes a fool's errand.

Dependent Origination

One of the Buddha's central messages is that we are ignorant of our selfless self, of the fact that we are only made up of impersonal qualities. Thinking that we have a self creates the condition to cling to our experience: this is happening to *me*. This clinging, along with the karma that goes with it, literally creates the person and perpetuates rebirth. The Buddha called this dependent origination. So central is this doctrine that the modern Buddhist master Buddhadasa refers to it as the "core of Buddhism."[33] In one famous sutra, the Buddha describes it thus:

> And what, bhikkus, is dependent origination? With ignorance as condition, volitional formations come to be; with volitional formations as

---

[31] *Samyutta Nikaya* 14.34.

[32] *Samyutta Nikaya* 22.60.

[33] Buddhadasa, *Under the Bodhi Tree: Buddha's Original Vision of Dependent Co-Arising*, ed. and trans. Santikaro (Boston: Wisdom Publications, 2017), 3.

> condition, consciousness; with consciousness as condition, name-and-form; with name-and-form as condition, the six sense bases; with the six sense bases as condition, contact; with contact as condition, feeling; with feeling as condition, craving; with craving as condition, clinging; with clinging as condition, existence; with existence as condition, birth; with birth as condition, aging-and-death, sorrow, lamentation, pain, displeasure, and despair come to be. Such is the origin of this whole mass of suffering. This, bhikkhus, is called dependent origination. But with the remainderless fading away and cessation of ignorance comes cessation of volitional formations; with the cessation of volitional formations, cessation of consciousness . . . [and so on to] the cessation of existence. . . . Such is the cessation of this whole mass of suffering.[34]

The Buddha continues then to describe the various kinds of existence, kinds of clinging, classes of craving, classes of contact, and so on—this, the Buddha discovered on the night of his enlightenment.[35]

This is the process of samsara (literally "wandering"), going from one birth to another. We die ignorant of the fundamental truths of impermanence, nonself, and suffering, and this ignorance conditions karma, the glue that keeps us in a conditioned state and binds us to our next life. One can imagine dependent origination as the relationship between spokes of a wheel that spin simultaneously, the wheel depending upon all the spokes. While each condition is dependent on and, in that sense, caused by the previous condition, no one condition exists without the others. The whole wheel arises and spins together. If one were to take a single condition out, the whole wheel collapses.

To continue the above metaphor, ignorance is placed first because it is the only spoke capable of being taken out of the wheel. In the Four Noble Truths, the cause of *duhkha* is desire or thirst. This is the central problem of life: we thirst because we do not know that there is no essential self experiencing anything. Ignorance gives the mental formations little choice but to crave, since they misunderstand the dynamic of craving. An ignorant mind naturally craves, and ignorance is the cause of all formations, craving included.

The Buddha attributes a great deal to the dynamics of karmic energy. It is either the producing condition or the decisive conditioning support for all that creates a human being and causes rebirth. It is literally that which

---

[34] *Samyutta Nikaya* 12.1.

[35] *Samyutta Nikaya* 12.10.

generates the aggregates. Karma literally means "action" in Sanskrit, and *karma-vipaka* refers to the results of that action. The Buddha emphasized one's intention and its result rather than the action itself. This is surely because every emphasis is on the dynamic relationship karma has on the aggregates. For example, the sensation aggregate experiences something physical as pleasant or unpleasant. Considering that this is happening to *me*, I will either experience craving for it or aversion toward it. Either way, I identify with the experience and react. The same can be said of the perception aggregate, which assesses mental and emotional states. Those pleasing or unpleasant conditions create a chain of reactivity.[36] Whether I want more of the experience or try to evade it, I still deludedly think it is happening to some substantial self. My mental formations are the source of my will, always running to the pleasing and evading the unpleasant. My intentions can even be wholesome, creating good karma and thus potentially good future experiences or rebirths, but because of my deluded sense that there is a substantial self, I am still trapped in a karmic world. Ironically, the process of craving keeps my mind from seeing clearly the very reactivity and self-identification that keep me in the vicious cycle of karma.

Such ignorance causes and shapes the craving mind, and thus leads to even more volitions. This is what the Buddha means by volition: an intention involving craving. Of course, someone who is enlightened surely *intends* things. But this intention is neither caused by nor cultivates attachment or narcissistic craving. In this sense, it is as though wisdom itself acts. There is no self behind the action, and when one realizes this truth at its core, then karma ceases to be produced. Without karma there is no energy in the consciousness aggregate for rebirth. The cessation of creating karma is how one escapes the wheel of rebirth and attains Nirvana.

The Pali texts refer to intending and acting without creating karma as the opposite of "fabricating" or "concocting." Buddhadasa describes "unconcoctability" as both being loosened from the control of one's experience as well as acting in the perfect freedom from karma formations:

> Unconcoctability is very powerful because it means that neither positive nor negative can be concocted. With *atammayata* (uncon-cotability) mind is in a state or condition that nothing can affect or concoct . . . the state of being that is so free that positive and negative can never affect or concoct. . . . When there is unconcoctability as both insight and realization, when life is above all influence of

[36] Both the sensation and perception aggregates can also experience something as neutral, which leads to lethargy, though this would be relatively rare.

> positive and negative, concepts of self and soul cannot arise. . . . Mind will be free, beyond concocting by positive and negative, beyond all ego and selfishness, unaffected by all things that once disturbed, hurt, and annoyed. This is the essence or heart of Buddhism.[37]

As we have seen, according to the Buddha the three fundamental characteristics of all phenomenal reality are impermanence, nonself, and dissatisfaction. All the aggregates are impermanent and thus represent interrelated processes that are constantly changing. And they are always being reformed by karma derived from craving. All the aggregates' arising are interdependent. This is a central tenet of the Buddha's dependent origination.

We see three fundamental truths from a Buddhist point of view regarding Buddhist anthropology. These truths, not coincidentally, correspond to the three characteristics of all phenomenal reality. By impermanence we see that everything is always in flux. Impermanence teaches that even rebirth is simply another, albeit dramatic, flux of the aggregates. Since they are always in flux, always involved in the dynamics of impermanence, rebirth is not qualitatively different from the moment-to-moment changes that happen even in a given lifetime.

The second truth in dependent origination concerns nonself. There is simply no singular, underlying essence of a person. There is only a collection of interrelated, always changing, ever impersonal aggregates, wandering moment to moment, lifetime to lifetime. A crucial element in the Buddhist path to enlightenment involves insight into this doctrine of nonself, so that what appears to be a solid mass or an essential self is experienced in Buddhist practice as not solid at all with nothing of an eternal essence.

The third truth in dependent origination is the concept of dissatisfaction (*duhkha*). This selfless process of life is experienced as *duhkha* when experienced in a manner based on ignorance. Such ignorance gives rise to unwholesome mental formations that need to be eliminated in following the path.

A Selfless Self

What then are we to make of the selfless self? Who or what is the self that discovers it is nonself so as to attain Nirvana, that ultimate refuge for the self? And how is this nonself related to Nirvana? The Buddhist response

[37] Buddhadasa, *Under the Bodhi Tree*, 29–31.

to these questions is that they are poorly framed. The Buddha himself taught that his doctrines are meant for the attainment of Nirvana, and nothing more. They have instrumental use, and in this sense they are assuredly true. But they are only conventionally true. They are *samvriti-satya*. Ultimate truth, *Paramartha-satya*, references that which cannot be conceptualized. Thus nonself is absolutely true, but only conventionally so.

In a famous dialogue with the Buddha, the monk Malunkyaputta questioned the Buddha about why he refused to answer questions as to whether or not the world was eternal, finite, or infinite; whether the soul was the same or different from the body; whether the Buddha existed after death or not; and so on. The Buddha responds with the story of a man wounded by a poisoned arrow, whose friends and family take him to a surgeon to pull out the arrow. But the man refuses to be treated until important answers are given, such as the characteristics of the person who shot him, the kind of bow and arrow used and their various characteristics, and so on. "All this would still not be known to that man and meanwhile he would die." The Buddha then repeats the monk's questions, assuring him that the answers would not support the noble quest, but only slow down the aspirant. "Malunkyaputta, if there is the view 'the world is eternal,' the holy life cannot be lived; and if there is the view 'the world is not eternal,' the holy life cannot be lived. Whether there is the view 'the world is eternal' or the view 'the world is not eternal,' there is birth, there is aging, there is death, there is sorrow, lamentation, pain, grief, and despair, the destruction of which I prescribe here and now."[38]

In one sutra, the Buddha explained the right posture for appropriating the Dharma through the use of two similes—a poisonous snake and a raft. Regarding the snake, one ought to grasp it skillfully in order not to get bitten. Regarding the raft, one uses it to get to the other side of the river, but then abandons it and continues his travel. "So I have shown you how the Dharma is similar to a raft, being for the purpose of crossing over, not for the purpose of grasping."[39]

While the Buddha's framework of enlightenment hinges on the insight of nonself, this view that there simply is nothing more to the human being than this impersonal collection, it would be erroneous to conclude that enlightenment means extinction after death. One would also be in error to conclude that there must be a *superself* or soul not associated with these impersonal changes, as if there were some sort of nonobjectifiable soul. To

[38] *Majjhima Nikaya* 63.

[39] *Majjhima Nikaya* 25.10–14.

the Western mindset it must be one or the other. Either we have a soul or we do not have a soul. For the Buddha, this remains an inappropriate question.[40]

To speculate on religious views that are not inherently conducive to the path of enlightenment is considered virtually immoral, since speculations lead away from enlightenment and not toward it.[41] In this sense, the Dharma is always considered a path or raft and nothing more. The Dharma, as articulated in doctrine, is truth, but it only represents the truth about phenomenal existence. It is appropriate only for understanding the phenomenal world. From the point of view of Nirvana (a *supramundane* or transcendent reality), such views no longer apply. There is another problem with the natural tendency to speculate about Nirvana: such speculation leads to a dualistic mindset. The Buddha taught, "This world leans on duality: upon the belief in existence or nonexistence. . . . Avoiding these two extremes, the Perfect One shows the doctrine of the middle: Dependent on ignorance are the *karma*-formations. . . . By the cessation of ignorance, *karma*-formations cease."[42]

Nirvana

The distinction between conventional truth and absolute truth is helpful in trying to wrap one's imagination around the concept of Nirvana, a term whose etymology is something like "extinguished," in the sense of extinguishing a candle. The Buddha used other names to indicate this goal—thirty or so in all—and they frequently denote the essence of what it is not. It is *uncaused*, *unformed*, *signless*, *unfabricated*, *deathless*. It is also regularly

---

[40] For an overview of different interpretations of the self and the various schools of thought, see Y. Krishan, "Buddhism and Belief in *atma*," *Journal of the International Association of Buddhist Studies* 7, no. 2 (1984): 117–35. For an overview on some modern Buddhalogists' opinions regarding the self, see Lynn A. de Silva, *The Problem of the Self in Buddhism and Christianity* (London: Macmillan Press, 1979), 50–71.

[41] Buddhists have called such speculations *ditthi*, which translates as "views." Of course, there are doctrines in Buddhism that are taken seriously, and on the path they are taken absolutely. But *ditthi* is a pejorative term reflecting an error in procedure. When one is engaged in *ditthi*, one is not engaged skillfully on the path. Sometimes the sutras use a play on words to reinforce the Buddhist critique of speculations. *Mana* (conceit) is connected to and played off of *mannati* (to conceptualize). See Takeuchi Yoshinori, *The Heart of Buddhism: In Search of the Timeless Spirit of Primitive Buddhism*, trans. and ed. James Heisig (New York: Crossroad, 1983), 3–7.

[42] *Samyutta Nikaya* 12.15. When charged with being a nihilist the Buddha responds that he is merely teaching suffering and the cessation of suffering (see the *Alagaddupama Sutra*). Ultimately the teaching on *anatta* is not about ontology but liberation.

represented as freedom from something bad, for example, disturbance or unhappiness. Nirvana is *unfabricated*, that is, it does not correspond to causality, form, or conditioned phenomenal existence.[43] Language, being fabricated, cannot do justice to or even directly correspond to Nirvana.[44] Consider the following classic Fire Sermon:

> Bhikkus, all is burning. And what, bhikkus, is the all that is burning? The eye is burning, forms are burning, eye-consciousness is burning, eye-contact is burning, and whatever feeling arises with eye-contact is burning, and whatever feeling arises with eye-contact as condition—whether pleasant or painful or neither-painful-nor-pleasant—that too is burning. Burning with what? Burning with the fire of lust, with the fire of hatred, with the fire of delusion burning with birth, aging and death; with sorrow, lamentation, pain, displeasure, and despair, I say. [And repeated with the ear, the mind.][45]

Nirvana is the blowing out of such a fire, that is, of craving and a psyche conditioned by lust, ill will, and delusion. Nirvana is not simply the absence of craving. The great Buddhist synthesizer Buddhaghosa, whom we address in the next chapter, argues vigorously that Nirvana is a reality. It is not something that can be produced through meditation or any other cause. It is both a *void* and something that can be apprehended and realized—a *supramundane* reality.[46]

In the *Aggivacchagotta Sutra*, the Buddha illustrates the enigmatic nature of Final-Nirvana in his conversation with his disciple Vaccha, who asks him whether one who has died reappears in some eternal form. The Buddha denies this: "The term 'reappears' does not apply." He then asks if the answer then is: does not reappear. Again this is denied. Then "both reappears and does not reappear" and then "neither reappears nor does not reappear." Each is denied by the Buddha.

---

[43] For canonical descriptions of the literary use of Nirvana, see Rune Johannson, *The Psychology of Nirvana* (London: Allen & Unwin, 1969).

[44] See Steven Collins, *Selfless Persons: Imagery and Thought in Theravada Buddhism* (Cambridge: Cambridge University Press, 1982), 83ff., and Richard Robinson, Willard Johnson, and Thanissaro Bhikkhu, *Buddhist Religions*, 5th ed. (Belmont, CA: Wadsworth, 2005), 19–20.

[45] *Samyutta Nikaya* 35.28.

[46] See Bhadantacariya Buddhaghosa, *The Path of Purification* (*Visuddhimagga*), 5th ed., trans. Bhikkhu Nanamoli (Kandi: Buddhist Publication Society, 1991), 1.32; 14.15; 16.70; 16.67; 21.18; 21.37; 21.124; 22.5; 22.127.

Buddha: What do you think, Vaccha? Suppose a fire were burning before you. Would you know: This fire is burning before me?

Vaccha: I would, Master Gautama.

Buddha: If someone were to ask you, Vaccha: What does the fire burning before you burn in dependence on?—being asked thus, what would you answer?

Vaccha: Being asked thus, Master Gautama, I would answer: This fire burning before me burns in dependence on grass and sticks.

Buddha: If that fire before you were to be extinguished, would you know: This fire before me has been extinguished.

Vaccha: I would, Master Gautama.

Buddha: If someone were to ask you, Vaccha: When that fire before you was extinguished, to which direction did it go: to the east, the west, the north, or the south?—being asked thus, what would you answer?

Vaccha: That does not apply, Master Gautama. The fire burned in dependence on its fuel of grass and sticks. When that is used up, if it does not get any more fuel, being without fuel, it is reckoned as extinguished.

Buddha: So too, Vaccha, the Tathagata has abandoned that material form by which one describing the Buddha might describe him; he has cut it off at the root, made it like a palm stump, done away with it so that it is no longer subject to future arising [rebirth]. The Tathagata is liberated from reckoning in terms of material form, Vaccha, he is profound, immeasurable, unfathomable like the ocean. The term "reappears" does not apply, the term "does not reappear" does not apply, the term "both reappears and does not reappear" does not apply, the term "neither reappears nor does not reappear" does not apply.[47]

In this text, and many other places, the Buddha thus denies that Nirvana is nihilism (as extinction pure and simple), and he denies that Nirvana represents eternalism (as some ultimate realm of existence).

The End of the Buddha's Life and Buddha Worship

Rather universally attested, the Buddha spent forty-five years teaching the Dharma in the Ganges region of northern India. The *Mahaparinibbana Sutra* recounts his final year. Most scholars see this chronicle as more than

[47] *Majjhima Nikaya* 72.15–20.

a mere historical telling, for it also describes (and justifies) the beginning of the cult of the Buddha's relics. After the Buddha's final rains retreat[48] and while staying in a forest shrine, he tells Ananda, his faithful attendant, that he could, if he were asked, remain alive on earth for the entire earth-age (kalpa). But Ananda does not realize that he is seeking to be asked: "Even with such a broad hint, such a plain sign, was given by the Blessed One, still the venerable Ananda could not understand it. He did not beg the Blessed One . . . so much was his mind under Mara's influence." The Buddha raises this three times, each of which Ananda fails to ask. Then alone Mara approached Gautama and told him that his time had come for his Final-Nirvana. He had established the Dharma and created an order of monks who were competent to continue the mission. After Mara's plea, the Buddha replied, "You may rest, Evil One. Soon the Perfect One's attainment of Final-Nirvana will take place. Three months from now the Perfect One will attain Final-Nirvana."

This announcement conditions an earthquake, which startles Ananda, who now asks the Buddha what it meant. The Buddha gives him many reasons, the final of which is that he is about to enter Final-Nirvana. "Lord," Ananda begs, "let the Blessed One live out the age, let the Sublime One live out the age, for the welfare and happiness of many, out of compassion for the world, for the good, the welfare and happiness of gods and men." "Enough, Ananda," he replied, "do not ask that of the Perfect One now; the time to ask that of the Perfect One has now gone by."

That same evening the Buddha met with his monks to rehearse the essentials of his teaching. Soon after the Buddha took his last meal at the home of Cunda, a goldsmith, and contracted food poisoning. The dying Buddha then entered the eight states of meditative absorption (which we address in the next chapter), and then returned to the fourth level, that of perfect equanimity and one-pointedness. From this perfect equanimity, he died, passing into the enigmatic Final-Nirvana. Earthquakes marked his passing.

The people of Kusinagari come the next day and hold a six-day wake for the Buddha, offering him garlands. On the seventh day, eight chiefs of the Malla clan carry his body to a shrine just outside of town. But devas interrupt the procession, and will not allow the pyre to catch fire until the arhat Mahakashypa arrives with five hundred monks. These monks circle the pyre with hands raised, worshiping the Buddha's feet and head. The funeral pyre then spontaneously bursts into flames, leaving no ashes, but only bones.

---

[48] A three-month annual retreat during the wet season.

They worship the relics for seven more days until the chiefs of seven other kingdoms come to worship and take claim of the relics. Finally, after a great deal of contention, they divide the relics into ten parts, eight with his bones, one being his urn, and one for the embers from the pyre. Returning to their homes, they build ten stupas or burial mounds as shrines. The sutra ends with a hymn that does not exactly follow the narrative, but is striking:

> *Eight portions of relics there were of him,*
> *The All-Seeing One. Of these, seven remained*
> *In Jambudipa with honor. The eighth*
> *In Ramagama's kept by naga kings.*
> *One tooth the Thirty Gods have kept,*
> *Kalinga's kings have one, the nagas too.*
> *They shed their glory o'er the fruitful earth.*
> *Thus the Seer's honored by the honored.*
> *Gods and nagas, kings, the noblest men*
> *Clasp their hands in homage, for hard it is*
> *To find another such for countless eons.*

Perhaps the most startling part of the Buddha's biography is his death and the reaction his followers had to his death: Buddha veneration to the point of Buddha worship, particularly with regard to his relics. Recall from above that the Buddha commended a kind of revulsion toward each of the skandhas: "Seeing thus, bhikkhus, the instructed noble disciple experiences revulsion towards form, revulsion towards feeling, revulsion towards perception, revulsion towards volitional formations, revulsion towards consciousness. Experiencing revulsion, he becomes dispassionate."[49] In commending various meditational practices, the Buddha also commended "the perception of unattractiveness [of the body] . . . the perception of the repulsiveness of food . . . the perception of nondelight in the entire world . . . the perception of a skeleton . . . the perception of a worm-infested corpse . . . the perception of a livid corpse . . . the perception of a fissured corpse . . . [and] the perception of a bloated corpse."[50] Here the purpose is to lose any "intoxication" with one's life as one sees its clear and grotesque outcome. A further strategy the Buddha taught was to deconstruct the body by its parts so as to experience repulsiveness toward it:

---

49 *Samyutta Nikaya* 22.59.

50 *Anguttara Nikaya* I.42. Unless otherwise noted, I am using *The Numbered Discourses of the Buddha: A Translation of the Anguttara Nikaya*, trans. Bhikkhu Bodhi (Boston: Wisdom Publications, 2012).

> Again, bhikkhus, a bhikkhu reviews this same body up from the soles of the feet and down from the top of the hair, bounded by skin, as full of many kinds of impurity thus: "In this body there are head-hairs, body hairs, nails, teeth, skin, flesh, sinews, bones, bone-marrow, kidneys, heart, liver, diaphragm, spleen, lungs, large intestines, small intestines, contents of the stomach, feces, bile, phlegm, pus, blood, sweat, fat, tears, grease, spittle, snot, oil of the joints, and urine."[51]

How do these and many other teachings of the Buddha square with the veneration of his dying and then dead body?[52]

We might also wonder about several other verses that seem to contrast veneration to the Buddha. In one famous teaching, the Buddha said,

> Bhikkhus, dwell with yourselves as an island, with yourselves as a refuge, with no other refuge; with the Dharma as an island, with the Dharma as a refuge, with no other refuge.[53]

The Buddha used virtually the exact same words to his disciple Ananda soon before the Buddha died. He further reflected on devas singing in homage to him and trees dropping blossoms on him:

> Ananda, these *sal*-trees have burst forth into an abundance of untimely blossoms . . . [and there is] divine music and song from the sky in homage to the Tathagata. Never before has the Tathagata been so honored, revered, esteemed, worshiped, and adored. And yet, Ananda, whatever monk, nun, male or female lay-follower dwells practicing the Dharma properly and perfectly fulfills the Dharma-way he or she honors the Tathagata, reveres and esteems him and pays him the supreme homage.[54]

---

[51] *Majjhima Nikaya* III.91.7.

[52] Consider also the Buddha's teaching about how to meditate on the aggregates. There are forty ways, he taught in the *Patisambhidamagga Sutra* (II.238). Consider the aggregates as impermanent, suffering, disease, boil, arrow, evil, sickness, alien, crumbling, calamity, danger, fear, misfortune, unstable, disintegrating, inconstant, without protection, without shelter, without refuge, null, vain, empty, without self, dangerous, mutable, without essence, root of evil, murderous, unprosperous, with taints, compounded, prey of Mara, subject to birth, subject to decay, subject to ailment, subject to death, subject to sorrow, subject to grief, subject to despair, and subject to corruption.

[53] *Samyutta Nikaya* 22.43.

[54] *Digha Nikaya* 16.5.3. Unless otherwise noted, I am using *The Long Discourses of*

Is Buddha veneration or worship thus a corruption of the Buddha's mission, something that actually undermined his ultimate message? For sure, the developing cult of the Buddha as well as worship of him at stupas represents something of an addition to his message, but there is plenty in the sutras, even those whose scholarly consensus puts them early, to suggest that the issue is more complicated. We have already seen in the prehistory of the Buddha that the role of other Buddhas was crucial in his success in ultimately becoming enlightened. Further, it is clear that the Buddha himself, and not just his Dharma, was important. Many stories in the sutras reference the Buddha's psychic powers in facilitating realization in his monks. In some, we find that he reads the minds of those before him, so as to best help them conquer spiritual roadblocks. In others, he supranormally appears before monks who are far away in order to support their future enlightenment.[55] Further, in the very *Mahaparinibbana Sutra* where he tells Ananda to be an island to himself and to reverence the Buddha by following the path diligently, he *also* stipulates how his body is to be cremated and that his relics ought to be dispersed. He even ordered the practice of pilgrimages to the four locations most central to his life story: the places of his birth, enlightenment, first sermon, and death. How reliable this material is to the historical Buddha is difficult to say, but those memorizing and ultimately compiling the canon saw no necessary contradiction.

The Buddha was a power figure and continued to be so after his death, after seemingly he was not available to his devotees. In the *Mahaparinibbana Sutra*, he requested (commanded?) that his relics be preserved and that the four great pilgrimage sites be created. He even promised that reverence at a stupa would produce great merit (karma). This is how it is framed in the sutra in a conversation between the Buddha and Ananda:

> "But Lord, what are we to do with the Tathagata's remains?" "Ananda, they should be dealt with like the remains of a wheel-turning monarch." "And how is that, Lord?" "Ananda, the remains of a wheel-turning monarch are wrapped in a new linen-cloth. This they wrap in teased cotton wool, and this in a new cloth. Having done this five hundred times each, they enclose the king's body in an oil-vat of iron, which is covered with another iron pot. Then having made a funeral-pyre of all manner of perfumes they cremate the king's body, and they raise a stupa at the crossroads. That, Ananda,

the Buddha: A Translation of the Digha Nikaya, trans. Maurice Walsh (Boston: Wisdom Publications, 1995).

[55] Robinson et al., 33.

> is what they do with the remains of a wheel-turning monarch, and they should deal with the Tathagata's body in the same way. A stupa should be erected at the crossroads for the Tathagata. And whoever lays wreaths or puts sweet perfumes and colors there with a devout heart will reap benefit and happiness for a long time."

One sees that several other aspects of devotion to the Buddha at stupas are found in the Buddha's own burial. For example, we find Mahakasypa circumambulating around the Buddha's body, which will then model the practice for stupa festivals. Further, when the Mallans come to pay their last respects, Ananda proclaims their family names out loud to the deceased body of the Buddha. The sutras detail how this was the proper way of showing respect, the devotee here being asked to be remembered. In many Indian monuments, donors' names are inscribed on the structure as a way of remembering their gifts. This would also be the case for stupas, yet Buddhism has long kept the practice of putting some donors' names inside the stupa, where no one would see this (except perhaps the Buddha?). Finally, the songs and dances, the gifts of garlands and perfumes that both humans and devas offer to the Buddha and his dead body are repeated as central aspects of stupa festivals.[56]

The Buddha and his relics constitute an unexcelled merit field called a Buddha-field. One finds elaborate descriptions of Buddha-fields in the *avadana* literature. While such texts were produced several centuries after his death, the concept of Buddha-fields goes back to the earliest strata of the canon. Unlike the Jataka tales, which principally sought to explain how the Buddha or arhats developed in past lives the perfections necessary for their current attainment, the avadana stories emphasized the boon that came to these figures when they showed veneration to past Buddhas. They planted seeds in the Buddha-field that ripened just when they needed them, thus encouraging later disciples of the historical Buddha to do the same.[57] So, while the Buddha might not be accessible in the same way as when he was alive, his disciples believed that there was still merit to be made by their continued devotion to him.

From the time of the Buddha's earliest mission, becoming a follower meant taking on the Three Refuges. They commit to taking the Buddha as refuge, the Dharma as refuge, and the Sangha or monastic community as refuge. These are the Three Jewels. It would be a grave mistake to

---

[56] Ibid., 40–42.

[57] Ibid., 70.

imagine that, once the Buddha died, taking refuge in him ought to be conflated with his Dharma alone. Although he continues to be a protector, how dynamically involved he is in the life of a disciple is complicated, and surely Theravada and Mahayana traditions will break on this and many other questions. Mahayana itself will ultimately provide a dizzying array of perspectives, not all of which are commensurate with each other. Still, in all forms of Buddhism, the Buddha himself and deep devotion to him personally remain crucially important.

Final Word

The Buddha left no written record of his teachings nor a centralized authority to adjudicate them. Indeed, even during his lifetime there were monastic disputes. Not surprisingly, various lineages developed in the first few centuries after his Final-Nirvana. Traditionally, there were eighteen distinct monastic lineages, of which Theravada is the sole surviving representative. Each lineage claimed to preserve orally the accurate teachings of the Buddha, and it would not be until around the first century BCE when the Pali canon was written down. What is striking is that there appear to be only relatively minor differences among the eighteen in terms of what he taught, that is, his sutras. Some of the differences had to do with minor practices or with monastic rules; others were more substantive and involved philosophical disputes or philosophical reflections on his message. While Mahayana followers will add many more sutras to their canon, a relatively consistent collection of sutras are shared by both Theravada and Mahayana traditions.[58]

[58] They are divided into sections called *Nikayas* or *Agamas*. The four Nikayas recognized by all the early lineages are the Long Discourses (*Dirgha*), the Medium Discourses (*Madhyama*), the Connected Discourses (*Samyukta*), and the Numerical Discourses (*Ekottara*). Some lineages, including the Theravada, also include a fifth (*Khuddakapatha Nikaya*) of short passages, stories, and anthologies of verse. These are the Dhammapada, Udana, Itivuttaka, Sutra Nipata, Vimanavatthu, Petavatthu, Theragatha, Therigatha, Jataka, Niddesa, Patisambhidamagga, Apadana, Buddhavamsa, and Cariya-pitaka.

Chapter 3

The Path of Purification and the Dark Night

Buddhaghosa and John of the Cross

Buddhaghosa (Fifth Century CE)

As we saw in the last chapter, the massive canon was for centuries only preserved orally, with various monks being responsible for memorizing and reciting parts of the canon verbatim.[1] How accurately it was preserved is an impossible question to answer, particularly as variants in some of the canonical material seem to reflect differences among the emerging sects. The history of the written Pali canon is aligned to the history of Sri Lanka. In the third century BCE, the Sinhalese founded a royal dynasty that allowed for political and cultural ties to northern India. According to tradition, King Ashoka (ruled c. 268–232 BCE) sent missionaries to Sri Lanka, including his son, Mahinda, and later his daughter Sanghamitta, who would form a community of nuns. Sinhalese King Tissa accepted the faith (c. 247 BCE), becoming a robust patron to Buddhism and building a large monastery, Mahavihara, in his capital city of Anuradhapura. In the first century BCE, southern Indian forces invaded Sri Lanka and the oral transmission was nearly lost. In response, the monks of Mahavihara took to preserving the

[1] For much of this chapter's material I am drawing on my doctoral dissertation, "Interrelatedness: A Comparison of the Spiritualities of St. John of the Cross and Buddhaghosa for the Purpose of Examining the Christian Use of Buddhist Practices" (Ph.D. diss., Graduate Theological Union, Berkeley, CA, 1996). See also Peter Feldmeier, *Christianity Looks East: Comparing the Spiritualities of John of the Cross and Buddhaghosa* (New York: Paulist Press, 2006).

canon and commentaries in writing. The term "Pali" probably means "text," and was likely a language (similar to Sanskrit) created in order to regularize the language of the canon.

In the fifth century, an Indian Buddhist monk and scholar came to Mahavihara in order to collect and collate various Sinhalese commentaries of the canon; this is Bhadantacariya Buddhaghosa, *the* master in Theravada Buddhism. Beyond his massive output, we know little about him with historical certainty.[2] The most important source concerning Buddhaghosa is a Sinhalese historical chronicle, the *Mahavamsa*, where chapter 37 is devoted to him. Beyond this, we also have material from Burmese hagiography. According to the *Mahavamsa*, Buddhaghosa was a brilliant Indian brahmin. As a young man, he came upon a Buddhist monk who questioned him. Unable to offer satisfactory responses to his many questions, the monk encouraged him to become a Buddhist, to which he agreed. As Mahavihara was something of the center for Theravadin orthodoxy, he eventually traveled to Sri Lanka in order to collect and translate Sinhalese commentaries. Before agreeing to give him full access to their texts, the elders of Mahavihara tested him with a riddle: How does one untangle the tangle with which one is entangled? His massive and magisterial *Visuddhimagga* (*Path of Purification*) represents his answer to that riddle, which he is said to have written in one sitting. In order to demonstrate his wisdom, a deva made his commentary invisible, forcing him to write it again. The deva then made his second attempt invisible, again forcing a third manuscript. When he presented this third manuscript to the elders of Mahavihara, the deva then revealed the earlier two and they found all three to be identical.[3]

According to the Burmese tradition, Buddhaghosa was said to have been living in a deva realm when a Burmese monk traveled to that realm through meditation and petitioned him to enter the human realm for the purpose of spreading the Dharma. This deva agreed. The tradition has him even more than merely precocious. He had memorized the Vedas by the age of seven and demonstrated insight beyond all other brahmins. When he realized his true identity and purpose for his human life he set out for Sri Lanka to study and translate the Sinhalese commentaries. On his boat trip a fellow passenger asked him the aforementioned riddle. In order to pass the

[2] E. W. Adikarem, *The Early History of Buddhism in Ceylon* (Dehiwala, Sri Lanka: Buddhist Cultural Centre, 1946), 3.

[3] Bimala Charan Law, *The Life and Work of Buddhaghosa* (Delhi: Nag Publishers, 1976), 2–3.

time, he wrote the Visuddhimagga, but a deva stole his copy. He then wrote a second copy, which again was stolen. By lamplight, he then immediately wrote a third copy, which he presented to his traveling companion. As in the first story, the deva then revealed the hidden two, both of which were exactly the same as his final manuscript.[4]

The Burmese tradition is more mythical, though it precedes the *Mahavamsa*, and could very well have been the source material for the Sinhalese tradition. Both accounts stretch historical credulity.[5] And yet both point to the fact that the Theravada community regards the work as destined, essentially perfect, inspired, and definitive.

Buddhaghosa claimed to be merely collating and organizing the tradition, and it appears that when he asserts his own opinion he marks it as such. But, because we have none of the Sinhalese source commentaries, there is no way to assess this claim. With regard to the sutras, however, we do know that he represents a development for the Theravadin tradition. He does not simply repeat the material from the sutras and even contradicts some of them (as they themselves seem to do *intra-sutra*). For example, he clearly distinguishes the aims of *samadhi* or meditations of mental absorption from *vipassana* or insight meditations. These are often conflated in the sutras, including the Buddha's own enlightenment experience. He also drops the canon's emphasis on whole-body breath awareness as a *samadhi* practice, framing it as an insight practice. Thus, if he is merely a collator and not an innovator, his work nonetheless expresses some development from the sutras to what would become mainstream Theravada Buddhism. On the other hand, my opinion is that Theravada Buddhism is the closest living tradition to those sutras shared by the vast majority of Buddhists, and Buddhaghosa's distillation of this tradition represents less a divergence from the sutras and more a systematic way of presenting them with clarity. As Winston King summarizes the Visuddhimagga, "This has always been the standard authoritative text book on meditational theory and practice, and mentioned in the next breath after the canon when meditation is spoken of."[6]

---

[4] Ibid., 26ff.

[5] Buddhaghosa's life also follows what may have been considered paradigmatic of an auspicious and destined life. Law points to how both of these biographical traditions reflect the same life story as that of Nagasena, the famous monk who converted King Milinda by his erudition. See Law, *Life and Work of Buddhaghosa*, 44.

[6] Winston King, "Theravada in South East Asia," in *Buddhist Spirituality I: Indian, Southeast Asian, Tibetan, Early Chinese*, ed. Takeuchi Yoshinori (New York: Crossroad, 1995), 81.

Buddhaghosa's Path to Nirvana

In both legendary accounts of Buddhaghosa's life, he was given the challenge to answer the riddle: *How does one untangle the tangle with which one is entangled?* His answer would be the *Visuddhimagga* or Path of Purification. His shorthand answer is,

> *When a wise man, established well in virtue,*
> *Develops consciousness and understanding,*
> *Then as a bhikkhu ardent and sagacious,*
> *He succeeds in disentangling this tangle.*[7]

The path (*magga*) is the key to understanding Theravada Buddhism. As we saw above, Buddhist doctrine has a twofold purpose. First, it is conceived of as an absolutely accurate description of conditioned reality. Second, it has a functional value; it is used to assist the aspirant on the path. The path is everything regarding the attainment of Nirvana. Buddhaghosa writes in his Introduction that the one who disentangles the tangle possesses six things: virtue (*shila*); concentration (*samadhi*); the threefold understanding (*prajna*) of nonself, impermanence, and dissatisfaction;[8] and ardor. Thus, with ardor presumed, Buddhaghosa's aim is to describe how virtue, concentration, and understanding lead one to enlightenment. This is the path.[9]

Virtue

Buddhaghosa sees the path of purification as principally one of meditation, but the first training is virtue. It is "the necessary condition for the triple clear vision."[10] Buddhaghosa presumes a monastic audience. This means that, in addition to the five moral precepts that all Buddhists observe,[11] there exist 227 rules ordering the lives of Buddhaghosa's monastic readers.[12] As with the

---

[7] Bhadantacariya Buddhaghosa, *The Path of Purification—Visuddhimagga*, trans. Bhikkhu Nanamoli, 5th ed. (Kandy, Sri Lanka: Buddhist Publication Society, 1991), 1.1.

[8] *Prajna* literally means "wisdom." Here, one is wise only to the extent that one realizes the very nature of conditioned reality and, of course, the cessation of karma formations, i.e., Nirvana.

[9] *Visuddhimagga* 1.7.

[10] *Visuddhimagga* 1.11.

[11] These are abstaining from taking life, from taking what is not offered, from sexual misconduct, from false speech, and from intoxicants.

[12] Edmond Pezet, "Vois de contemplation dans Bouddisme Theravada," in *Médi-*

five precepts, the ethos of the rules is that of providing a mental culture of restraint. Virtue is physical, verbal, and mental restraint, and its function is to stop misconduct on each of those levels.[13] Their purpose, he writes, is to "eliminate sensual desire, since they manifest the opposite."[14] The experience of asceticism is not to be seen as a burden, but as an opportunity for the mind to be free from burdens. If, for example, one has a sensuous personality disposition, then a rigorously ascetical lifestyle is going to be challenging initially, but only then. The very insecurity that represents a craving mind is replaced by a kind of sensitivity of spirit. Buddhaghosa promises that as one grows in the virtue of restraint, one becomes more alive, ever more filled with energy and happiness.[15]

Concentration

Once virtue is established, Buddhaghosa next describes how the mind cultivates a spiritual posture through meditations designed for concentration.[16] They are intended for several ends. First and foremost, they suppress and lessen that which keeps the mind from being self-possessed. These impediments are the *five hindrances* of lust, ill will, torpor, agitation, and uncertainty.[17] Such hindrances undermine both concentration and insight. Further, concentration meditations support strengths in the psyche. And, conversely, they can reverse unskillful mental habits or traits. Buddhaghosa writes, "When a man cultivates what is unsuitable, his progress is difficult and his direct-knowledge sluggish. When he cultivates what is suitable, his progress is easy and his direct-knowledge is swift. This refers to both severing of impediments and to the object choices of meditation."[18] If one had, for example, a *faithful* personality profile, then meditations on qualities of the Buddha would be easy, agreeable, and follow one's strength. If one had a *sensuous* personality, then meditations on the *foulness of the body* would counter both one's attachments to the body and one's predilections toward physical pleasure.

---

tation dans le Christianisme et les autres religions, ed. Mariasausai Dhavamony (Rome: Gregorian University Press, 1976), 67.

13 *Visuddhimagga* 1.21–22.

14 *Visuddhimagga* 2.12.

15 *Visuddhimagga* 2.1, 83.

16 Theravada also knows concentration as *shamatha*, meaning calm or tranquil.

17 *Visuddhimagga* 4.104.

18 *Visuddhimagga* 3.116.

Collating the canon's many scattered expressions of meditation, Buddhaghosa derived a list of forty meditation subjects, categorized in seven headings.

1. *Ten Kasinas*: These meditation subjects are visual aids intended to allow the mind to enter into deep levels of concentration or absorption.
2. *Ten Kinds of Foulness:* These meditations are meant to encourage nonattachment to the body and a kind of repulsion to sensual pleasures.
3. *Ten Reflections:* These meditations range from qualities of the Buddha, Buddhist virtues, and body awareness.
4. *Four Divine-Abidings:* These are meditations on lovingkindness, compassion, sympathetic joy, and equanimity. Collectively, they produce a proper and balanced Buddhist relationship to other beings.
5. *Four Immaterial States:* These meditations develop advanced levels of concentrative absorption.
6. *One Perception:* This is a meditation on food consumption in order to avoid attachment to eating.
7. *One Defining*: This meditation strategy involves discerning primal elements (earth, water, fire, air) in a given object or within oneself.

Buddhaghosa lists eight levels of meditative absorption or eight *jhanas.*[19] We noted in chapter 2 that as the Buddha was dying, he entered into all eight, and then settled into the fourth just before his passing. The following is an example of how a meditation brings various levels of absorption. I use the meditation of an earthen disk (*kasina*) as it can demonstrate all eight. One begins meditation by mental preparations, such as arousing the desire to be liberated from the senses and dispelling any of the above-mentioned hindrances. Then one looks intently at the disk, representing earth. Once the mind is sufficiently concentrated, one recognizes qualities of the initially absorbed mind. These qualities are applied thought, sustained thought (staying focused), happiness, bliss, and one-pointedness of mind. Collectively they represent the first *jhana*. Here the *sign* of "earth" becomes the mind's absorption. The attainment of the three next higher levels of *jhana* consists in recognizing the grosser factors of mind, and disinclining from

[19] *Jhana*, which literally means "to burn up," is said to burn up opposing states of mind. It can be translated simply as "meditation," but Buddhaghosa uses it to reference levels of *samadhi.*

them by focusing on the more subtle factors. So, to enter into the second *jhana* is to avert from applied and sustained thought and focus on happiness, bliss, and one-pointedness. When the quality of absorption is only these three, one has entered into the second *jhana*. Then happiness is recognized as a grosser factor than the other two, and so averting from happiness and focusing on the mental qualities of bliss and one-pointedness, one enters into the third *jhana*. Finally, one recognizes bliss to be the grosser mental factor of the remaining two. Averting from bliss, one remains simply in one-pointedness. One-pointedness remains constant, while equanimity enters to replace bliss. Thus, one is utterly focused and centered while experiencing an extraordinary sense of equanimity.

While cognitions are barely occurring, the meditator has the intuition that, if the grosser factors were gone, there would be more tranquility, subtlety, and sublimity. There is some kind of executive function of the mind operating here. The mind recognizes its own state of existence and can choose to move mentally to the next level. Such is the case with the next set of *jhanas*, the *arupa-jhanas* or formless states. These are the *four immaterial states* mentioned in the list above. Unlike the former absorptions, these do not vary in compositional factors of consciousness. What is different is that the *object* of consciousness changes. The fifth level (first *arupa-jhana*) occurs when one extends the *kasina* to the limits of one's imagination. And then to the sixth level (second *arupa-jhana*) by mentally removing the *kasina*'s sign and concentrating on the space left behind. The seventh level (third *arupa-jhana*) is achieved when the nonexistence of boundless space becomes the object of concentration. The eighth and final level (fourth *arupa-jhana*) is called the base of neither-perception-nor-nonperception. Here, in focusing on the mental components of one's current state, the meditator averts to the base via a mantra, like *peaceful, peaceful, peaceful*. This is the highest and deepest level of concentration or *samadhi*.[20] We might remember here that the Buddha had learned of these last two levels of concentration by two different masters before his enlightenment.

According to Buddhaghosa, *samadhi* practices are utterly important for progress. These practices infuse the Buddhist aspirant with virtues and values inherent to Buddhism; they develop the mind exquisitely and prepare it to practice deep insight.[21] Ultimately, however, these meditations are

---

[20] The Theravada tradition also holds another meditation known as *nirodha*, the entire cessation of feelings and perception. See Paravahera Vajiranana Mahathera, *Buddhist Meditation in Theory and Practice* (Kuala Lumpur, Malaysia: Buddhist Missionary Society, 1975), 108.

[21] *Visuddhimagga* 12.1.

fundamentally inadequate. While they do serve a purpose in purifying the mind to some degree, they do not eliminate attachments or impurities but only suppress them. With the exclusive use of them, one comes to a deeply happy and serene life as well as an excellent rebirth. But one cannot get off the wheel of samsara through them. Liken the situation to being in a prison cell. One can dress up the cell, making it comfortable and pleasing. Yet it is still a prison. The only way to escape is through insight.

Understanding or Insight

Samadhi practices cannot bring one to attain Nirvana. They do not have the capacity for seeing reality for what it is (impermanent, nonself, and dissatisfying), and in fact suppress this knowledge for the sake of concentration. Further, Buddhaghosa writes that true knowledge is not merely perception but "penetration of the characteristics as impermanent, painful, and not-self."[22] So, the issue is not merely accepting that all conditioned things (especially the aggregates that make up oneself) have these qualities, nor is the issue a mere recognition. One has to deeply penetrate the core of this reality. Buddhaghosa will spend half of his massive tome on the specifics of insight.

It would be laborious to detail every step of insight meditation, and I think unnecessary. A brief outline will suffice for our purposes, for the meditator practicing *vipassana* goes through a series of levels of insight. Each series is but a deeper penetration of self-understanding into the three qualities of existence. It is this penetration that allows one to be liberated from the karma produced by desire.[23]

Buddhaghosa places the first experience of deep insight through meditating on the aggregates that constitutive the person. One discerns them as consisting of impersonal elements and recognizes the self to be nonconstitutive.[24] Here in meditation one may perhaps watch one's breath or analyze the energy flow through the body. Experiences arise and dissipate, and one

---

[22] *Visuddhimagga* 14.3.

[23] The Buddha's *Sattipatthana Sutra* (Four Foundations of Mindfulness) is central here. In this famous sutra, the Buddha outlines various ways to consider the body, particularly the breath, in order to penetrate the impersonal qualities of the aggregates. Modern commentator Thera Nyanaponika, in summing up the role of *sattipatthana*, describes it thusly: "All the Buddha's methods ultimately converge in the way of mindfulness." See *The Heart of Buddhist Meditation* (York Beach, ME: Samuel Weiser, 1965), 7.

[24] This is *purification of view*. One sees in the aggregates the four elements of the universe: earth, wind, fire, and water.

realizes that there is no essential self behind them. The second purification occurs when one realizes through bare attention how the karma process works in real time. One literally sees how desire creates the conditions for the furtherance of the aggregates.[25] In the third stage of progress, one understands how impermanence is painful and afflictive.[26] This is the result of penetrating the inner drama of how one reacts to the rise and fall of these impersonal experiences. One inclines one's attention to the rapid dissolution of all mental and physical arisings; arising is suffering, nonarising is bliss. The next phase is that of intense desire for Nirvana.[27] The final stage of insight leading to total liberation is a *change-of-lineage knowledge*, whereby the cycle of rebirth has been broken.[28]

John of the Cross (1542–1591)

We know much more about John of the Cross than we do about Buddhaghosa. And yet, even here, there are some problems with his biographical material. His first biographies were written more than thirty years after his death and were influenced by the cultural view of sanctity common to sixteenth- and seventeenth-century Spain.[29] This includes, for example, reports about St. John at the end of his life as having lights emitting

---

[25] This is *purification of overcoming doubt*. Here one sees that the pleasure or pain that arises does not last. The meditator brings oneself to the point where, without clinging to experience, feelings of pleasure or pain are allowed to simply be, arising and falling without any reactivity.

[26] This is *purification by knowledge and vision of what is the path and what is not the path*.

[27] This is *purification by knowledge and vision of the way*. The great desire for liberation comes when one painfully realizes that there is no refuge in phenomenal reality. Such a realization is overwhelming and often terrifying.

[28] This is *purification by knowledge and vision*. There are four levels here: that of a *stream-enterer* (guaranteed to attain Nirvana in the next seven lifetimes), that of a *once-returner* (guaranteed to attain Nirvana in the next human lifetime), that of a *nonreturner* (guaranteed to attain Nirvana in the next rebirth though as a being in a higher plain of existence), and finally that of an *arhat*, or one who has now attained Nirvana. The difference among these noble states is not great but refer to very subtle distinctions in psychic predilections to desire. Buddhaghosa believes that one could progress through each of these levels quickly, even in one sitting.

[29] See Teófanes Egido, "Contexto historico de San Juan de la Cruz," in *Experiencia y pensamiento en San Juan de la Cruz*, ed. Federico Ruiz (Madrid: Editorial de Espiritualidad, 1990), 336–38; and "San Juan de la Cruz: de hagiografía a la historia," in *Juan de la Cruz, espiritu de llama: estudios con occasion del cuarto centenario de su muerte (1591–1991)*, ed. Otger Steggink (Kampen, The Netherlands: Kok Paros, 1991), 7ff.

off his body, aromatic odors from his confessional, and levitations during prayer.[30] While these reports may or may not be historically factual, most of his life story is generally recognized as quite accurate.[31]

Juan de Yepes was born in a small Castilian town of Fontiveros in 1542. His father died while he was a child and left the family poor. Happily, he received a primary education in a school for the poor. Because of his impressive intellect, his further education was supported by a free Jesuit school. In 1563, when St. John was twenty-one, he entered the Carmelite Order and began formal studies in 1564 at the University of Salamanca. Even as a student his life was marked by significant asceticism and devotion to prayer.

After leaving the university and becoming ordained a priest he spent his twenty-three-year ministry working with the newly reformed Carmelite order—the Discalced Carmelites. There he was assigned a number of highly responsible positions, such as novice master, student master, prior, spiritual director, rector, provincial, and counselor to the vicar general of the order. Thus, in the man who would teach a highly individualistic journey of the soul to God, we find also an energized priest in active ministries.

To situate St. John's writings in the context of his life, one must see how he related to and was experienced by others. He was known for his humor, gentleness, and joy.[32] He enjoyed numerous friendships, and his letters are filled with warmth and compassion. He also had a deep love of the liturgy. This is important, since he appears to teach that all meditative or symbolic prayer ought to be left aside as one progresses contemplatively. His biography tells us, however, that he incorporated a sacramental piety with his contemplative agenda. He was also interested in art. His poetry is regarded as among the Spanish classics, and he spent time cultivating gardens, decorating chapels, and creating his own paintings and carvings.[33]

---

[30] See Gerald Brenan, *St. John of the Cross: His Life and Poetry* (London: Cambridge University Press, 1973), 34ff.

[31] The most authoritative, critical study of his life is still that by Crisógono de Jesús Sacramento, *San Juan de la Cruz, vida y obras* (Madrid: Biblioteca de Autores Cristianos, 1955). I am relying on the translated text by Kathleen Pond, *The Life of St. John of the Cross* (London: Longmans, 1958).

[32] Thomas Kane, *Gentleness in John of the Cross* (Oxford: SLG Press, 1985), 1. See also Olivier Leroy, "Quelques traits de Saint Jean de la Croix comme maître spirituelle," *Carmelus* 11 (1964): 7–8.

[33] See Frederico Ruiz and Crisógono de Jesús Sacramento, eds., *God Speaks in the Night: The Life, Times, and Teachings of St. John of the Cross* (Washington, DC: ICS Publications, 1991), 309–10.

Thus, an all-too literal interpretation of his works, especially those commending *leaving the world*, has to be reframed to allow for a much richer embrace of life and the world. Certainly, he was an austere and ascetical man, and he was unremittingly rigorous in his approach to the spiritual life. But he was also a gentle man, one who loved the world generously and enjoyed it liberally.[34]

St. John's Path to Union with God

The Carmelite community began as a group of monks who resided in small individual hermitages on Mount Carmel in the Holy Land. Throughout the history of Carmel, the original impulse for deep contemplative prayer has always remained a challenge and inspiration. St. John diagrammed a sketch of Mount Carmel as a metaphor for climbing the contemplative peak to the summit of union with God. What does the summit look like? St. John surrounded the summit with the terms "peace, joy, happiness, delight, wisdom, justice, fortitude, charity, [and] piety" where "glory means nothing to me" and "suffering means nothing to me," "only the honor and glory of God dwells on this mount."[35]

What are the possible ways to travel? One failed way in this diagram is to seek the "goods of the earth, possessions, joy, knowledge, consolation, [and] rest." Not these, he assures. A second failed way is to seek the "goods of heaven, glory, joy, knowledge, consolation, [and] rest." Likewise, not these. Regarding what these two ways seek, he writes, "Now that I least desire them, I have them all without desire." The only way to the summit, the "path of Mount Carmel the perfect spirit," is "nothing, nothing, nothing,

---

[34] For example, St. John refers to the *world* as the enemy of the soul and ugly compared to God (*Ascent* I.4.4). Instead of loving others, we seem to be told to withdraw our affection from everything and everyone so as to focus solely on God (*Ascent* II.6.4). And the body is often described as a prison from which we must detach ourselves (*Ascent* I.3.3; I.15.1; II.8.4). Much of this is hyperbole, but even if not all, this seemingly negative language needs to be put into perspective in light of his overall agenda.

[35] I am relying on two texts. Principally, I draw on John of the Cross, *The Collected Works of Saint John of the Cross*, revised, trans. Kieran Kavanaugh and Otilio Rodriguez (Washington, DC: ICS Publications, 1991). For checking on the primary source, I use San Juan de la Cruz, *Obras Completas: Edicion Critica* 14th ed., ed. Lucinio Ruano de la Iglesia (Mardrid: Biblioteca de Autores Cristianos, 1994). These collections include *The Sayings of Light and Love*, *The Ascent of Mount Carmel*, *The Dark Night*, *The Spiritual Canticle*, and *The Living Flame of Love*.

nothing, nothing, nothing, and even on the Mount nothing." At the base of his sketch he writes a series of axioms:

> *To reach satisfaction in all, desire satisfaction in nothing.*
> *To come to possess all, desire the possession of nothing.*
> *To arrive at being all, desire to be nothing.*
> *To come to enjoy what you have not, you must*
> *go by a way in which you enjoy not.*
> *To come to the knowledge you have not, you must*
> *go by a way in which you possess not.*
> *To come to be what you are not, you must go*
> *by a way in which you are not.*
> *When you delay in something, you cease to rush toward the all.*
> *To go from the all to the all, you must deny yourself of all in all.*
> *And when you come to the possession of the all, you*
> *must possess it without wanting anything.*
> *In this nakedness, the spirit finds its quietude and rest,*
> *For in coveting nothing, nothing tires it by pulling it up,*
> *and nothing opposes it by pushing it down,*
> *because it is in the center of its humility.*[36]

Let us begin with several premises crucial to understanding St. John's path.[37] The first is that the psyche—he will call it the *soul*—is naturally designed to negotiate the created world. To know something or be in relationship with something is to know it as another object. The second is that God is not an object among other objects of the universe. Rather, God, as the Transcendent Absolute, the Absolute Mystery, cannot be known *naturally*. This does not mean that God cannot be experienced in the context of the world, but this would be God mediated through our psyche as it engages the world. God cannot be known *as God* through conceptualizations, as we can only conceptualize objects in the created world. St. John will divide the soul into *sensory faculties*, knowing through the senses, and *spiritual faculties*, knowing through intellect, memory, and will. These latter three ways of knowing correspond to the theological virtues of faith, hope, and love.

---

[36] John of the Cross, *Collected Works*, 111.

[37] A running dictum that St. John employs is that God draws each soul uniquely. Thus, the spiritual path, even as he outlines it in a linear and progressive way, is understood ultimately as unique in each individual (*Dark Night* I.14.4–6). See also *Ascent* II.17.2; III.39.1; *Dark Night* I.2.6; *Living Flame* 3.59.

The final premise is that the human soul (psyche) is extraordinarily narcissistic. In many ways, things matter only because they matter *to me*, that is, only as they affect *me*. Just as we saw in the teachings of the Buddha, I like something because it gratifies *me*; I dislike something because it is afflictive to *me*. I become attached to gratifications, even authentically spiritual ones. And I run from my aversions. So, in order to attain union with this Absolute Mystery, I will have to travel a path that undermines my attachments, my narcissism, my reactivity. And I will have to engage God in the darkness of mystery. For St. John, this engagement renounces searching for and clinging to satisfactions and desires, and goes the way we know not. The paradox, as he makes clear, is that in doing so one actually finds every authentic satisfaction without seeking it.

Active and Passive Night of the Senses

In the Prologue of *The Ascent of Mount Carmel*, St. John says that he wrote the book to alert souls to what may be happening to them as God draws them into a deep contemplative experience. He sought to keep them from regressing and to encourage them to embrace the kinds of abandonment into which God is inviting them.[38] He states that his teaching is only to those "whom God favors by putting on the path leading to this mount [of union] . . . Because they are already detached to a great extent from the temporal things of the world, they will more easily grasp this doctrine on nakedness of spirit."[39] He calls these souls *beginners* or *novices* (*principiantes*) as in those beginning to enter the mystical life. Beginners truly love and know God, but they only know God in a mediated way, a *natural* way. He also saw them as unconsciously focused on the gratification of the self, where personal satisfaction is the central motivating force in their piety.[40] Compared to mystical knowledge of God, what they enjoy of the divine is like eating "morsels" from God's table, or eating the "rind" of the fruit instead of the heart of the fruit itself.[41] In order to truly free them for deeper contemplation, he calls for an *active night of the senses*, one in which they withdraw from the comforts and attachments they generally rely on.

---

38 *Ascent* Pro.3–7.

39 *Ascent* Pro.9.

40 *Dark Night* I.6.6.

41 *Ascent* II.14.4; II.16.11; II.17.5.

Withdrawing from normal comforts primarily refers to "disordered appetites," as he explains in chapter 3 of book 1 in *The Ascent*. But this is not entirely the case. He also challenges the reader to deep asceticism.

> *Endeavor to be inclined always:*
> *Not to the easiest, but to the most difficult;*
> *Not to the most delightful, but to the most distasteful;*
> *Not to the most gratifying, but to the less pleasant;*
> *Not to what means rest for you, but to hard work;*
> *Not to the consoling, but to the unconsoling;*
> *Not to the most, but to the least;*
> *Not to the highest and most precious, but to the lowest and most despised;*
> *Not to wanting something, but to wanting nothing. . . .*
> *Desire to enter into complete nakedness, emptiness, and poverty in everything in the world.*[42]

So far in their spiritual lives God had been self-communicating to them in a "sensory" or mediated way. They must prepare themselves for deeper contemplation. Ultimately, it is God who must draw them into deep contemplation, or the *passive night of the senses*. In *The Ascent* he describes signs that this is happening: (1) one cannot make discursive meditation or receive the satisfaction it once provided, (2) one lacks the desire to fix the imagination on anything, and (3) one desires to stay in simple loving awareness of God without particular considerations.[43]

The passive night of the senses is a process whereby God brings *sensible* dryness to the soul and begins to communicate to it more directly. As one progresses through this passive night, one experiences increasing awareness of God's general loving presence.[44] The passive night of the senses may seem dry to the *sensory* part of the soul, but it is also energizing to the *spiritual* part.[45]

---

[42] *Ascent* I.13.6. This is not asceticism for asceticism's sake. Clearly, it is for the primary purpose of shaking off the stranglehold that our attachments have (see also *Ascent* I.4.1; II.7.7). I see a secondary purpose here. Such a minimization of pleasurable experience tends to center the soul for contemplative prayer. Sensory overload, even if one is detached, is very disturbing to deep contemplation. See Alain Cugno, *St. John of the Cross: Reflections on Mystical Experiences*, trans. Barbara Wall (New York: Seabury, 1982), 50–71.

[43] *Ascent* II.13.2–4. In *Dark Night* he also offers a slightly different set of signs, where the soul experienced profound dryness and deep solicitude toward God (*Dark Night* I.9.4). The difference is whether the soul initially recognizes the subtle presence of God in contemplation or not.

[44] *Ascent* II.13.2–4; *Dark Night* I.9.2–8.

[45] *Dark Night* I.8.2; I.9.4–6.

This dark night brings one from the stage of *beginners* to that of *proficients* (*aprovechados*), traditionally described as the "illuminative way." The soul lives many years as a proficient, becoming increasingly liberated. A proficient regularly finds within serene, loving communication with God that is quite direct and typically delightful.[46] Proficients become increasingly attuned to a whole realm of the spiritual life that had formerly been blocked. Progressively, what had initially been a vague awareness of God in contemplation continues to intensify, occasionally even into powerful experiences of absorption in God's love. Now that the proficients are far less motivated by sensory and religious gratifications, they become free to live selflessly for God and others. Their attachments, which they once believed provided emotional support and security, are now recognized for what they are: the cause of restlessness, anxiety, and insecurity of spirit. The proficient now knows a deep freedom of the soul.

Active and Passive Night of the Spirit

Recall the spiritual faculties of intellect, memory, and will. Like the sensory faculties, they are limited in and of themselves to their natural operations in the created world. But, unlike the sensory faculties, they have the capacity to know God directly in an infused or supernatural way. For the many years when souls are proficients, they have been engaging God in a nonconceptual way. We have ideas of who God is and how God works. Our memory both aids us in how we expect God to work, based on our past experience, and who we are, our identity. Further we can only *naturally* will toward what we understand. Proficients strive to let go of all of this, particularly in contemplative prayer. The will is active in averting from one's attachments, and the soul continues to strive to desire what God desires. In both intellect and memory, the soul practices a kind of radical emptiness and availability to God. There can be no self-interest, and indeed the *self* that one thinks one is has to be undermined. Here God is an absolute mystery, the soul's core is an absolute mystery, and direct encounter with God will have to be shrouded in absolute mystery. Cultivating this "denuding" of self unto God is the active night of the spirit.

The *passive night of the spirit* represents what God does to such prepared souls; that is, God empties the soul of any self-identity and purges it fully. This is the transition period from being a proficient to entering into full union

---

[46] *Dark Night* II.1.1.

(which St. John calls the *perfect*)—this is the "high state of perfect union with God."[47] Here God personally empties the spiritual faculties. St. John writes,

> It [the passive night of the spirit] puts the sensory and spiritual appetites to sleep, deadens them, and deprives them of the ability to find pleasure in anything. It binds the imagination and impedes it from doing any good discursive work. It makes the memory cease, the intellect becomes dark and unable to understand anything, and hence it causes the will also to become arid and constrained, and all the faculties empty and useless.[48]

The dark night of the spirit is the most intense and difficult period of the spiritual journey. God literally strips the soul and undermines any of its *natural* moorings; this process can take years.[49] He compares any former experiences of detachment as mere pruning compared to what is now a ripping out of those attachments by the roots. St. John's advice is to continue to abandon the *natural* self in faith, hope, and love. In the dark night of the spirit, God sometimes communicates so powerfully that these experiences can be difficult to take. God, who is love, is not the cause of the pain exactly; rather it is one's imperfections being purified that make the soul suffer. Not all experiences of the night of the spirit are challenging. Even before the full state of union one may have profound, but not overwhelming, experiences of God. At other times, however, experiencing this divine love is not so subtle. St. John uses the image of an assailing arrow or dart afire with the love of the Holy Spirit. When the soul is pierced with that dart, the flame of love gushes forth suddenly and overwhelmingly; the entire universe becomes a sea of love.[50]

Union

Union with God, which St. John also refers to as *spiritual marriage*, is nothing less than the divinization of the soul through participation in the divine life. His dictum, "love produces equality and likeness,"[51] comes to fruition. The soul, he says, is transformed into the Beloved; it is a total

---

47 *Living Flame* 2.27: *alto estado de perfección de unión de Dios.*

48 *Dark Night* II.16.1.

49 *Dark Night* II.7.4.

50 *Living Flame* 2.8.

51 *Ascent* I.5.1.

possession of God who totally possesses the soul.[52] The quality of transformation that St. John describes can hardly know a superlative. He says that all things of both God and the soul become one. In terms of natures, the divine remains divine and the human remains human. But by participation in the divine life, the soul is made divine *relationally*.[53] He offers images that are particularly telling. In terms of fire, for example, he says that the flames of love between God and the soul are now a single flame, indistinguishable from each other; it is the soul's splendor and glorification.[54]

A second description is in the form of a song verse that he imagines God singing to the soul: "I am yours and for you and delighted to be what I am so as to be yours and give myself to you." He frames this as the absolute divine humility, that it pleases God to make the soul his equal by this "exchange of selves."[55]

What does the soul know of God now? In one sense, the soul knows everything; it sees and knows God *as* God. But it knows this in a supernatural way and cannot convey what it knows to the natural operations of the intellect. Thus, knowledge of God remains a *dark wisdom*, and all that is communicated to the soul continues to dwell in mystery.[56]

Buddhaghosa and John of the Cross Compared

One way to compare the message of these two masters could be to recognize obvious doctrinal differences. Buddhaghosa, like the Buddha, appears to have no room for or little interest in a belief in God. There is no grace, and the individual is an island unto herself. While St. John surely believes in an eternal soul, we find nonself as the discovered truth in Theravada Buddhism. The philosophical *principle of noncontradiction* tells us that one cannot hold two premises that are either directly opposed or allow no conceptual room for each other. Either there is God or there is not God, either there is a self or there is not a self. These two worldviews seem decidedly incommensurate. Such a comparative framing does not seem particularly fruitful, though it does clarify that we are dealing with very different spiritual paradigms.

Another possible way of comparing them might lead us to challenge that these conceptual differences are not important or meaningful. Both

[52] *Spiritual Canticle* 22.3; *Living Flame* 3.6; 3.24–25; 4.14.

[53] *Living Flame* 2.33–34.

[54] *Living Flame* 3.10.

[55] *Living Flame* 3.6.

[56] *Ascent* II.26.3–8.

are paths to liberation, and perhaps these are just two different lenses in seeing the same thing. Or perhaps it is simply not important that one view is theistic, for example, and the other is not. And yet, they certainly seem important to both Buddhaghosa and John of the Cross. So, to ignore such differences under some cloak of irrelevance strikes me as odd. They don't matter? Recognizing that we are dealing with very different anthropologies and metaphysical claims, how might we set a different course?

Who and What Are We?

Given that the assumptions and paths hold very different claims, what is striking is that both Buddhaghosa and St. John see the person in many of the same ways. Both recognize the will as the great concern, for it is constantly craving. For St. John, the will is disordered due to original sin. For Buddhaghosa, the disordered will is caused by ignorance, and craving due to our ignorance produces karma formations that themselves condition future grasping. Yet, for both, the unreformed mind is a reactive one, assessing experience on whether it is pleasant or not. On the most base level, we crave and cling to pleasing experiences. We make attachments. Our relationship to afflictive experiences has its own kind of attachment; we are attached to the experience. Something bad is happening to *me*, and *I* do not want it. Both spiritual masters realize that attachments to what pleases and to what afflicts is a prison that arrests any deep spiritual progress.

In both spiritual agendas, narcissism is a core problem. Both describe how unwittingly the *self* makes it the center of all things. St. John argues that God is the true center, and for Buddhaghosa there seemingly is no center. None of that really matters for the unreformed will. The unpurified psyche sees all things as ultimately about oneself. While the Buddhist might say that there is nonself, and while the Christian might say that "Jesus is Lord," the unpurified soul experiences all things as though the self and its experience are central. On deep levels of the unpurified Christian soul, God is loved because God does good things for the soul. It is as though God is a satellite revolving around one's own narcissism. And until one is freed from that narcissism, "Jesus is Lord" is more a slogan than a reality.

We tend to think of our attachments as gratifying or comforting, but are they really? Both masters recognize that craving undermines the soul. Instead of bringing actual comfort, they agitate the soul and cloud its vision. This is the case with all inordinate desires: When/how will I get well fed? When/

how will I be comforted? When/how will I be recognized and praised? When/how will I get what's coming to *me*? Both masters also recognize that nothing we experience can actually satisfy in any sustained way. We are bottomless pits of gratification. And the more we rely on these superficial comforts, the deeper we get ingrained in our delusions. This is why both recommend determined asceticism. As we saw above, asceticism is not a value in itself, but it does lower the fever, and surprisingly it allows more mental and emotional energy to come to the fore. Asceticism, for them, is neither body-denying nor world-denying. Both Buddhaghosa and St. John see the opposite: it frees the body and mind to engage life more fully.

On a conceptual level, the anthropologies of Buddhaghosa and St. John are far apart. Buddhaghosa recognizes the self as an impermanent, impersonal collection of aggregates, and experiencing this utterly is how one becomes liberated. All spiritual practices are ultimately to achieve this end. For St. John, the various faculties of the soul as well as the life of the body constitute a substantial human being. This soul is called to love and be united to God completely. On a level of practice, however, they share much of the same agenda: deconstruction of what and who you think you are. Buddhaghosa reflects the Buddha's message that denies both eternalism and nihilism: there is not an eternal soul and there is not nothing after Final-Nirvana. To this paradox, we are instructed to see all our experience as not the self. I do not see this as much different from the aims of St. John's deconstruction project. The way is "nothing, nothing, nothing, nothing, nothing, nothing, and even on the Mount nothing." If there is a final identity in union with God it is also a paradox, this of recognizing self as both nothing and at the same time identical with God (in some sense). The only way to realize this paradox is to undermine everything we thought was our self. Even in union with God there is a paradoxical emptiness.

In perhaps his most mature book, *New Seeds of Contemplation*, the modern mystic Thomas Merton describes the paradox. Collectively, the following medley of citations addresses this mystery:

> The secret of my full identity is hidden in God. . . . To say that I am made in the image of God is to say that love is the reason for my existence, for God is love. Love is my true identity. Selflessness is my true self. Love is my true character, Love is my name. . . . [One] lives in emptiness and freedom, as if one had no longer a limited and exclusive *self* that distinguished oneself from God and other people. . . . What happens is that the separate identity that is *you* apparently disappears and nothing seems to be left but a pure freedom indistinguishable

> from infinite Freedom, love identified with Love. . . . God is the *I* who acts there. God is the one Who loves and knows and rejoices.[57]

Where is the distinct *I* in all of this? For St. John, the full realization of the self is a kind of paschal death to the self, something that can only come from grace by the passive night of the spirit. In a very real way, we are utterly emptied of the self. Both traditions posit something of selfless selves.

Nirvana and Union with God

The divinization St. John writes about is consonant with broad Christian assumptions, particularly highlighted in the Orthodox and Roman Catholic traditions. Consider, for example, the *Catechism of the Catholic Church*, where we read, "By participation of the Spirit, we become communicants in the divine nature. . . . For this reason, those in whom the spirit dwells are divinized. . . . The purpose of the Incarnation is that humanity might become divine. . . . Grace makes us partakers of the divine nature. . . . Grace deifies us."[58] In a similar manner, Buddhaghosa frames Nirvana in a way broadly agreed upon in Theravada Buddhism. These are not idiosyncratic voices of their traditions, but representative voices. Nirvana (and, by extension, Final-Nirvana) represents the absolute, transcendent principle and goal. There is nothing higher or better. In a similar manner, union with God and the divinization of the soul collectively represent the absolute, transcendent goal. What ought one to make of the differences between the *summum bonum* of Nirvana and that of Mystical Union with God?

One of the more striking similarities in achieving these goals is that those who do achieve either of them share many of the same transformative traits. As we have seen, Buddhaghosa thinks Nirvana is a reality and not simply a mode of existence. It is also ineffable and beyond conceptualization. For the most part, he describes Nirvana not positively but negatively. It is the removal of those qualities, such as greed, hatred, and delusion that once ravaged the mind. Nirvana includes the state of existence without such qualities. One exists in Nirvana with perfect purity of mind and heart. If there are two concepts that best depict such purity, they are peace and freedom. With all clinging gone, nothing disturbs the mind. With no more

---

[57] Thomas Merton, *New Seeds of Contemplation* (New York: New Direction, 1961), 33, 60, 210, 283, 286–87 (with exclusive language adjusted).

[58] See *Catechism of the Catholic Church*, rev. (New York: Doubleday, 1995), nos. 1988, 1996–99.

grasping, the arhat lives in absolute freedom. Recall that the liberated mind is free from *volitions*. This does not mean that the arhat does not intend things, but rather that there is no grasping or craving in those intentions. It is as though wisdom itself is working through the arhat's mind. She simply acts compassionately, spiritually and morally skillfully, wisely, perfectly. And she does this because all impediments to compassion and wisdom are completely removed.

One could say that this same dynamic is found in St. John's depiction of union with God. The soul becomes one with God through love. She is in perfect harmony with God, with herself, and with the created world. With no sense of a self to advance or defend, the soul in union lives in perfect peace. Just as Buddhaghosa understood an arhat living in perfect wisdom, so now the soul in union lives in and through God. It is as though the Holy Spirit is performing the saint's actions personally.

> What the soul calls death is all that goes to make up the old self. . . . In this new life that the soul lives . . . all the inclinations and activity of the appetites and faculties . . . become divine. . . . The intellect becomes divine, because through its union with God's intellect both become one. And the will . . . is now changed into the life of divine love. . . . By means of this union God's will and the soul's will are now one.[59]

This does not, of course, mean that the person in union no longer acts as an actual agent and is somehow God's automaton. Rather, the soul acts in and through her union with God. She loves with God. There is now perfect synergy between the soul and God.[60]

Are Nirvana and union with God fundamentally the same? Two particularly important proponents of versions of universal faith, Wilfred Cantwell Smith and John Hick argue decidedly *yes*. As we saw briefly in chapter 1, pluralists—Smith and Hick are certainly these—strive to see all or most religions doing fundamentally the same thing or about the same project. Smith writes, "My submission would be this: faith differs in form, but not in kind."[61] Smith particularly highlights similarities in transformation. Adherents are "saved from nihilism, from alienation, anomie, despair; from the bleak despondency of meaninglessness. Saved from unfreedom; from being the victim of one's own whims within, or pressures without; saved

---

[59] *Living Flame*, 2.33–34.

[60] *Ascent* III.20.2–3.

[61] Wilfred Cantwell Smith, *Towards a World Theology: Faith and the Comparative History of Religion* (Philadelphia: Westminster Press, 1981), 168.

from being merely an organism reacting to its environment."[62] Of course, such salvation takes on the particular qualities of one's given religion: "The Muslim has been saved by Islamic faith; the Buddhist by Buddhist faith, the Jew by Jewish."[63] So there are patterns, flavors, styles, but the same kind of salvation project. Surely, we see evidence of this in our comparison between Nirvana and union with God.

John Hick certainly agrees. Religious traditions are indeed different and so religious experiences will be different, some impersonal and some personal, all associated with how religious practices form the psyche and avail oneself to the Absolute:

> People formed by different religious traditions become aware of the Transcendent in significantly different ways. . . . The various God-figures and the various non-personal foci of religious meditation are, according to our big picture, different transformations of the impact upon us of the ultimately Real. But that reality, in itself beyond the range of conscious human experience, does not fit into the systems of concepts in terms of which we are able to think.[64]

This *Real* could be understood interpersonally: "If our tradition has conditioned us to think of the Transcendent in personal terms, and to practice I-Thou prayer and worship, we shall be conscious of a divine presence. . . . But if, on the other hand, our tradition has taught us to think of the Ultimate in non-personal terms and to practice a non-I-Thou type of meditation, our religious awareness will take one of the quite different forms described in eastern mystical literature."[65] In comparing Western and Eastern metaphysics, Hick argues, "Both conceptions are speculations in which we impose our human categories on the unknown."[66]

It would be hard to imagine Buddhaghosa and John of the Cross agreeing here. Nirvana is Nirvana; it is not a spiritual union with the divine. Union with God is radically personal, and the love and presence of God are palpable and indeed the agent of transformation; it is certainly not merely the cessation of karma formations. St. John describes union in a dynamically relational way. Union—and indeed the entire path—involves knowing and

---

[62] Ibid.

[63] Ibid.

[64] John Hick, *The Fifth Dimension: An Exploration of the Spiritual Realm* (London: Oneworld, 1999), 46.

[65] Ibid., 47.

[66] Ibid., 227.

loving God more directly and intimately. Union is relational. True, this is not a relationship like other relationships. A *personal relationship with God* is language by analogy. God is Absolute Mystery and Being itself, not another being among other beings in the universe. Still, union is indeed *personal*. It is a true, loving communion, an intimate knowledge of and sharing between divine lover and beloved, a possession of each other in love. This loving union or sharing of selves is not reflected in any way by the descriptions of Nirvana. While it is indescribable, it is utterly impersonal. One does not have a *relationship* with Nirvana. To suggest a real personal encounter is to sabotage the very philosophical and religious foundations through which a nirvanic experience is interpreted.

As we saw in chapter 1, Mark Heim has criticized both Smith and Hick in their pluralistic assumptions. It is this *force-fitting* that fails to take religions, their representatives, and their intrinsically unique experiences seriously. What pluralists fail to do, he argues, is look at the extremely radically different ways religions pose themselves. He writes, "What in my view is incoherent is any supposition of a neutral 'meta-theory' of judgments made from above the religious rather than among them."[67] In challenging Hick, he argues Hick's "thesis is distinctly a meta-theory of religion, like those derived from Freud and Marx. Its plausibility depends on the claim to transcend the frame of reference of the religions, to speak not from among them but above them."[68] Heim has a point. Nirvana simply does not seem to look like union with God.

On the other hand, are his criticisms justified? Heim again: "Hick's thesis rests on two sweeping assumptions, each questionable: a metaphysical dogma that there can be but one religious object, and a soteriological dogma that there can be but one religious end. Together they lead to conclusions which are even shakier."[69] Heim's insistence on the uniqueness of various religions is surely valid. It could be, however, that he overshoots his critique. What is striking, particularly with regard to John Hick, is that Hick *does* distinguish differences among religions, their unique paths and unique experiences.[70] Hick indeed holds the two sweeping dogmas that Heim claims him to have. And yet, I find them rather reasonable. The first is the most central: there is only one Absolute, Transcendent Reality. Why wouldn't it

---

[67] S. Mark Heim, *Salvations: Truth and Difference in Religion* (Maryknoll, NY: Orbis Books, 1995), 4.

[68] Ibid., 30.

[69] Ibid., 23.

[70] See Hick's *Fifth Dimension* and *An Interpretation of Religion: Human Responses to the Transcendent*, 2nd ed. (New Haven, CT: Yale University Press, 2004).

be reasonable to argue that various paths, if they be authentically religious, would be engaged in that one Reality? And if that is true—one Absolute by definition of *Absolute*—then the being drawn into or radically aligned to that Absolute would be the most authentic religious end.

Heim, who as a Christian believes that God is Trinity, argues for allowing different religious ends. "I want to point out that the 'finality of Christ' and the 'independent validity of other ways' are not mutually exclusive. One need not be given up for the sake of the other unless we insist there can only be one effective religious goal. One set of ways may be valid for a given goal, and thus final for that end, while different ways are valid for other ends."[71] And yet Heim cannot seem to shake that personal union with God is in fact the ultimate and singular human *summum bonum* for all humanity. Heim writes,

> The actual ends that various religious traditions offer as alternative human fulfillments diverge because they realize different relations with God. It is God's reality as Trinity that generates the multiplicity of dimensions that allow for that variety of relations. God's threefoldness means that salvation necessarily is a characteristic communion in diversity. It also permits human responses to God to limit themselves within the terms of one dimension. Trinity requires that salvation be communion. It makes possible, but not necessary, the realization of religious ends other than [Christian] salvation. Humans can concentrate their response to the divine in a particular dimension of the divine life, and if this channel of relation is maintained in isolation from others it can lead to a distinct religious end.[72]

Are these other modes of spiritual realizations deficient? He would say *yes and no*. Yes, they are deficient, since the fullest expression of salvation is a radical personal union with the Trinity. But do all saved Christians attain this? It appears not. In heaven, we encounter what we are prepared to encounter and perhaps only to the depth we are prepared to encounter it. As Heim notes, "Each person retains a unique profile with God and relation to others. . . . Indeed, this variety is an occasion for continual delight."[73] In this sense, Buddhist Nirvana or other non-Christian religious ends are "*higher up and further in* in specific ways that no Christian

---

[71] Heim, *Salvations*, 3.

[72] S. Mark Heim, *The Depth of Riches: A Trinitarian Theology of Religious Ends* (Grand Rapids: Eerdmans, 2001), 280–81.

[73] Ibid., 281.

can approximate . . . In heaven, people perceive that there are others in some respects better than they, who have better knowledge of some (or all) aspects of God. They can see this also in those attaining other religious ends. Within the communion of salvation, they rejoice in these differences and are nourished by them."[74]

What we see here is that Heim actually embraces Hick's two dogmas (one Absolute, one salvation). The difference is that Heim imagines heaven as a limited experience of the Absolute, limited by what each religious seeker prepares herself for within the context of her religion. So, Nirvana *is* union with God for Heim; it is the experience of "a feature of the inner-trinitarian relations of the divine persons."[75] "God is not static," he argues, as there is an "exchange among the divine persons." What the Buddhist experiences and unites to is the "flux itself . . . contact with the impersonality of the divine."[76]

I have wrestled with these questions for decades. Is Nirvana a limited kind of salvation project? Is Nirvana a *form* of union with God? Is God both personal and impersonal and beyond these categories such that both Nirvana and union with God amount to the same thing? And what ought one to make of Heim's versions of salvation, all to be understood as various experiences of the Trinity? I simply do not know. But I would like to offer two possibilities for future investigations, both coming from Lynn de Silva. The first alignment addresses Nirvana and the Kingdom of God. He writes,

> Whatever *Nibbana* [Nirvana] means, at least it means two things: the extinction of desire (which includes all defilements) and the experience of well-being, the latter being the outcome of the former. . . . Self-negation is an essential aspect of this experience. This does not mean annihilation of the self but an experience in which the notion of "I," "me," and "mine," of separate individuality disappears. Since "self" is at the heart of man's problem, the "self" must be conquered if the goal is to be realized. The egocentric life of craving and self-interest must be put to an end by the deliberate denying of the self.[77]

De Silva sees both in the Gospels and in the Christian mystical tradition this call to self-emptying as a radical one, such as we have seen in John of the

---

[74] Ibid., 284.

[75] Ibid., 186.

[76] Ibid., 186–87.

[77] Lynn de Silva, *The Problem of the Self in Buddhism and Christianity* (London: Macmillan Press, 1979), 125.

Cross. "The experience of self-negation is a state . . . when nothing is left but Divine Reality. In this I-Thou relationship one loses oneself completely, and in losing oneself one finds oneself. This state . . . reaches its ultimate state in the Kingdom of God."[78] He concludes, "In the idea of the Kingdom of God, I suggest, we have an answer to the Buddhist quest for self-negation as well as a form of self-fulfillment, without one contradicting the other."[79]

How might the role of love, so central to Christian salvation and seemingly so marginal in descriptions of Buddhism, find its place in such a comparison? De Silva again:

> Because love on the one hand implies the total surrender of self (centrifugal love), in the final state exclusive individuality will be completely negated. Self-contained, self-conscious individuality disappears. Centrifugal love therefore leads to the extinction of the self—the dying-out of separate individuality. We could therefore speak of this goal as *Nirvana*. In the end we cease completely to be individuals. In love, *tanha* (craving) and the notion of I-ness which is at the basis of *tanha* are conquered. . . . On the other hand, to speak of total self-negation would amount to nihilism (*uccheda ditthi*). However, centripetal love overcomes this contradiction. . . . Love is neither union nor absorption, but communion. In communion, love integrates being with being and being with Being. There is a perfect integration of the self with the eternal in which individuality disappears.[80]

De Silva's second possibility is to imagine possibilities between Nirvana and God. He points to a famous passage where the Buddha was expounding on Nirvana:

> *There is, bhikkhus, a not-born, a not-brought-to-being, a not-made, a not-conditioned. If, Bhikkhus, there were no not-born, not-brought-to-being, not-made, not-conditioned, no escape would be discerned from what is born, brought-to-being, made, conditioned. But since there is a not-born, a not-brought-to-being, a not-made, a not-conditioned, therefore an escape is discerned from what is born, brought-to-being, made, conditioned.*[81]

---

78 Ibid., 129.

79 Ibid., 130.

80 Ibid., 135.

81 *Udana* 8.3. I am using *The Udana and the Itivuttaka: Two Classics from the Pali Canon*, trans. John Ireland (Kandy, Sri Lanka: Buddhist Publication Society, 1997).

From this canonical passage de Silva argues,

> The implication underlying this passage is that the Unconditioned Reality is indispensable if man is to escape the conditioned. . . . If man is absolutely *anatta* [nonself] the hypothesis of the Unconditioned or some such other hypothesis becomes absolutely necessary if the error of nihilism (*ucchedaditthi*) is to be avoided. Apart from the Unconditioned Reality there can be no emancipation for that which is conditioned. . . . Nagarjuna, making a specific reference to this Udana passage, emphatically states that without the acceptance of the Ultimate Reality (*Paramartha*) there can be no deliverance (*Nirvana*) from conditioned existence. . . . It is clear that Nagarjuna makes a distinction between the Paramartha and Nirvana. According to him the attainment to the state of Nirvana is possible because there is an Ultimate Reality (*Paramartha*). *Nirvana* is an experience related to the Absolute and is not the absolute in itself.[82]

Here, we may have come full circle back to Heim's insights, including that Nirvana is different from full union with God, but implies and is related to it.

Buddhist Meditations for Christians

Vipassana (Insight) Practices

Theravada Buddhist practices have everything to do with the attainment of Nirvana, something that is simply not the agenda of Christians, or at least those seeking St. John's union with God. Could they, however, actually assist the Christian alongside the teachings of St. John of the Cross? Buddhism recognizes that all phenomenal reality is conditioned and relative. Buddhaghosa's philosophy teaches this, and insight (*vipassana*) practices clarify it by direct experience. This insight corresponds profoundly with St. John's spirituality. Of course, for him the created universe is valuable, and one certainly would not seek the kind of repulsion described by the Buddha. But the world is valuable for St. John only insofar as it is related to God as source and end of all meaning. His spirituality intends to break the aspirant from attributing any ultimate value to anything but the glory of God. The way is "nothing, nothing, nothing, nothing, nothing, nothing, and on the Mount nothing." The active night of the senses renounces all gratifications that are

[82] Lynn De Silva, *The Problem of the Self*, 141.

not aligned to God's glory and the active night of the spirit directly intends to deconstruct any ideas of both self and God.

The practice of *vipassana* meditation has the ability to bring this insight to decisive clarity, one that even a *proficient* would not have before union. *Vipassana* meditation is a comprehensive set of meditation techniques that demonstrate by direct experience the relativity of one's experience. *Vipassana* profoundly aligns with the agenda of the active nights of the senses and spirit.

In the first book of *The Dark Night*, St. John takes the typical seven capital sins and spiritualizes them regarding the *beginner*. Thus, for example, greed is understood as craving for comforting spiritual experiences, and anger has to do with impatience with one's own spiritual progress. Things can get pretty subtle, and attachments can seem like authentic religious interests. Through *vipassana* practice, one comes to increasingly subtle awareness of the impermanence of all reality. Here, the inclinations of an unreformed soul are substantially reduced. One sees with great clarity the arising and dissolution of all thoughts, both virtuous and sinful. There is nothing to cling to here. Further, one sees not only the ever-changing nature of desire but also the illusory value of the objects of desire. Through *vipassana* practice, one loses one's attachments to the very things that keep us from being free and available to God. We literally see these thoughts with utter clarity, as we watch them arise and dissipate.

In modern Christian literature, one regularly comes across the terms *false self* and *true self*. We are called to die to our false self or break the illusion of our false self so that the true self might emerge. As we saw above, St. John describes this as a real crucifixion of the *false* self. The narcissism of the *old man* has to die so that the transformed divinized self can emerge. What we imagined to be ourselves, conditioned by our experience, our roles, our various identities, are all illusions to the truth of the mystery of the self, found only in the mystery of the divine. As we have seen, even in union with God there is no self-identification or objectification. Buddhist insight practices consistently undermine that objectified self, which St. John demands needs to be negated.

Samadhi (Concentration) Practices

Buddhist concentration practices could also assist the Christian life. As we saw, Buddhist *samadhi* practices are intended to strengthen the mind and infuse it with skillful ideals. This is not Christian contemplation, but means of skillfully manipulating the mind to healthy ends. Consider, for example, the divine-abiding meditations. We saw that Buddhaghosa recommended these sets of meditations in order to create a wholesome, balanced engagement with the world. Again, they are lovingkindness, compassion, sympathetic joy, and equanimity. One might imagine that these would be an impediment to St. John's agenda. He argued that, once the *beginner* is taken into the contemplative life by God's grace, then she ought to let go of discursive prayer. I would argue that these would not be an impediment. They provide a kind of beautifully engaged way of being that is also nonattached. Take lovingkindness, for example: one imaginatively extends the *sign* lovingkindness to a universal level. Absorbed in lovingkindness for all beings, one then remains in an absorbed state of lovingkindness. This lovingkindness then is complemented by compassion, which attends to the suffering of the world and its hoped-for dissipation, culminating with an absorbed mind in compassion. Then, taking joy in the flourishing of others not only keeps one from comparing oneself to others but infuses the mind with real happiness for others' sake. And finally, equanimity balances everything, so that one remains unattached and free from any kind of controlling quality of the mind. The mind infused thereby is nonjudgmental and accepting of reality as it is.

One could even utilize the meditative technique along the lines of Christian beliefs. For example, one might take a Christian concept of the universal presence of Christ's love, and utilize the same strategy as we saw in the divine-abidings meditations. One could begin with the realization of Christ within, extending that realization progressively and universally. The meditation would be wholly Christian and sufficiently nondiscursive so as to avoid St. John's warnings about the liabilities of discursive prayer.

Because this is a concentration exercise, it would not be properly Christian contemplative prayer. On the other hand, it would be a way to infuse a Christian truth deeply into the consciousness. And it would create, on a highly subtle level, a deep sense of universal love and gratitude.[83] One could even imagine this practice as helping the Christian cultivate nonattachment, since the soul would visualize the love of Christ as divinely gratuitous and universal. There is no pride when the soul believes herself existing only by grace and living in the same love as the rest of the universe. The soul sees that it drinks from the same gratuitous well as all other beings.

---

[83] On the widespread value of divine-abiding meditations, see Claudia Eppert, "Heart-Mind Literacy: Compassionate Imagining and the Four Brahmaviharas," *Paideusis* 19, no. 1 (2010): 17–28.

Chapter 4

Nagarjuna and the Christian *Via Negativa*

From Mahasanghika to Nagarjuna

No religion stays static, and Buddhism surely never did. We have already seen developments in what became known as the Theravada tradition in the works of Buddhaghosa. Even canonical texts, which claimed absolute fidelity to the Buddha's teachings, show doctrinal developments. On the one hand, followers of the Buddha memorized his teachings and ultimately created a canon (or canons). They believed these to be faithful to the Buddha's original teachings. On the other hand, some of the sutras demonstrate a decidedly polished form that addressed later controversies. That is to say, even the earliest canons were products of developments. Buddhists also preserved and later developed codes for monasticism in canonical works called the *Vinaya*. A further development was the *Abhidharma*, which represents compilations of Buddhist philosophy and psychology. Here we find a robust attempt to analyze and systematize psychological and spiritual phenomena. These works became codified and canonized between the third century BCE and the third century CE.

Buddhaghosa's *Vissuddhimagga* is a noncanonical form of abhidharma. As we saw, he created a systematic way to understand and practice virtue, concentration, and insight so as to attain Nirvana. He also provided a detailed analysis of how one ought to interpret experience. He stipulates, for example, twenty-four classifications of the materiality aggregate, fifty-two concomitants of consciousness, eighty-nine types of consciousness, and so on. Knowing what one is experiencing and how to interpret it dominates the Theravada path to Nirvana. The great Buddhologist Edward Conze describes the essence of this path as "*mystically tinged rationalism*."[1]

A new form of Buddhism became increasingly distant from the Theravada school. Initially, Buddhist elders convened a council shortly after the Buddha's Pari-Nirvana in order to settle on the Buddha's teaching. This was in Rajagriha. The second council in Vaishali (c. 386 BCE) was convened to reconcile differences in monastic discipline. This was principally an exchange between the Sthavira school and the Mahasanghika school. The third council became far more decisive in Buddhists taking distinctive positions that would eventually send schools of Buddhism into decidedly different directions. This was in Pataliputra (c. 250 BCE). How the Mahasanghikas developed what would become Mahayana Buddhism is little known. What is clear is that between 100 BCE and 100 CE, Mahayana slowly emerged as a very different form of Buddhism than that of Theravada.[2] This would include such seemingly novel beliefs as the Buddha retaining a supramundane (that is, spiritual) existence with a limitless body, limitless power, and perpetual life; the Buddha abides eternally. Further, the Mahasanghikas believed that a bodhisattva can voluntarily be born in the lower realms of existence to soothe the torment of beings in hell states or to expound the Dharma to other beings. Here bodhisattvas were even claimed to be able to share their good karmic fruit (merit) to those in need.

Between 50 and 150 CE, representatives of what later became Mahayana produced a number of sutras on the "Perfection of Wisdom" (*Prajnaparamita*). These texts fundamentally launched the Mahayana movement. The *Prajnaparamita* sutras are overwhelmingly concerned with the question of Ultimate Reality or the Unconditioned and served as a critique to the Theravada path, which they imagined represented anything from a limited enlightenment to a deformed enlightenment to nothing other than a collection of perverse views preventing enlightenment. These sutras advocated higher stages in the path, particularly transcendental knowledge of or

[1] Edward Conze, *Buddhist Thought in India: Three Phases of Buddhist Philosophy* (Ann Arbor: University of Michigan Press, 1967), 201.

[2] Paul Williams writes, "The earliest use of the word 'Mahayana' in Indian inscriptions dates from the sixth century CE. . . . This is a very long time after the earliest Mahayana literature, and indicates that while doctrinally there may have been a growing idea of the Mahayana as an alternative aspiration and spiritual path from, say, the first century BCE, nevertheless the notion of a clear and separate identity among Mahayana followers, represented by their using a separate name for themselves as a group, took centuries to develop. To a monk in the first or second century CE the Mahayana as a visible institution may have been scarcely evident." See Paul Williams, *Mahayana Buddhism: The Doctrinal Foundations*, 2nd ed. (London: Routledge, 2009), 29–30.

direct experience with the Unconditioned. Conze, who frames the Theravada path as "mystically tainted rationalism," argues that Mahayana ought to be considered "rational mysticism."[3] Or as Frederick Streng observes, "The aim of articulating this religious vision, however, was to 'realize' it—not simply to talk about it."[4]

The most central tenet in the *prajnaparamita* literature is that everything is empty (*shunya*) or has the quality of emptiness (*shunyata*). On the surface, this is not highly dramatic or controversial. In one text Ananda inquired of the Buddha, "In what way, venerable sir, is it said, 'Empty is the world'?" The Buddha responded, "It is, Ananda, because it is empty of self and of what belongs to self that it is said, 'Empty is the world.'"[5] Further, as we have seen, the Buddha constantly taught that all conditioned phenomena are impermanent. Thus, all things are changing and are without an essential self. I think it is safe to say that essentially *all* Buddhists understand that no phenomenal reality has an *essential* self. But Mahayana emptiness goes much further.

In the abhidharma tradition, monks defined and classified various realities, mental states, and experiences (collectively *dharmas*).[6] Utmost in importance is seeing by direct experience how the aggregates (*skandhas*) relate to the arising and dissipation of experiences. It appears that the Theravada abhidharma understood these momentary arisings as representing something real, something that had an inherent existence. This is what makes *dharmas* able to be assessed, even as they are also impermanent.[7]

Prajnaparamita sutras challenge anything like this. Everything is empty, including *dharmas*. Conze describes the newly framed ontological status of *dharmas* according to the following: (1) All *dharmas* as regard their "own being" are empty, not facts in their own right, but merely imagined and falsely discriminated as distinct things; (2) *dharmas* are ultimately nonexistent, in the sense that they do not have their own-being; (3) *dharmas* have a purely nominal existence as products of conventional words; (4) *dharmas* are without distinctive property, thus not separate from other *dharmas*; and (5) *dharmas* have never been produced, never come into existence

[3] Ibid.

[4] Frederick Streng, *Emptiness: A Study of Religious Meaning* (Nashville: Abingdon Press, 1967), 40.

[5] Theravada *Salayatanasamyutta Sutra*, *Samyutta Nikaya* 35.85.

[6] *Dharma* can refer to "teaching" or even "way." The term also refers to any "thing"—and is used here as such.

[7] See Christopher Key Chapple, "Abhidharma as Paradigm for Practice," in *Pali Buddhism*, ed. Frank Hoffman and Deegalle Mahinda (London: Curzon Press, 1996), 79–101.

(as self-entities), and thus never left the original emptiness.[8] *Dharmas* are simply not amenable to theoretical knowledge.

The Theravada school understands *dharmas* as conditioned realities. They arise and dissipate due to conditions. They are no refuge because they suffer the three characteristics of impermanence, nonself, and dissatisfaction. They are thus in contrast with Nirvana, which is the Unconditioned Reality, the true and absolute refuge. Mahayana will have none of this, for such a position misunderstands that there are no *dharmas* as actual references. Further, if they have never been produced and thus have never left the original emptiness, they cannot act as a contrast to Nirvana. Further, if all things are empty, and if Nirvana is to be understood as meaningful, then Nirvana itself is empty. Therefore, how then can they contrast?

Nagarjuna (c. 150–250 CE) and the Stanzas on the Middle Path

Nagarjuna, founder of the Madhyamika (Middle School) philosophy, tasked himself with providing the philosophical basis for Indian Mahayana Buddhism. Central to his philosophical agenda is to provide an *apologia* for emptiness and a logic to the axiom *form is emptiness, emptiness is form*. His most influential work is the *Mulamadhyamakakarika* (Stanzas on the Middle Path; hereafter MMK).[9] The MMK, consisting of 450 verses over twenty-seven chapters, is a systematic and logical deconstruction of any dependent relationships or inherent essences. There is, ultimately, nothing to discriminate or interpret or know. "Suchness" (*tathata*), now for Nagarjuna a technical term, alone lies outside of delusion. To seize on anything as permanent or impermanent or both-permanent-and-impermanent or neither-permanent-nor-impermanent is to fall into delusion. On the surface or at least read literally, his series of theses seem more than challenging to understand. Consider the following:

- The great ascetic [Buddha] said: "The extreme limit of the past cannot be discerned." Existence-in-flux (samsara) is without bounds; indeed there is not beginning or ending of that [existence]. How could there be a middle portion of that which has no *before* and *after*? It follows that *past*, *future*, and *simultaneous events* do not obtain (11.1–2).

[8] Conze, *Buddhist Thought in India*, 220–22.

[9] I am relying on a translation of the Stanzas of the Middle Way as preserved in Candrakirti's Prasamnapada and as provided by Frederick Streng, *Emptiness*, 183–220.

- A nonstationary time cannot be grasped, and a stationary time which can be grasped does not exist. How then, can one perceive time if it is not grasped? Since time is dependent on a thing, how can time [exist] without a thing? There is not any [essential] thing which exists; how, then, will time become? (11.5–6).
- If the one who desires would exist before desire itself, then desire may be disregarded. When desire becomes related to one who desires, then desire comes into existence. If there is no one who desires, how then will desire come into being? [And the questions] whether desire exists or does not exist likewise hold true for one who desires (6.1–2).
- Space does not exist at all before the defining characteristic of space. If it would exist before the defining characteristic, then one must falsely conclude that there would be something without a defining characteristic. In no instance has anything existed without a defining characteristic. If an entity without a defining characteristic does not exist, to what does the defining characteristic apply? (5.1–2).
- Therefore space is neither an existing thing nor a nonexisting thing, neither something to which a defining characteristic applies nor a defining characteristic. Also, the other five irreducible elements can be considered in the same way as space. But those unenlightened people who either affirm reality or nonreality do not perceive the blessed cessation-of-appearance of existing things (5.7–8).
- The producer proceeds being dependent on the product, and the product proceeds being dependent on the producer. The cause for realization is seen in nothing else. In the same way one should understand the acquiring on the basis of the giving up, etc., of the producer and the product. By means of [this analysis of] the product and the producer all things should be dissolved (8.12–13).
- It is impossible that there is an arising of that which exists, of that which does not exist, and of that which exists and does not exist (7.20).
- We say that you do not comprehend the purpose of emptiness. As such, you are tormented by emptiness and the meaning of emptiness. The teaching of the doctrine by the Buddha is based upon two truths: truth related to worldly convention and truth in terms of ultimate fruit. Those who do not understand the distinction between these two truths do not understand the profound truth embodied in the Buddha's message. Without relying upon convention,

the ultimate fruit is not taught. Without understanding the ultimate fruit, freedom is not attained (24.7–10).

- An action is that whose "self" is desire, and the desires do not really exist. If these desires do not really exist, how would the action really exist? (17.26).
- Action and desire are declared to be the conditioning cause of the body. If action and desire are empty, what need one say about *body*? (17.27).
- If the producing action, etc., do not exist, then neither can the true reality (*dharma*) nor false reality (*adharma*) exist. If neither the true reality nor the false reality exists, then also the product born from that does not exist. If there is no real product, then there also exists no path to heaven nor to ultimate release. Thus it logically follows that all producing actions are without purpose (16.5–6).
- *Nirvana* has been said to be neither eliminated nor attained, neither annihilated nor eternal. [To have] neither disappeared nor originated (25.3).
- There is nothing whatever which differentiates the existence-in-flux (samsara) from *nirvana*; And there is nothing whatever which differentiates *nirvana* from existence-in-flux (samsara) (25.19).

What ought one to make of such assertions that seem to argue against the possibility of ending samsara, that deny reality, deny temporality, deny the attainment of Nirvana, and that then seemingly equate Nirvana and samsara? Conze seems to throw up his hands: "Nagarjuna's arguments . . . seem to be invalidated by equivocations."[10]

In assessing interpretations of Nagarjuna's philosophy, David Cooper recognizes three interpretive camps.[11] One is the transcendentalist position. Here Nagarjuna seeks to lead the reader beyond all conditioned forms to where there is an Absolute, Unconditioned Real—something Nagarjuna calls Emptiness, but also identifies as Suchness (*tathata*). Applied to forms, the Absolute is without self-being (or own-being). But applied to Suchness, the Absolute references a realm with "nothing in it of conditioned existence, one that is outside the samsaric processes. Samsara and Nirvana ought not to be set apart as samsara is the matrix where Nirvana is expressed, but there is a transcendental realm of Emptiness/Suchness."[12] He cites Robert Thurman's

[10] Conze, *Buddhist Thought in India*, 206.

[11] David Cooper, "Emptiness: Interpretation and Metaphor," *Contemporary Buddhism* 3, no. 1 (2002): 7–20.

[12] Ibid., 8–9.

framing of this position as the *monist-absolutist* camp. Here Emptiness and Suchness refer *mystically* to an inexpressible Absolute.[13]

Cooper's second interpretive stance is one of nihilism. The ultimate truth is that of "reality-less-ness," where everything is understood as empty illusion. It is, citing Thurman again, the *existential-relativism* position: "the goal is to realize that there is no Goal."[14] Consider this the nihilist camp. And finally, there is the *quietist* interpretation. This, Cooper claims, is the prevailing scholarly camp where the *prajnaparamita* goal is to realize Suchness is emptiness, and thus everything should be left as it is. Cooper places himself in the nihilist camp. No matter how imperatively Nagarjuna claims it is not, there is no rational conclusion but nihilism.

My reading of the tradition and both ancient and modern interpreters tells me that Cooper is not right to conclude existential relativism as the dominant interpretation. It strikes me that the transcendentalist position is the most reasonable and most broadly accepted, though Thurman may have overshot his description as monist-absolutist. Clues of the transcendentalist interpretation in both the MMK and other *prajnaparamita* literature have to include the many synonyms for the Absolute that tell us they refer to something more than relativism or nihilism. These include *Suchness*, the *signless*, the *absence of marks*, *nonduality*, the *realm of non-discrimination*, *non-production*, the *true nature of Dharma*, the *Inexpressible*, the *Unconditioned*, the *Unimpeded*, *cessation*, *Nirvana*, *Buddhahood*, *Wisdom*, *Enlightenment*.[15]

In understanding Nagarjuna and indeed the whole *prajnaparamita* project, we might start by reminding ourselves how difficult it is to discuss Nirvana and what it means to attain it. Recall the Buddha's response to the disciple Vaccha regarding his anticipated Pari-Nirvana. After delineating all of his own aggregates as "cut off at the root," he said, "The Tathagata is liberated from reckoning. . . . He is profound, immeasurable, unfathomable like the ocean. The term *reappears* does not apply, the term *does not reappear* does not apply, the term *both reappears and does not reappear* does not apply, the term *neither appears nor does not reappear* does not apply."[16]

It seems logically necessary to hold one of those views, but the Buddha rejects them all. A corollary could be: Nirvana exists; Nirvana does not exist; Nirvana both exists and does not exist; Nirvana neither exists nor does not exist. None of these positions is appropriate. We might also recall that *clinging to views* is an error in Buddhism. The Dharma is for crossing

[13] Ibid.

[14] Ibid., 9.

[15] Conze, *Buddhist Thought in India*, 226.

[16] *Majjhima Nikaya* 72.15–20.

over, not for clinging on to. The Buddha called these speculations *ditthi*, which translates as *views*. *Ditthi* is a pejorative term reflecting an error in procedure. When one is obsessed with *ditthi*, one is not engaged skillfully on the path. Sometimes the sutras play on two similar words: *mana* (conceit) and *mannati* (to conceptualize).[17] Perhaps what we see in Nagarjuna and the *prajnaparamita* is this procedure on steroids.

Much of the Buddha's teaching was aimed at eliminating mental defilements (*klesha*). On this, everyone agrees. These are, of course, various forms of lust, ill will, and delusion. Among other *prajnaparamita* claims, the defilements due to delusion (or ignorance) also include mental constructs (*kalpana*) of many kinds. And these constructs arise from *prapanca*, or conceptualizations. Nagarjuna writes, "On account of the destructions of the pains (*klesha*) of action there is release; for pains of action exist for him who constructs them. These pains result from conceptual proliferation (*prapanca*); but this conceptual proliferation comes to a stop by emptiness" (18.5).[18] *Prapanca* refers to words, meaning represented by words, and objects of words. When one realizes that there are no *essential* things in the universe, one also realizes conceptualizations of them are, in the end, artificial and illusory. It is the clinging to *prapanca* that must be put to cessation.[19] Nagarjuna ends his treatise with, "The cessation of accepting everything [as real] is a salutary cessation of *prapanca*" (25.24). Candrakirti (c. 600–650), the great commentator on Nagarjuna, writes,

> By not recognizing that all things have no essence, when people cling to things as real, they are caught in the net of fabricating. But, since things are really without essence and are empty . . . if those burning with desire did not cling to things as real, then they would not be caught in the net of fabricating and regard such things as objects to be known. And, not being caught in the net of fabricating, neither would they be caught in the net of projected images, which arise by taking such fabrications as objects. And, not being caught in the net of projected meanings, they would not give rise to the passions, which are based upon the belief in self, which in turn gives rise to clinging to *me* and *mine*. Therefore, basing themselves

---

17 See Takeuchi Yoshinori, *The Heart of Buddhism: In Search of the Timeless Spirit of Primitive Buddhism*, trans. and ed. James W. Heisig (New York, Crossroad, 1983), 3–7.

18 Here my translation of *prapanca* differs from the text I have been using.

19 Tachikawa Musashi, "Mahayana Philosophies: The Madhyamika Tradition," in *Buddhist Spirituality I: India, Southeast Asian, Tibetan, Early Chinese*, ed. Takeuchi Yoshinori (New York: Crossroad, 1995), 189.

> on emptiness, upon the absence of essence, they sever fabricating, images are exterminated. . . . Therefore emptiness, because it is the extermination of fabricating, is called cessation.[20]

Is emptiness then the Absolute? Surely, Nagarjuna used it to express the nature of Ultimate Reality, but also with a deep awareness of the problems involved in discussing something supramundane or transcendent. Consider emptiness as a term Nagarjuna uses to undermine any attempt at rarifying anything, including anything that might be understood as the *Absolute*.[21] Frederick Streng interprets emptiness as having a "dialectical function, which seeks to destroy absolute dependence on the logical and discursive structure in speech for expressing Ultimate Truth."[22] Streng concludes, "Thus, the analytical procedure was quite usable in attaining wisdom, but if it became an end in itself, or if the analysis led to absolutizing *a conclusion*, then it became detrimental speculation."[23]

In chapter 22 of Nagarjuna's MMK he analyzes the referent *tathagata* (thus gone). This was a common reference to the Buddha and could refer to anyone who has attained Nirvana. The chapter is a dizzying set of propositions where the reference *tathagata* cannot be obtained nor nonobtained, neither existent nor nonexistent. "That image of *nirvana* [in which] the Buddha (*tathagatha*) either *is* or *is not*—by him who [so imagines *nirvana*] the notion is crudely grasped" (22.13). Nagarjuna ends this chapter with, "The self-existence of the *fully completed* [being] is the self-existence of the world. The *fully completed* [being] is without self-existence [and] the world is without self-existence" (22.16). Streng concludes about the meaning of absolute *prajna*: "It is wisdom without an object of knowledge. . . . True knowledge should not be regarded as some absolute information which is revealed every now and then. The knowledge of *emptiness* is not conceived as an expression of *something*, it is not a proposition about something. Rather it is a power which spontaneously operates throughout existence (or non-existence, both or neither)."[24] Emptiness is a way of recognizing the true nature of things that have no essential selfhood. In this sense, it is simply a mundane truth. Emptiness is also a recognition that our very analysis must be recognized as problematic if we rarify our concepts (including the concept of emptiness!) in that very analysis. But relinquishing any fabrications of things or the mind thinking things leads us to a

20 Cited in Streng, *Emptiness*, 134.
21 Ibid., 22.
22 Ibid., 35.
23 Ibid., 40.
24 Ibid., 82–83.

transmundane cessation. This is the Absolute. And yet, this Ultimate Absolute does not obtain as a rarified *something* either. But it can be realized in the very context of the mundane.

The Christian *Via Negativa*

Gregory of Nyssa (335–395)

Christianity knows little of Nagarjuna's philosophy of emptiness as Nagarjuna frames it. God is assuredly an actual referent. And while Christianity has worked with paradoxes and such framings as the *coincidentia oppositorum*,[25] I find no easy parallel. This does not mean, however, that Nagarjuna cannot be a useful dialogue partner. From the beginning Christians have wrestled with the problem of God's radical transcendence. In Gregory of Nyssa's classic work, *The Life of Moses*,[26] he sketches out his understanding of the spiritual ascent to union with God. Here Gregory draws on the exodus story to discuss how a Christian ought to understand progressive union with God. As is typical of the patristic church and later medieval church, he thought that the biblical text could be read in different ways. Some texts ought to be read literally, others morally, others analogically, and still others anagogically (representing how the text reveals ultimate things or ends). Of course, many texts could be interpreted through more than one of these lenses. The *fourfold* method of interpretation tended to be quite fluid. Most of the exodus story Gregory took as historical/literal. The deeper meaning of the text, however, is what he was interested in. So, when Moses took off his sandals before the burning bush, this refers to the Christian's need to remove normal sense perceptions if one were to deeply engage God. Pharaoh represents the hardened will, and the plagues represent the work of the passions. Crossing the Red Sea is mystically understood as baptism, and so on.

The most profound religious expression in the story is that of Moses ascending Mount Sinai to receive the Law. Here Moses experienced God

---

[25] Nicholas of Cusa first coined this term in his *De doctrina ignorantia* in 1440—literally, "a coincidence of opposites" or a unity of opposites. It may refer to the notion of nonduality, in the sense of two coexisting conditions that are dependent upon each other yet also in tension.

[26] Gregory of Nyssa, *Life of Moses*, trans. Abraham Malherbe and Everett Ferguson (New York: Paulist Press, 1978). Part of this description follows my work in *Christian Spirituality: Lived Expressions in the Life of the Church* (Winona, MN: Anselm Academic, 2015), 83–86.

as directly as one could in this life. The top of the mountain is covered in a thick cloud, which Gregory calls the *dark cloud*. God can only be known in a kind of *unknowing*. Gregory's path is a progressive one. And most of his treatise involves ongoing purification in virtue, eradication of sin, and prayer. God's grace carries the Christian through it all. "His way to such knowledge is purity. . . . This means that one who would approach the contemplation of Being must be pure in all things so as to be pure in soul and body, washed stainless of every spot in both parts, in order that he might appear pure to the One who sees what is hidden and that visible respectability might correspond to the inward condition of the soul."[27] Contemplation of Being, then, becomes one of stripping our perceptual apparatuses: "He who would approach the knowledge of things sublime must first purify his manner of life from all sensual and irrational emotion. He must wash from his understanding every opinion derived from some preconception and withdraw himself from his customary intercourse with his own companion, that is, with his sense perceptions. . . . When he is so purified, then he assaults the mountain."[28] This is no easy thing, as Gregory reflects: "The knowledge of God is a mountain steep indeed and difficult to climb—the majority of people scarcely reach its base."[29]

Gregory tells his readers that early in the spiritual life God can be known through our senses and life experiences. God mediates himself through these. These experiences, because they are mediated, are not direct experiences of God. In these mediated experiences, God reveals himself as light, that is, something to be known. Still, God *as* God transcends them all and is different from them all. "What does it mean that Moses entered the darkness and then saw God in it? What is now recounted seems somehow to be contradictory to the first theophany, for then the Divine was beheld in light but now he is seen in darkness. . . . But as the mind progresses and, through an ever greater and more perfect diligence, comes to apprehend reality, as it approaches more nearly to contemplation, it sees clearly what of the divine nature is uncontemplated."[30] Here is his fuller explanation:

> For leaving behind everything that is observed, not only what sense comprehends but also what the intelligence thinks it sees, it keeps on penetrating deeper until by the intelligence's yearning for understanding it gains access to the invisible and the incomprehensible, and

[27] *Life of Moses* II.154.
[28] *Life of Moses* II.157.
[29] *Life of Moses* II.158.
[30] *Life of Moses* II.162.

> there it sees God. This is the true knowledge of what is sought; this is seeing that consists in not seeing, because that which is sought transcends all knowledge, being separated on all sides by incomprehensibility as by a kind of darkness.[31]

God simply cannot be known to the created intellect. God is, in the end, incomprehensible to the intellect. In this dark and blind unknowing Gregory is not saying that the soul cannot *know* God or *know* it is experiencing God, but rather that we have to rely on our *spiritual senses* to comprehend what our natural senses cannot. It appears that Gregory believes that there is a faculty of the soul that has the ability to know the Divine, even if one's conscious intellect cannot. This leads Gregory to seemingly paradoxical assertions where God is seen by not seeing and God is contemplated in the context of being uncontemplated.

Gregory believed that every concept related to God is, in the end, a false likeness, even an idol.[32] One can skillfully speak of God, so long as one also realizes that all words and concepts fall short of and distort who God is *as* God. Gregory taught that, since God is infinite, one can never engage God fully. Even in apophatic contemplation one could never exhaust the infinite. Rather, one continues to penetrate the inexhaustible Divine life. In his *Commentary on the Song of Songs* he writes, "The bride (soul) never ceases going in or going out, but she rests only by advancing towards that which lies before her and by always going out from what she has contemplated."[33] This apparently remains true in heaven where the beatific vision is not simply a static union with God but a paradoxical rest by eternal advancement. What we find in Gregory, then, is that union with God is conceptually *dark*, that God is an incomprehensible mystery, and that knowing God *as* God is one of not-knowing, of nonconceptuality.

Gregory is not alone in maintaining the utter incomprehensibility of God. This has always been a standard assumption. As Augustine once quipped, *Si comphrehendis non deus est* (If you understand, it is not God).[34] The path to union with that incomprehensible Absolute as one of *unknowing* is also typical.

---

[31] *Life of Moses* II.163.

[32] *Life of Moses* II.165.

[33] Gregory of Nyssa, *Commentary on the Song of Songs* 5.6, as cited in Bernard McGinn, *The Foundations of Mysticism: Origins to the Fifth Century* (New York: Crossroad, 1992), 141.

[34] Augustine, *Sermons,* 52.

Pseudo-Dionysius (c. Fifth–Sixth Centuries)

Another helpful patristic sounding is Pseudo-Dionysius, initially imagined to be the convert Dionysius in Acts 17:34, but since widely challenged. Dionysius authored a number of seminal texts.[35] These are *The Divine Names*, which presents a philosophical interpretation of the many names of God found in the Bible; *Mystical Theology*, which summarizes Dionysius's understanding of how one would come to spiritual knowledge; *The Celestial Hierarchy*, which discusses the types of angels or celestial beings and how they reflect both God and spiritual progress; and *The Ecclesiastical Hierarchy*, which addresses the hierarchy and sacraments within the church as an expression of the Divine life.

A central theme in all of Dionysius's writings is the Neoplatonic framing of creation and redemption as an *exitus* and *reditus*, coming from God and returning to God. How do human beings understand themselves as having come from God? What kind of participation does created reality have with the Uncreated? How does one return to God, given the answers to these first two questions? Such issues dominate all of Dionysius's writings.

Dionysius was convinced that if everything came from God, including the church and its structure and worship, then these are real manifestations of God and reveal a way of knowing God. Dionysius saw hierarchy everywhere. For example, in *The Celestial Hierarchy* he borrows New Testament texts to posit nine classes of celestial beings or versions of angels. Along with many biblical texts referring to seraphim, cherubim, archangels, and angels, Paul mentions five more that came to be interpreted as separate classes of angels.[36] Dionysius sees the whole spiritual world as one of a hierarchy of triads: (1) seraphim, cherubim, and thrones; (2) dominations, powers, and authorities; and (3) principalities, archangels, and angels. *The Ecclesiastical Hierarchy* presents a hierarchy of (1) liturgical expressions of anointing, Eucharist, and baptism; (2) bishops, priests, and deacons; and (3) monks, laity, and those Christians not fully in communion.

All of these created things symbolize and manifest God's truth and presence in the world. They teach human beings about God and provide ways of transcending their created limitations to encounter the uncreated God. Like the other exemplars in this chapter, Dionysius believed that God is invisible, ultimately imperceptible, and incomprehensible. These symbols, along with the names of God, draw the soul into the truth of God. God is both similar

---

[35] See likewise my treatment in Peter Feldmeier, *Christian Spirituality: Lived Experience in the Life of the Church* (Winona, MN: Anselm Academic, 2015), 91–94.

[36] Eph 1:21; 3:10; 6:12; Col 1:16; 2:11, 15.

to them as they manifest the Divine, as well as dissimilar in that they can never actually address God as God really is. One begins with the perceptual appearances of symbols to rise higher to their conceptual meaning. Yet, Dionysius insists, even the conceptual meaning has to be transcended:

> Sometimes the mysterious tradition of the scriptures represents the sacred blessedness of the transcendent Deity under the form of "Word," "Mind," and "Being." It shows thereby that rationality and wisdom are, necessarily, attributes of God, that he is also to be deemed a true subsistence and the true cause of the subsistence of every being, and that he may also be represented as light and hailed as life. Now these sacred shapes certainly show more reverence and seem vastly superior to the making of images drawn from the world. Yet they are actually no less defective than this latter, for the Deity is far beyond every manifestation of being and of life; no reference to light can characterize it; every reason or intelligence falls short of similarity to it.[37]

As one engages God's revelation, one becomes imbued in contemplation of its truth. From the perceptual, such as liturgical rites, one can experience the truth they manifest. Encountering their truths more fully requires negating their perceptual limitations and experiencing these truths on the conceptual or immaterial level. This becomes a deeper appropriation of their truths. Yet the conceptual is itself still a problem, for God is not only similar to them but also dissimilar. The conceptual has to be transcended. Dionysius's final goal is union with God, a God beyond and in some way dissimilar to everything one can say or think about him.

Dionysius's treatises express both *kataphatic* theology, affirming true revelation about God, and *aphophatic* theology, negating any conceptions about God who is beyond them. Such a negation brings the soul into the silence of the Divine.

> The fact is that the more we take flight upward, the more our words are confined to the ideas we are capable of forming; so that now as we plunge into the darkness which is beyond intellect, we shall find ourselves not simply running short of words but actually speechless and unknowing. . . . [W]hen it has passed up and beyond the

[37] Pseudo-Dionysius, *The Celestial Hierarchy*, 140C. Translations of Pseudo-Dionysius are taken from *Pseudo-Dionysius: The Complete Works*, trans. Colm Luibheid (New York: Paulist Press, 1987).

> ascent, it will turn silent completely, since it will finally be at one with him who is indescribable.[38]

Dionysius believed that even these negations themselves must be negated. Pure negation would imagine God as unrelated to the world: "The Cause of all is . . . not inexistent, lifeless, speechless, mindless."[39] God is real and related to the created world, but God is not merely the infinite expression of truth; God is also radically unique. Dionysius's theology holds a kind of *both-and* in tension. God is both the absolute expression of the good and true, and God is different from any considerations about goodness and truth.

For Dionysius, theology and spirituality are not disciplines to acquire knowledge about God, but means to experience that which surpasses all understanding. His spirituality entails embracing God's manifestations and using them to ascend even higher. Unlike a purely "negative way," his ascent takes seriously God's manifesting descent into the world. His is a school of contemplation that fully embraces the created world and gifts of the church, all the while using them to discover the Divine incomprehensibility that ultimately grounds their meaningfulness.

Thomas Aquinas (1225–1274)

The imperative among many Christian theologians and spiritual masters—that in order to know God *as* God, one must transcend and even reject conceptualizations about God—is broad-based and typical. It is also philosophically necessary. In an excellent treatment comparing Nagarjuna to Christian thought, James Fredericks leads us philosophically through the works of Thomas Aquinas, particularly Aquinas's *Summa Theologiae* and *Commentary on the Gospel of John*. In Aquinas's *Commentary* he discusses the Johannine verse "No one has ever seen God; it is the Only Begotten Son, who is in the bosom of the Father, who has made him known" (Jn 1:18). Aquinas reflects here on what it might mean to see or to know. For Aquinas, seeing and knowing all come through the senses. Further, our cognitional structure is set up to see and know "things," objects in the created world. Herein lies the problem: "Nothing finite can represent the infinite as it is."[40]

---

[38] *Mystical Theology* 3.1033B–C.

[39] *Mystical Theology* 4.1040D.

[40] Cited in James Fredericks, *Buddhists and Christians: Through Comparative Theology to Solidarity* (Maryknoll, NY: Orbis, 2004), 74.

Even visions of the Divine that come from God cannot actually represent God *as* God: "But the vision of the Divine essence is not attained by any of the above visions: for no created species . . . is representative of the Divine essence as it is."[41]

The problem of seeing or knowing God *as* God is twofold. The first is that, if God really is infinite, then knowing God fully or completely—comprehending God—would mean that we would have to encompass God. This is a problem even in the beatific vision in heaven. Fredericks notes, "If God were ultimately comprehensible in the beatific vision, then by completely comprehending God the human mind would in effect transcend God."[42]

The second problem, as noted above, is that the human mind working naturally is designed to know objects, and God is no object. Objects are created things, dependent things, caused things, contingent things. In contrast, Aquinas understands God as *ipsum esse subsistens* (God is his own existence). We simply cannot know that which cannot be known.

> In God alone is there unrestricted existence; He is existence, *ipsum esse subsistens*. Here we have an argument for the fact that God's essence is his existence, because His essence is *not* a restriction of *esse* to a finite expression or character. And yet it remains true that while we know the facts, we do not know the why of the fact because knowledge of God's essence remains unknown to us.[43]

Thus, even experiencing the Divine essence directly does not remove God's incomprehensibility. Aquinas asserts, "No created intellect which does see the Divine essence, can comprehend it in any way."[44]

Fredericks notes that Aquinas also argues, seemingly paradoxically, that if we ultimately can never know God's essence, even in the beatific vision of heaven, then our deepest desire for beatitude is left unmet. And this cannot be. Aquinas also argues, "It is necessary that the Divine essence be seen."[45] How does one reconcile this conundrum? Fredericks writes, "If Aquinas is to succeed in affirming the human's unlimited potential for beatitude, he must locate the incomprehensibility of God in God's infinite

---

41 Ibid.

42 Ibid., 79.

43 "Saint Thomas Aquinas" in *Stanford Encyclopedia of Philosophy*, 11.3; https://plato.stanford.edu/entries/aquinas/#EssExi.

44 Fredericks, *Buddhists and Christians*, 76.

45 Ibid., 75.

capacity to be known."[46] Thus, like Gregory of Nyssa, heaven for Aquinas is the perpetual engagement with the infinite and infinitely revealing divine nature.

Comparing the Messages

What we find in all three of our Christian soundings is not a Christian version of Mahayana emptiness. Rather, we find resonance that both emptiness and divine incomprehensibility drive the human soul beyond any objectifications, beyond any attempts to rarify the Absolute. Both *shunyata* and divine incomprehensibility place us in a strategy to know through unknowing. For Gregory, one can truly or fully know God, but only insofar as one is willing to let go of all ideas of God, all idols of the mind. You can know God, but you do not know a *thing*. Like Nagarjuna's demand for a constant deconstruction of all conceptualizations through and into *shunyata*, Gregory demands a like deconstruction for God.

For Dionysius, one moves increasingly beyond what can be known or said. One moves from the perceptual to the sacramental to the abstract. And even there, one has to negate any abstract formulations of the Divine. Finally, one negates the negation in a kind of affirmation in the context of negation. This is where God *as* God is met and known. And how does one describe this negation of negation? Surely, it is not yet some higher affirmation (of some *thing*). Rather, the Divine registers as that which is known by unknowing. Thomas Aquinas assures us that this kind of divine incomprehensibility is no negative framing, but the positive posture of deep and endless encounter with the Absolute.

Nagarjuna's emptiness is, for him, a necessary component to a Buddhist's awakening. Emptiness is a strategy to help the mind withdraw from any fabrications. It is also an extraordinarily positive statement about the state of affairs. Here Nirvana becomes not a goal *out there*, but the simultaneous mundane and supramundane life in the context of samsara. Human fulfillment is right here, right now, if we would only stop rarifying anything, from our minds to objects of experience to ultimate religious goals. It is less a dogma—the problem of views—than it is a descriptor of authentic life. And the very fact that emptiness is also "empty of emptiness" guards us against making emptiness some kind of Absolute. As Nagarjuna writes, "One may not say that there is *emptiness*, nor that there is *non-emptiness*. Nor that both

---

[46] Ibid., 81.

[exist simultaneously], nor that neither exists; the purpose for saying [*emptiness*] is for the purpose of conveying knowledge" (MMK 22.11).

Emptiness, thus understood, has resonance with Christian beliefs about the absolute transcendence of God: *Si comprehendis non Deus est.* The paradox of emptiness can give added wisdom and dimension—an additional layer—to divine incomprehensibility. Christians can talk about God's transcendence and the divine mystery, but all conceptualization even of these terms are laden with a human perspective. We talk about eternity but end up imagining it in the only context we have—that is, *time.* We speak about God as Absolute and Other and Pure Subject, and yet can only do so as an objectified (in one way or another) reference. Here, Buddhist emptiness becomes a nonnegotiable and constant deconstruction of all conceptualizations. It becomes a constant *cloud of unknowing.*

Shunyata is akin to the life of the Christian mystic. When Gregory warns that God-talk is a kind of idolatry, he wants his readers to keep letting go, constantly letting go. God is known only in darkness where nothing can be said, and *no thing* can be known. Dionysius likewise takes us on a tour of affirming, negating, affirming something higher, negating that higher perspective, and ultimately negating negation unto the Absolute Mystery where silence (and nonthinking) reign. In this sense, Christian mysticism reinforces Buddhist wisdom.

Buddhists may also begin to appreciate Christian philosophical and theological commitments more deeply. For the vast majority of people, Buddhists included, God is imagined something like a great being, in fact the greatest. God is a being among other beings. It is also the case that religious theists typically recognize God acting as a causative agent in the universe, much like other causes. To such conceptualizations, Buddhists generally respond as nineteenth-century astronomer Pierre-Simon de Laplace did to Napoleon who asked him why God did not figure into his explanation of the universe. Laplace was said to have replied, "*Je n'ai pas besoin de cette hypothèse.*" And neither do Buddhists. For them, talk of God is an unnecessary discussion, a distraction, or more typically a false view. Yet, what "God" is being rejected? Laplace saw the working of the cosmos as a series of facts about the natural world. God would be an unnecessary add-on. This is how most Buddhists think about theism.

This is not the God we see in our philosophical or mystical heritage. All three Christian "dialogue partners" assure us that this kind of God is an idol, a projection of the human mind. In no way does this mean for Christians that there is no revelation or truths that can be meaningfully said about God. Rather, it means that all conceptualizations, all rarifying tactics, all objectifications must in the end be deconstructed if one were to truly consider the being or essence of God. Mahayana Buddhists claim that Nirvana and samsara are one, that the transmundane is lived in the mundane. Christians could say the same thing. A Christian corollary is that God's eternity is the condition of possibility for God's ubiquity. God is everywhere, interpenetrating the universe precisely because God is nowhere, not spatially present. The claim to God's eternity is also the claim that God is not one among us dwelling in time and space. God's radical presence is only that when it is realized that God is not here or there or everywhere. We might say, following Nagarjuna's frustrating sets of affirmations and rejections: The universe is filled with the divine because God is everywhere and nowhere.

Can we say more? Emptiness is, for sure, a strategy for stilling the mind of all fabrications. Fredericks describes it as such:

> Properly used, emptiness is a tool for prying loose attachments generated by a feverish mind. . . . In using a term like "emptiness," what Nagarjuna wants to communicate is not another theory about the ultimate nature of reality, but to impress the Buddhist wisdom of freedom through non-attachment. His emptiness is completely in the service of promoting the Buddhist diagnosis of our human predicament—attachment to false views.[47]

For Fredericks, this is Nagarjuna's "only purpose."[48]

Shunyata (emptiness) is more; it is the context, the condition of possibility, and in some sense, the very content of Nirvana. Recall some of the synonyms that Nagarjuna and the *Prajnaparamita* sutras use and regularly substitute for each other: *Emptiness*, the *true nature of Dharma*, the *Inexpressible*, *Enlightenment*, and so on. Emptiness references something more than just a strategy to quiet the mind. Consider the terms *tathagatha* and Nirvana. Nagarjuna certainly deconstructs *how* they might be understood, but they are still meant to be meaningful. As noted above, Nagarjuna says that the "image of *nirvana* [in which] the Buddha (*tathagatha*) either *is* or *is not* . . . the notion is crudely grasped" (22.13). Certainly, we should not attempt to grasp that image. But Nirvana and *tathagatha* are real references.

What ought the Christian make of this? Is there such a transcendental life that is being described here, one where "emptiness" and "Nirvana" reference such a life? These questions takes us back to chapter 3's discussion and rhetorical conflict between the ideas of pluralists such as John Hick and

[47] Ibid., 77.

[48] Ibid.

inclusivist—albeit a unique one—Mark Heim. Recall that for reasons of the singularity of God and soteriological universality, Hick identified various salvations as the same thing even if expressed and experienced somewhat differently. Heim cried *foul*, as he alleged that pluralists like Hick are simply not seriously attentive to very different truth claims and experiential reports. On the other hand, Heim conjectured how a Buddhist salvation project worked through his Christian lens. Functionally, he saw the Buddhist as experiencing something of the emptiness of the "space" between the persons of the Trinity. This is quite a conjecture, and one that ironically parallels Hick's univocal soteriology, though in a nuanced way.

As I stated above, Buddhist emptiness and Nagarjuna's Nirvana do not seem to look like a Christian salvation project. And if they are indeed different, could they both be true? If so, how? Or is it the case that they really are the same thing, but the differences in the language and practices are so great that they appear different? Could it be that they reference the same transformation in light of union with God, understood either personally for the Christian or impersonally for the Buddhist? What ought the Buddhist make of a Christian apophatic absorption into the incomprehensible Divine? Is it the same thing, but with a kind of paradoxical divine person who is not a person, a divine referent who cannot be a direct referent or object of discourse? We may get closer to answering these questions, even if tentatively, in our next chapter regarding the Mahayana bodhisattva and the works of Meister Eckhart.

Chapter 5

Emptiness, Buddha-Nature, Bodhisattvas, and Meister Eckhart

From Arhat to Bodhisattva

Poring through the massive Pali canon, one sees virtually no interest in the Buddha's ministry of encouraging others to become a Buddha like himself. Nirvana, the highest and singular aim of his preaching, was available to anyone karmically ready and willing to enter deeply into the threefold practice of virtue, concentration, and wisdom. To realize utterly the three qualities of existence (impermanence, nonself, and dissatisfaction) was to be free from karmic production and thus liberated from samsara. This is the arhat. In *this* sense, there is no difference between a Buddha and an arhat; Buddhas and arhats are emancipated. Both have eliminated all defilements, destroyed the possibilities of more fabrications, are free, and upon death will attain Final-Nirvana (whatever exactly that may be).

All this is not to suggest, however, that Buddhas and arhats are equivalent. Recall from chapter 2 that throughout the eons a few virtuoso practitioners of the Dharma will decide to take on the enormously arduous bodhisattva path to become a Buddha. This will involve countless rebirths in order to practice the *ten perfections* to the utmost degree and finally residing in the *tushita* heavenly realm in a penultimate existence until the time is ripe to become reborn as a human and attain the fullest realization of Buddhahood. Even Buddhahood has degrees, from a nonteaching or "private Buddha" (*pratyekabuddha*) to a Buddha that desires to work for the liberation of others, such as Gautama. As we saw in chapter 2, the Buddha himself questioned whether it would be wise for him to teach anyone about the Dharma, it being so lofty.

Among arhats there are also differences, where some have only become liberated by wisdom while others have attained levels of higher knowledge, supernormal states of consciousness, or other expressions of spiritual mastery.[1] All arhats are said to have perfected the *ten powers*, which collectively pivot around the practice and realization of the Dharma.[2] In the *Mahasihanada Sutra*, we learn that Buddhas carry ten additional powers. These include knowing their past lives, the kinds of actions that lead to various rebirths, extraordinary clairvoyance, and all knowledge of causal connections between actions and their karmic fruits, past, present, and future.[3]

If Nirvana is the singular goal and *summum bonum* of existence, why would one place oneself on the bodhisattva path? One might say that a Buddha's enlightenment is actually higher or more exquisite. Perhaps it is simply a better Nirvana. The lowest Nirvana would then be that of the arhat, a middling Nirvana would be that of a *pratyekabuddha*, and the ultimate nirvanic experience would be that of a Buddha. This became known as *apratishthita nirvana* (unrestricted Nirvana). Some Mahayana texts argue along these lines.[4] The *Rastrapalapariprccha Sutra*, for example, is devoted to comparing the superiority of Buddhas and their Nirvanas to arhats and their Nirvanas, and argues for the imperative to seek the bodhisattva path.[5] Once

---

[1] Lily de Silva, "Nibbana as Living Experience / The Buddha and The Arahant: Two Studies from the Pali Canon" in *Access to Insight (BCBS Edition)*: http://www.accesstoinsight.org/lib/authors/desilva/wheel407.html.

[2] Qualities of all arhats are (1) seeing all component things as impermanent; (2) seeing all sense pleasures as a pit of burning embers; (3) being inclined to seclusion and renunciation; (4) having developed the four stations of mindfulness; (5) having developed the fourfold right exertion; (6) having developed the four bases of psychic powers; (7) having developed the five spiritual faculties; (8) having developed the five spiritual powers; (9) having developed the seven factors of enlightenment; and (10) having developed the eightfold path. See Lily de Silva, "Nibbana as Living Experience."

[3] These totally are (1) knows possibility and impossibility for what they are; (2) knows the causal connection of all actions, past, present, and future; (3) knows the course of action leading to all states of existence; (4) knows all worlds composed of various and diverse elements; (5) knows the spiritual propensities and dispositions of human beings; (6) knows the maturity levels of the spiritual faculties of human beings; (7) knows the attainment of all levels of meditation, with the defilements and purities associated with them and the means of their arising; (8) knows past lives extending to several eons and can recall past details; (9) has clairvoyant powers with the ability to see beings dying and being reborn in high or low states according to their karma; and (10) knows the complete destruction of defilements in this very life. See *Majjhima Nikaya* 12.9–21.

[4] See Mark Siderits, *Buddhism as Philosophy* (Indianapolis: Hackett, 2007), 142–44.

[5] See Daniel Boucher, *Bodhisattvas of the Forest and the Formation of the Mahayana:*

the bodhisattva literature matured in Mahayana, we find two related exhortations. The first is to reject the Nirvanas of the arhat and *pratyekabuddha*, and strive for the greatest Nirvana, that of a Buddha. In this rendering, the former Nirvanas are something less than full. Additionally, they are considered only self-interested or deficient in compassion for others. One is implored to strive for the Nirvana of a Buddha because only here does one achieve the fullest Buddhist ideal, that of perfect freedom due to wisdom and perfect compassion due to serving the Dharma for the good of all sentient beings. Hints of why this is better actually come from the Theravada text discussing the powers of a Buddha. Here one finds the additional excellences of the Buddha, almost all of which are geared toward what would be most helpful for knowing how to liberate others. A second rendering found, for example, in the famous *Shrimaladevisimhanada Sutra* (The Lion's Roar of Queen Shrimala), claims that arhats and nonteaching Buddhas do not, in fact, attain any kind of Nirvana, but will need to be reborn to continue the path.[6] Thus, these paths are simply deficient.

Typical to many college textbooks as well as popularizations of the bodhisattva is the depiction that a bodhisattva renounces Nirvana in order to spend eons upon eons of rebirths serving the needs of all sentient beings and vowing to withhold one's own attainment of Nirvana until all other beings attain it first. Certainly, there are numerous Mahayana sutra passages that suggest this. Consider the crucial *Ashtasahasrika Prajnaparamita*: "Great compassion . . . takes hold of him. He surveys countless beings with his heavenly eye, and what he sees fills him with great agitation. . . . And he attends to them with the thought that: 'I shall become a saviour to all those beings, I shall release them from all their sufferings!'"[7] A. E. Burtt reflects the same dynamic in his medley of sutra citations:

> I take upon myself the burden of all suffering. . . . At all costs I must bear the burdens of all living beings. . . . All beings I must set free . . . I must not cheat all beings out of my store of merit. . . . It is better that I alone should be in pain than that all these beings should fall into the states of woe . . . and with this my own body I must experience, for the sake of all beings, the whole mass of all

A Study and Translation of the Rastrapalapariprccha Sutra (Honolulu: University of Hawaii Press, 2008).

[6] Paul Williams, *Mahayana Buddhism: The Doctrinal Foundations*, 2nd ed. (London: Routledge, 2009), 105.

[7] Edward Conze, *The Perfection of Wisdom in Eight Thousand Lines and Its Verse Summary* (Bolinas, CA: Four Seasons Foundation, 1973), 238–39.

> painful feelings. . . . In reward for all this righteousness that I have won by my works . . . May I be balm to the sick, their healer and servitor. . . . May I be in the famine of the ages' end their drink and meat . . . and unfailing store for the poor.[8]

In these beautiful aspirations, one certainly sees overwhelming compassion, inexhaustible love, and an unending hero's journey. Such sentiments do reflect the bodhisattva way. But the depiction of bodhisattvas renouncing Nirvana for the sake of all others, and *only* attaining it after all have been liberated, is simply not cogent. For example, if numerous beings have taken the bodhisattva vow, how would any, save one, achieve it? One could imagine something like a great entrance into Nirvana many eons from now with only bodhisattvas on the other side each insisting that the others enter first and refusing to enter until the rest do. Or consider the odd scenario: everyone who has *not* become a bodhisattva would attain Nirvana; this before bodhisattvas. How would/could they? This is particularly an issue as the theology of the bodhisattva developed in Mahayana where the *lesser* Nirvanas had come to be seen as not Nirvana at all.

A second real problem is how one *could* hold off Nirvana. This would be a question for the Theravadin commitment of bodhisattvas as well. Once one fully recognizes the three qualities of phenomenal reality and stops clinging, then karma is simply not created anymore. Thus, there would be no karmic energy to the next rebirth. Recall how dependent origination works. Among the spokes that keep a being in samsara, only ignorance can be taken out. But once that has happened the whole wheel collapses. Once you see/realize this, you cannot unsee/unrealize it. We even saw in Buddhaghosa that a stream-enterer is so far along that she cannot *not* attain Nirvana in the next several lifetimes at longest. Further, Buddhaghosa believed that one could move from one stage of stream entry to another (or even all simultaneously) in a given meditational sitting. One is simply so close that the final realizations come quickly with diligent practice.[9] A further problem would

[8] E. A. Burtt, *The Teachings of the Compassionate Buddha: Early Discourses, the Dhammapada, and Later Basic Writings* (New York: New American Library, 1982), 109–18.

[9] The *Ashtasahasrika* tries to explain how this could happen in two ways, though these two reasons do not exactly cohere logically. On the one hand, the bodhisattva is said to use strategies and skillful means (*upaya*) to prevent himself from falling into arhatship. He practices not to eliminate, but keep under his control those factors that would lead to rebirths. On the other hand, it also argues that, since Nirvana and samsara are one, there is no really leaving the world to some *outside* Nirvana. It becomes something of a moot point.

be what to make of Buddhas who have indeed attained Nirvana. Were they less compassionate than bodhisattvas?

The best way to understand the bodhisattva vow, both in Theravada and Mahayana, is to see it as the desire for full Buddhahood. In short: a bodhisattva is a *mahasattva* (great being) who has taken the vow to be reborn again and again through the eons so as to attain complete and perfect Buddhahood. This is the bodhisattva's singular quest. It is also a quest that understands that the very nature of Buddhahood is to be for the benefit of all sentient beings. But this is just a start. As we may recall, Mahayana is something of a collective term that represents some rather broadly (and loosely) held Buddhist ideas. Not all the *prajnaparamita* texts agree with each other, use terminology in the same way, or have the same metaphysics. Further, while the Theravada understanding of Nirvana is enigmatic—*neither remains nor does not remain*, and so on—the Mahayana understanding is even more dizzying. As Williams reflects, "The landscape of Mahayana sutras is quite extraordinary, space and time expand and conflate, connections seem to be missed, we move abruptly from ideas so compressed and arcane as to verge on meaninglessness, to page after page of repetition."[10]

Suchness, Buddha-Fields, and Buddha-Nature

We simply have to get our Mahayana bearings if we are to make sense of the bodhisattva. Recall from chapter 4 that Nagarjuna's understanding of emptiness (*shunyata*) dominates his metaphysics. All *dharmas* are empty, reality is empty, Nirvana is empty, and emptiness is empty. I argued that this is not some form of nihilism or quietism, but rather a kind of mysticism. This mysticism insists on nonduality in all things. There is a Suchness (*tathata*) that lies outside of delusion, but it cannot be rarified as some "thing." Nirvana and samsara are one because Nirvana is not somewhere *out there*. Rather, it is realized in the context and perhaps in the content of the mundane. We see in Nagarjuna and other early *prajnaparamita* sutras that terms such as *emptiness*, *Suchness*, *nonduality*, *Unconditioned*, *Nirvana*, *Buddhahood*, and *true nature of Dharma* are used often as synonyms or otherwise conceptually conflated.

Understood this way, Final-Nirvana does not consist in exiting the universe, as Nirvana and samsara are one. The Buddha continues to be present, and thus taking refuge in the Buddha is taking a real refuge in an

[10] Williams, *Mahayana Buddhism*, 45.

actual reality, however conceived. As noted in chapter 2, Gautama continues to be a *natha*, a protector. Mahayana literature tends to be critical of stupa devotions, as though Gautama's bones create his Buddha-field (*Buddha-kshetra*). Now Buddha-fields ought to be understood as the realm where a Buddha ministers. I stated in chapter 2 that the Lotus Sutra assures us, "In order to save living beings, as an expedient means I appear to enter Nirvana but in truth I do not pass into extinction. I am always here, preaching the Law. I am always here, but through my transcendental powers I make it so that living beings in their befuddlement do not see me when close by. . . . I tell all living beings that I am always here."[11] Thus, the Buddha's mission essentially never ends. Due to his infinite compassion, he remains always leading us in the Dharma way.

There are many such Buddha-fields, an infinite number, all with Buddhas guiding sentient beings there along the path of Dharma. And these other fields are accessible as well for those sufficiently trained. Recall Nagarjuna's theses conflating time and space in the MMK:

- Existence-in-flux (samsara) is without bounds; indeed there is not beginning or ending of that [existence]. How could there be a middle portion of that which has no *before* and *after*? It follows that *past, future*, and *simultaneous events* do not obtain (11.1–2).
- Space does not exist at all before the defining characteristic of space. If it would exist before the defining characteristic, then one must falsely conclude that there would be something without a defining characteristic. In no case has anything existed without a defining characteristic. If an entity without a defining characteristic does not exist, to what does the defining characteristic apply? (5.12).
- Therefore space is neither an existing thing nor a nonexisting thing, neither something to which a defining characteristic applies nor a defining characteristic. Also, the other five irreducible elements can be considered in the same way as space. But those unenlightened people who either affirm reality or nonreality do not perceive the blessed cessation-of-appearance of existing things (5.7–8).

If everything is empty, and if time and space are not solid, then movement through various universes and various Buddha-fields is most possible. There are simply no hard edges in a universe (multiverse?) that is recognized as empty.

---

[11] Burton Watson, trans., *The Lotus Sutra* (New York: Columbia University Press, 1993), 230–31.

There is yet one more layer to add to this vertiginous cosmology. Mahayana sutras began to wrestle with an additional question: What creates the condition of possibility for becoming a Buddha? If everything is *empty* and yet has a Suchness to it, what constitutes our ability to recognize this? The answer, according to the *Tathagatagarbha Sutra* (third century) and the famous *Lankavatara Sutra* (fourth century) is that all sentient beings have a Buddha-nature (*tathagatagarbha*). This is a challenging term to define. As we have seen, Tathagata means "thus gone," and referred to one who has attained Nirvana, particularly a Buddha. *Garbha* is more complicated. According to Michael Zimmerman, *garbha* could mean "womb" or "seed" as well as the "innermost part" of something. Together we have a noun that refers to *seeds of awakening* or *awakening essence* or *awakening core*.[12] According to the Chinese version of the sutra, the Buddha sees with his divine eye:

> All the living beings, though they are among the defilements of hatred, anger, and ignorance, have the Buddha's wisdom, Buddha's eye, Buddha's body sitting firmly in the form of meditation. Thus, in spite of their being covered with defilements, transmigrating from one path . . . to another, they are possessed of the Matrix of the Tathagata, endowed with virtues, always pure and hence are not different from me. Having thus observed, the Buddha preached the doctrine in order to remove the defilements and manifest the Buddha-nature (within the living beings).[13]

According to the *Avatamsaka Sutra*, all beings have within them a Tathagata-awareness (*Tathagatajnana*). The point of enlightenment is to remove the defilements (kleshas) to see the eternally and inherently pure Buddha-nature shine forth.[14] The doctrine of the Buddha-nature gets even more developed in the Mahayana version of the *Mahaparinirvana Sutra*. Here we are taught that the Buddha-nature is nothing other than the *self*. The *self* is the meaning of *Tathagatagarbha*, this element that exists in all beings. Of course, the Buddha taught nonself, but this refers to the egoistic self, that self that clings or craves. But the *Tathagatagarbha* is that absolute truth of sentient beings. This sutra makes the most interesting juxtaposition.

[12] Michael Zimmerman, *The Buddha Within: The Tathagatagarbha Sutra—The Earliest Exposition of the Buddha-Nature Teaching in India* (Tokyo: International Research Institute for Advanced Buddhology, 2002), 39–46.

[13] Cited by Williams, *Mahayana Buddhism*, 56.

[14] Ibid., 105.

We find in many Theravada as well as Mahayana texts that the Buddha challenged his hearers not to imagine permanence where there is no permanence, or self where there is no self. Now in the *Mahaparinirvana Sutra* we are exhorted to not imagine impermanence where there is permanence, and nonself where there is self. This *self* is the immaculate Suchness, the Buddha-nature, the *Dharmakaya* (Buddha-body). In the *Ratnagotravibhaga Sutra* we learn that this reality is "unchangeable by nature, sublime, and perfectly pure. It is the *Dharmakaya* that pervades all, an unchanging reality.[15] This doctrine is furthered in the Chinese sutra known as the *Awakening of Faith* (*Dasheng Qixinlun*), where Buddha-nature is understood as the One Mind—the Mind as Suchness—Absolute Reality: "The true Mind is eternal, permanent, immutable, pure, and self-sufficient; therefore it is called non-empty."[16]

While one could only wonder how Nagarjuna might react had he lived in this progressing Mahayana cosmology, we ought to recognize that *Tathagatagarbha* is nondual, nonconceptual, beyond fabrication. It is also empty. We might ask, if the underlying reality is Buddha-nature, and if all sentiency is empty, do Buddhas, Buddha-fields, bodhisattvas, and the like actually exist, or are they empty manifestations of Buddha-nature with nothing behind them? The short answer is that they do indeed exist just as we do, *and* they certainly do not exist, as all is empty.

Becoming a Bodhisattva

According to the great eleventh-century Indian scholar Atisha in his classic *Bodhipathapradipa* (*A Lamp for the Path to Awakening*), the difference between the Theravada goal of arhatship and the Mahayana goal of achieving the bodhisattva path is not one of gaining the greatest Nirvana but has everything to do with the very motivation for attaining enlightenment. Arhatship is self-concerned. While it certainly involves the development of compassion as one of the brahma-viharas (lovingkindness, compassion, sympathetic joy, and equanimity), it lacks the fullness of compassion. Full Buddhahood represents inexhaustible wisdom and inexhaustible compassion. The difference is the development of *bodhicitta* (Awakened Mind), which is generated by the bodhisattva aspirant. *Bodhicitta* certainly includes the aspiration of wisdom, but its emphasis

---

15 Ibid., 108–10.

16 Cited in ibid., 116.

is compassion. Kamalashila, the great eighth-century Indian Buddhist scholar, describes Buddhas as those who attained their omniscience by their development of compassion, and that they remain in service of their Buddha-fields because of their compassion.[17]

Bodhicitta is the foundation for bodhisattva aspirants to pursue the arduous path to full Buddhahood, and it must be generated before one can even begin. Kamalashila's second *Bhavanakrama* (*Stages of Meditation*) describes how *bodhicitta* can emerge for the aspirant in a series of meditations whose end is to become positively determined to serve others in their suffering. It is called the *Six Causes and One Effect*. One begins by considering a friend, a neutral person, and an enemy. Given that we have all endured an infinite number of lifetimes, we realize that all of our friends were at some point enemies and all our enemies were themselves our friends in some past life. None is intrinsically friend or foe. Infinite lifetimes also assure that all beings were at one time also our mother. The six causes are then: (1) realizing that every sentient being was once my mother; (2) realizing that, as mothers, they suffered for my sake and were immensely kind to me; (3) realizing that right now my past mothers are undergoing great suffering themselves and I have an obligation to them; (4) realizing that if I do not attend to their suffering, I myself am guilty of conscience; (5) generating great love and compassion for my mothers, I desire to free them from suffering and its causes; and (6) I decide to take upon myself the responsibility for alleviating their suffering, and to do this I must become a fully enlightened Buddha. These are the six causes. The one effect is *bodhicitta*, the aspiration for full enlightenment for the benefit of all sentient beings.[18]

Once *bodhicitta* is generated deeply, the bodhisattva aspirant then actively pursues the bodhisattva path to full Buddhahood. There is no shortage in Indian, Tibetan, or Chinese texts that outline the bodhisattva path. Perhaps the most important is the *Dashabhumika Sutra* (*Ten Stages*), which appears alone as well as embedded in both the *Avatamsaka* and *Lankavatara Sutras*. It describes ten stages of training that correspond loosely to the traditional ten *paramitas* (perfections) that all Buddhists are supposedly committed to, though the Mahayana list was ultimately reduced to six. These ten perfections are (1) generosity, (2) morality, (3) renunciation, (4) wisdom, (5) energy/exertion, (6) patience, (7) truthfulness, (8) determination/resolution, (9) lovingkindness, and (10) equanimity.[19] The

[17] Ibid., 195.

[18] Ibid., 197.

[19] The traditional Mahayana list is generosity, mindfulness training, patience, perseverance, meditation, and wisdom.

ten stages are technically called *bhumis*, which literally translates as "place" or "region," and thus implies a firm place to stand or perhaps even a condition of life.[20]

The first stage in the bodhisattva path is called *Joyful*. Once the firm intent on full Buddhahood is established as grounded in *bodhicitta*, the aspirant practices generosity and self-sacrifice. Such giving is described as universal and nondiscriminative. Being filled with joy at the beginning of the path, one makes ten vows: to revere all Buddhas; to observe the discipline; to review the earthly career of the Buddha; to realize enlightenment; to establish all beings in the Dharma; to purify all Buddha-fields; to enter the path; to create a common purpose with all other bodhisattvas; to make useful all body, speech, and mental actions; and to achieve enlightenment so as to teach the Dharma.

The second stage, *Pure*, is engaged by gaining self-control, calm, and freedom from craving. All this is connected to morality; one overcomes impure actions by pure actions and reaches equanimity so as to act virtuously. In the third stage, *Luminous*, one's thoughts become pure, dispassionate, and resolute. Being purified by the vow of renunciation, one cultivates endurance, promotes the good of all, and overcomes any reactivity. Here the aspirant grasps the nature of impermanence and obliterates duality.

The fourth stage is *Radiant*, and it is here that the bodhisattva-to-be perfects the knowledge of and faith in the three refuges (Buddha, Dharma, Sangha), and deepens in understanding of impermanence. Continuing to develop the perfection of vigor, one terminates emotional and mental afflictions and cultivates the thirty-seven elements of enlightenment. In the fifth stage, *Difficult-to-Conquer*, one regards all principles of Buddhahood with pure thought, comprehends fully the Four Noble Truths, and realizes all things as empty. Now one is unconquerable by Mara. In the sixth stage, *Face-to-Face*, the aspirant understands the ten aspects of equality, that is, all things are without an essential essence. Being empty means that nothing has a particular higher or lower quality. It is imagined in the text that this is fundamentally the level of arhatship and that the bodhisattva-to-be could enter Nirvana if she or he wanted, but decides to continue the path of the bodhisattva for the welfare of others. As discussed above, such a framing is logically straining.

The seventh stage, *Far-Going*, represents the acquisition of wisdom in the sense of discovering skillful means (*upaya*) for the purpose of helping others

[20] Karl Olson, *The Different Paths of Buddhism: A Narrative-Historical Introduction* (New Brunswick, NJ: Rutgers University Press, 2005), 156. In the following description of the ten stages, I am primarily following Olson's depiction.

along the path. Here one also conquers all inner passions. The *Dashabhumika* states, "They become ultimately calm and tranquil due to removal from the fires of afflictions, yet they undertake to accomplish the extinction of the flames of affliction of lust, hatred, and delusion in all beings."[21] At this stage, the text assures that progress is irreversible and that the aspirant will, in fact, achieve full Buddhahood. In the eighth stage, *Immovable*, the aspirant is so well established in the practice that there is no possibility of being contaminated by false views or fabrications in the mind. Here one learns the processes of the universe, and acquires ten supranormal powers, for example, divine eye or clairvoyance. Now the bodhisattva practices without effort and can assume a variety of bodies in order to teach the Dharma.

The ninth stage, *Good Intelligence*, is where the bodhisattva knows the minds of others so as to help them mature quickly in the Dharma. She or he grasps all paths of Buddhism with perfect facility, and understands the nature of the bondage of others. The bodhisattva also perfects all states of meditation and trance. The tenth stage is represented as *Cloud of Dharma*. By mastering all states and knowledge, the bodhisattva enters the Cloud of Dharma (*dharmamegha*) and resides with a glorious body, one that can emit rays that destroy the pain and misery of others. According to a similar Tibetan source, the Sgam Po Pa, the bodhisattva at this stage "lets the Dharma fall like rain and extinguishes the very subtle flow of conflicting emotions held by sentient beings."[22] Williams writes,

> The Bodhisattva enters into meditation and appears upon a wonderful jeweled lotus seat known as the Great King of Jewels. Many other Bodhisattvas appear, and light rays permeate all the directions which relieve the misery and sufferings of sentient beings. After further miracles and wonders the Tathagatas consecrate our Bodhisattva to full Buddhahood. He can now put into one atom of dust an entire world region, or put innumerable sentient beings into one pore of his skin, without their suffering injury or indeed noticing. He can manifest all the deeds in the early life of a Buddha as many times as he wishes throughout innumerable worlds.[23]

It should be obvious that these stages are not exactly linear. A bodhisattva aspirant strives with several of them at the same time. One does

---

21 Cited in Olson, *Different Paths of Buddhism*, 158.

22 Cited in Williams, *Mahayana Buddhism*, 207.

23 Ibid.

not practice stage one for some time and then move on to stage two, and so on. Some practices imply each other in mutual development.

This is a many-eon project as it was for Gautama. One sees, too, that there is a great deal of repetition in them. This probably is due to the *Dashabhumika Sutra*'s attempt at correlating several traditions together. Finally, these stages strike me as somewhat odd. I fail to see, for example, why at the *radiant* stage one is not already at the level of arhat, having perfected the knowledge (*prajna*) necessary for arhatship. Or we find in the eighth stage that the fires of afflictions are removed. Were they not removed in the second stage? At any rate, one cannot help but be impressed and inspired by the aspiration of the bodhisattva vow and the herculean effort necessary to attain perfect Buddhahood; all this for the benefit of every sentient being.

Bodhisattvas and Buddhas

As a final note, the difference between a Buddha and a bodhisattva by the tenth stage is essentially nil. In a review of the literature, classical commentators, and the sutras themselves, one finds their qualities and ministries quite blurred. Avalokiteshvara (Bodhisattva of Compassion) takes on the ministries of a Buddha and the epithets of the Hindu divine Shiva, who for Shaivites is the very face of Absolute Brahman. Manjushri (Bodhisattva of Wisdom) is also widely known as a Tathagata, and apparently (and oddly) has not entered full Buddhahood because he understands emptiness so well that he realizes there is no full Buddhahood, as even this is empty. Thus, he has actually attained full Buddhahood in light of the emptiness doctrine. In the Tibetan tradition, Tara is also a Bodhisattva of Compassion who either acts as a companion to Avalokiteshvara or acts as the single Bodhisattva of Compassion. In the *Tara Tantra*, she is said to be the "Mother of all the Buddhas" and is regarded by many Tibetans as a fully enlightened female Buddha, even if she is still called a bodhisattva.[24]

All of them resemble gods who work throughout the many universes to hear and respond to prayers, to alleviate suffering, and to preach the Dharma. Given that Buddhas all have their own Buddha-fields of ministry, it could be that these (and many other) bodhisattvas are more popular and more important than Buddhas themselves. The reason is that they move through various Buddha-fields assisting any sentient being anywhere in the multiverse. They are constantly at rest and constantly working for the good

[24] Ibid., 221–29.

of all beings. They are beyond being affected, yet attend to the suffering of all beings. They are transcendent, and this allows them to be anywhere, anytime. They are within samsara because they have transcended samsara. They ultimately attain full, unrestricted Nirvana, realizing that it is empty, as are they, perfectly and happily.

The central axis of our comparative project in this chapter is not the role or the training of the bodhisattva, which we will deal with more in the next chapter. Rather, here our focus is on the Mahayana worldview out of which emptiness, Buddha-nature, and bodhisattvas make sense. We have here a world of paradox where endless wisdom and compassion come with recognizing the emptiness of all things as well as positing something (Buddha-nature and/or Suchness) that is eternal, all-pervading, unchanging, and nondual, underlying all sentiency, even as this too is said to be empty. It is a worldview where we find paradoxes such as: the ultimate goal of full Buddhahood is realized by Manjushri precisely by realizing there is no full Buddhahood.

Given that these claims are widely made by a venerable tradition with innumerable members who are of good will, intelligence, and presumably spiritual excellence, what ought one to do with them? Is the conceptually confusing language of Nagarjuna and the *Prajnaparamita sutras* merely designed to take us out of conceptuality? Is the problem language itself? Perhaps these texts take us to the limit of logical discourse and then throw us off the edge to where we can see what simply cannot be spoken of. Our previous chapter's work comparing Nagarjuna and the Christian *via negativa* does demand that if we want to get to the core of our religious Ultimate we will have to, in the end, abandon language and conceptuality. And then, as Dionysius reminds us, we will have to negate our negations as well into some kind of transconceptual world of an absolute depth-experience.

Meister Eckhart

In this chapter, we intend to further our Christian dialogue with the pioneering witness of Meister Eckhart,[25] whom Bernard McGinn has stated to be possibly the most influential and controversial mystic in the history of Christianity.[26] Born John (possibly) Eckhart von Hochheim around 1260 near

[25] Unless specifically cited, all of the following represent general, well-known biographical details about Eckhart.

[26] Bernard McGinn, *The Mystical Thought of Meister Eckhart: The Man from Whom God Hid Nothing* (New York: Crossroad, 2001), 1.

the German city of Erfut, he joined the Dominicans in late adolescence or early adulthood, where he went through formation and early studies at Erfurt and Cologne. Ordained in the early 1280s, he was sent to Paris for higher studies. While a brilliant student and teacher, he spent much of his ministry administrating priories and provinces for the Dominican Order throughout Germany. In 1311, he was sent back to Paris as *magister*, his second two-year stint there and an honor only given previously to Thomas Aquinas. In 1313, he was called to Strasbourg as special vicar for the Dominican Master General. It is here that he particularly plunged into the life of preacher and spiritual counselor. Around 1323, Eckhart left Strasbourg for the Dominican house at Cologne. Here the powerful archbishop, Henry II of Virneburg, who was striving to rid his diocese of *free-spirit* thinkers, laid his eyes upon Eckhart's works. With the help of some Dominicans suspicious of Eckhart's theology, he drew up two lists (and eventually a third) of passages from Eckhart's treaties and sermons and in 1326 demanded that Eckhart appear before an inquisitorial commission. The Dominicans were free of episcopal control and argued that the case could only be adjudicated by the papacy.

Eckhart was sixty-seven or sixty-eight years old when he and his Dominican delegation walked the five-hundred-mile trek to Avignon and to yet another formal inquiry under the authority of Pope John XXII. The resulting papal bull, *In argo dominico*, lists a number of propositions Eckhart was said to have preached. The first fifteen were deemed heretical, two of which he denied ever having preached, and the final eleven were deemed to have had an offensive ring but could "with many explanations and additions" be given or already have a Catholic sense. *In argo dominico* ends by assuring the Archbishop of Cologne that Eckhart had "revoked and also deplored the twenty-six articles which he admitted that he had preached . . . *insofar* as they could generate in the minds of the faithful a heretical opinion, or one erroneous or hostile to the truth."[27] Eckhart died in Avignon shortly after his recantation. It should be noted that he did not agree that these propositions were themselves heretical, but only recanted that which could be misunderstood as heresy.

Eckhart's writings continued to have influence after his death. His sermons and short treaties were copied and widely disseminated, and his legacy also lived among some of his famous pupils, including John Tauler and Henry Suso. Why were his writings challenged? Consider just a few of his more provocative claims:

---

[27] Emphasis mine. See Edmund Colledge, "Historical Data," in *Meister Eckhart: The Essential Sermons, Commentaries, Treatises, and Defense*, trans. and ed. Edmund Colledge and Bernard McGinn (New York: Paulist Press, 1981), 13–14.

- God's being is my life; since my life is God's being, God's essence is my essence.
- God's ground and the soul's ground are one ground.
- All creatures are one pure nothing. I do not say that they are a little something or anything, but that they are pure nothing.
- As long as the soul has God, knows God, and is aware of God, she is far from God. . . . The greatest honor the soul can pay to God [is] to leave God himself and to be free of him.
- The eye in which I see God is the same eye in which God sees me. My eye and God's eye are one eye and one seeing, one knowing, and one loving.[28]
- Man's last and highest parting occurs when, for God's sake, he takes leave of God. St. Paul took leave of God for God's sake and gave up all that he might get from God. . . . In parting from these, he parted with God for God's sake and yet God remained in him as God in his own nature . . . but more as an *is-ness* as God really is. Then he neither gave to God nor received anything from him, for he and God are a unit, that is, pure unity.[29]

God and Not God

One can see in some of these citations a dramatic witness to union with God as something by which there appears literally no difference between God and oneself. To say that the person is "pure nothing," that there is no difference between God's essence and one's own, and so on, strikes many readers as pantheistic. But this charge is denied by most of his serious interpreters.[30] Certainly, however, Eckhart goes much further than the typical framing of divinization in the Christian mystical tradition. As we saw in chapter 3, John of the Cross makes it clear that the soul in union is divinized, that is, lives the divine life as God lives the divine life, *while still remaining a creature*. By grace and not by nature we find union, St. John assures. Bernard of Clairvaux likewise insists that the substance of the person in union

---

[28] As cited in Bernard McGinn, *The Harvest of Mysticism in Medieval Germany* (New York: Crossroad, 2005), 104, 120, 137, 179, and 183, respectively.

[29] Meister Eckhart, *Meister Eckhart: A Modern Translation*, trans. Raymond Blakney (New York: Harper Torchbook, 1957), 204.

[30] See, for example, Burkhard Mojsisch, *Meister Eckhart: Analogy, Univocity, and Unity*, trans. Orrin Summerell (Ansterdam: B. R. Gruner, 2001), 154, and McGinn, *Mystical Thought*, 148

(*mane quidem substantia*) always retains its creaturely distinction from the Divine.[31] Further, while the mystical tradition speaks dramatically of a *kind* of indistinct union, it also holds this in a creative tension with a love mysticism where there is a bona fide I-Thou relationship. Such a tension seems to break down in Eckhart. Likewise, we have seen clearly in the *via negativa* Christian tradition that ideas of God cannot correspond to God *as* God. Several of the above citations align with this, and I believe it is what Eckhart meant by such terms as "taking leave of God." Still, Eckhart stretches this mystical axiom to the limit, and may even go beyond the limits of Christian orthodoxy.

It is difficult to make perfect sense of Eckhart. He does not always seem to use technical terms, for example, *esse* (being or existence), consistently. It is sometimes difficult to know when he is using analogy or making direct propositional claims. And his dialectical style of logic is used often for different ends; sometimes to conclude that which goes beyond linear thought, sometimes to draw the reader beyond language,[32] sometimes to assert a technical philosophical position, and sometimes to draw the conclusion that can only be solved by some sort of coincidence of opposites. Some have even called it a philosophy of paradox.[33] Mojsisch reflects on "how often one has been explicitly or implicitly advised just to leave off from interpreting Eckhart at all, precisely because this extraordinary thought (or non-thought) was known only unto itself, if at all, and allowed for no subsequent access."[34] I think, however, that if we were to survey his work *in toto*, rather than choosing random citations or focusing too much on any given Eckhartian argument, there are golden threads that can lead us to a provisional but responsible interpretation, one that can further our interfaith dialogue with Mahayana.

One of the most important terms Eckhart uses throughout his writings is *grunt* (ground). McGinn describes this protean term as what is inmost or most proper to a being—its essence. Among other things, *grunt* references the hidden depths of God.[35] The *grunt* represents the Divine *as* Divine. There is absolute unity in *grunt*; it represents "the indistinct nonrelative

[31] Bernard of Clairvaux, *De diligendo Deo* 10.28, as cited in McGinn, *Mystical Thought*, 33.

[32] McGinn writes, "His mystical language explores and sometimes explodes ordinary speech." See *Harvest of Mysticism*, 116.

[33] See, for example, Zbigniew Kazmierczak, "A Trial of Interpretation of Meister Eckhart's Thought on God and Man through the Analysis of Its Paradoxes," *Annals of Philosophy* 65, no. 1 (2017): 5–22. Mojsisch will call it a "paradox theory."

[34] Mojsisch, *Meister Eckhart*, 3.

[35] McGinn, *Mystical Thought*, 41.

'aspect' of God which is *absolutely* One."[36] As such, *grunt* lies deeper than the Trinity. Eckhart will also assert that God is nothing but one pure Being. God is Being itself.[37] This is something that technically lies deeper than the Trinity itself.[38] In and of itself, Divinity has no attributes other than itself. This will lead Eckhart to describe the "nothingness of God beyond God."[39]

The God beyond God is never static,[40] but necessarily outflowing. God's initial outflowing Eckhart calls *bullitio*, or "inner boiling." This boiling is an emanation that produces "pure nature" within, one that is equal to its source. God's *bullitio* emanates or is foundation for the Trinity. It is only here that "Father" makes any sense as the emanation represents itself as Father, Son, and Holy Spirit. Following Christian dogma, the Trinity is said to be eternal, where there was "never a Father without a Son (or Holy Spirit)." Presumably Eckhart does not deviate from this dogma. But he also wants us to understand that one can speak technically of a primal indistinct ground from which to make sense of the very fact of the Trinity.

From the initial and eternal *bullitio* comes *ebullitio*, the "boiling over" of divinity into creation. Unlike the emanation of the Trinity that is one with its source, Eckhart describes creation "in the manner of an efficient cause and with a view toward an end [final cause], by which something produces something else that is from itself, but not out of itself."[41]

Thus far, there is little innovation between Meister Eckhart and many other Christian Neoplatonists, who saw creation as a form of divine emanation. It is the nature of creation, particularly humanity which has intellect, and how humanity returns to the Divine that sets Eckhart off from most of his contemporaries. Eckhart sees the initial *bullitio* of the Trinity as an image of the *abullitio* of creation in key ways. *Esse* or existence in its proper sense (*esse simpliciter*) can only be predicated to God, not to creatures. This means that Being is the actuality of all things. We exist only in the sense that we participate in Divine existence and Divine Being. "God is nothing but one pure Being," Eckhart writes, "and the creature is from nothing and also has one being from the same Being."[42] Does he mean that we are God? Not exactly. Eckhart distinguishes the *esse hoc et hoc* (being this or that) of

---

36 Ibid., 81.

37 Mojsisch, *Meister Eckhart*, 51.

38 Ibid., 46.

39 Charlotte Radler, "Losing the Self: Detachment in Meister Eckhart and Its Significance for Buddhist-Christian Dialogue," *Buddhist-Christian Studies* 26 (2006): 111.

40 Ibid.

41 Cited in McGinn, *Mystical Thought*, 72–74.

42 Cited in ibid., 98.

created reality and the pure *esse indistinctum* of God. God is absolute existence (*esse absolutum*) and creatures represent "formally inherent existence" (*esse formaliter inhaerens*), but the reliance on God and the necessary activity of God as Being dominate his ontology.[43]

God does not merely create existence for us or hold us in being but impresses on us an emanation of the whole of the divine image. Eckhart writes, "Every created being radically and positively possesses existence, life, and wisdom from and in God and not in itself. . . ."[44] The difference between the Divine *grunt* giving birth to the Trinity and God giving birth to humans is that the Trinity is God's essence properly, while human creation is God's essence by participation. This whole of God's being impressing on or birthing humanity is the divine image. This is literally God in us. Eckhart asserts, "You should know that the simple divine image which is pressed onto the soul in its innermost nature acts without a medium, and the innermost and the noblest that is in [the divine] nature takes form in a most proper sense in the image of the soul."[45] McGinn notes, "Since there is no medium between God and the soul, their relation is one of formal emanation, not creation."[46] Eckhart again: "Here the image does not take God insofar as he is Creator; it takes him, rather, insofar as he is a being endowed with intellect, and what is noblest in [the divine] nature takes its most proper image in this image."[47]

Returning to the Source

It appears that humans are ontologically drenched in the divine, and indeed have something of the divine within us. McGinn notes that while Eckhart denied that there was something in the soul that is uncreated and literally divine, we see it asserted in many of his sermons.[48] The divine image impressed on the human soul parallels and is effected by the image of the Son. Eckhart writes, "The eternal birth occurs in the soul precisely as it does in eternity, no more and no less, for it is one birth, and this birth occurs in the essence and ground of the soul."[49] The eternal birth of the Son represents

---

[43] See McGinn, *Harvest of Mysticism*, 137; McGinn, *Mystical Thought*, 120; McGinn, "Introduction," in *Meister Eckhart*, 33; and Mojsisch, *Meister Eckhart*, 49.

[44] Cited in McGinn, *Harvest of Mysticism*, 137.

[45] Cited in McGinn, *Mystical Thought*, 109.

[46] Ibid., 108–9.

[47] Ibid., 109.

[48] McGinn, "Introduction," in *Meister Eckhart*, 42.

[49] Cited in McGinn, *Mystical Thought*, 60.

the foundation of our *exitus* or emanation from God. The task of humanity is the *reditus* or return back to the *grunt* that is the core of the Divine. The Son, in this sense, is not a distinct category, a divine Person. On the one hand, the human soul is distinguished from God, the Trinity, or even the Son. We are *esse hoc et hoc*, existence of this and that, while the Son represents something of the pure *esse indistinctum* of God. And Eckhart will also say that from the perspective of created beings we are sons by adoption and participation. But these categories are fluid as he also says in the same breath that there is only one Sonship. Insofar as there is only one Son of God, if we are sons, we are indeed identically the same Son.[50] "Since I am an only son whom the heavenly Father has eternally born, if then I have eternally been a son in God then I say: 'Yes and no.' Yes, a son, as the Father has eternally borne me, and not a son, as to being unborn . . . Out of the purity he everlastingly bore me, his only-born Son, into the same image of his eternal Fatherhood, that I may be Father and give birth to him of whom I am born."[51]

Eckhart's sermons and treaties are dominated by the idea of returning to that original *grunt* of God. This divine ground also represents the very ground of the soul that emanated from God. "Man is created to the image of the entire divine substance, and thus not to what is similar, but to what is one; hence it must return to the One from which it came forth and this alone satisfies it."[52] Thus, his mysticism is not one of raptures of divine love, but a new kind of awareness or consciousness of being indistinct from God in God's very ground. This is certainly one of the most uncompromised or purest forms of mystical identity in the Christian tradition, one that seeks a place where all duality vanishes and "there is a *unitas indistinctionis* in which there is no difference between God and human."[53] This is a place where Eckhart argues, "God's ground and the soul's ground is one ground."[54]

Detachment and Love

His fundamental strategy to allow God's grace to draw the soul into the divine *grunt* is detachment to the utter limit so as to dis-identify with any quality of the human person at every level. "Now know," he writes, "all

50 Ibid., 118.

51 Colledge and McGinn, *Meister Eckhart*, 194.

52 Ibid., 108.

53 McGinn, *Harvest of Mysticism*, 120.

54 Cited in ibid., 120.

our perfection and our holiness rests in this: that a person must penetrate and transcend everything created and temporal and all being and go into the ground that has no ground. We pray our dear Lord God that we may become one and indwelling, and may God help us into the same ground. Amen."[55] Interestingly, McGinn will call this a "deconstruction," much like we saw in Buddhaghosa and John of the Cross.[56] His synonyms for detachment include cutting off, leaving, resigning, unforming, dis-imagining, and unbecoming. And the soul successfully free is one imagined as empty, naked, dispossessed.[57] The soul even dispossesses herself of the Persons of the Trinity: "As long as the soul has God, knows God, and is aware of God, she is far from God. . . . [T]he greatest honor the soul can pay to God [is] to leave God himself and to be free from him."[58] Here there is an absolute union and identity with the One in the one *grunt* of God. One of Eckhart's most famous quotes, earlier noted, describes this: "The eye in which I see God is the same eye in which God sees me. My eye and God's eye are one eye and one seeing, one knowing and one loving."[59]

Seeing, knowing, and loving all become apiece here. Most scholarship focuses on Eckhart's "intellectual" way to God. But love also plays a central role. On the surface, this would seem like an impediment to the radical indistinction between God and the soul. Love presumes some kind of distinction for an I-Thou relationship, as we saw in John of the Cross. How can there be a love relationship with perfect unicity? Charlotte Radler has shown that Eckhart often taught of the necessity of loving God, even as this is the "God beyond God," and even if there must also be unicity in the divine *grunt*.

In his German sermon 41, Eckhart rhetorically asks, "What is God's love?" and he answers that it is God's nature and being. Clearly love, being, and nature are united in God in such a way that they can be commensurate in their simplicity.[60] In fact, Eckhart understood the Holy Spirit's role as that which melts the soul that it might be absorbed in God. "The Holy Spirit's being is that I become burnt in him and become wholly melted in him and become wholly love."[61] This kind of love, like Eckhart's whole vision of going

---

[55] Cited in ibid., 118.

[56] McGinn, *Mystical Thought*, 139.

[57] McGinn, *Harvest of Mysticism*, 166.

[58] Cited in McGinn, *Harvest of Mysticism*, 179.

[59] Cited in Charlotte Radler, "'In Love I am More God': The Centrality of Love in Meister Eckhart's Mysticism," *Journal of Religion* 90, no. 2 (2010): 185.

[60] Cited in ibid., 183.

[61] Cited in ibid.

beyond God unto God has a radical apophatic quality to it that extended beyond the love mysticism of his day. "You should love God apart from his lovableness, that is: not because he is lovable for God is unlovable as he is One not-god, One not-spirit; One not-person, One not-image, further: as he is a simple, pure, clear One, separated from all duality, and in the One we should eternally sink down out of something into nothing."[62]

Radler finds in Eckhart's commentary on the Song of Songs that there are four reasons the soul cannot name God whom it loves:

> First, God is nameless because God is above all names. Second, when the soul passes over into God through love and fades away in a fusion of identities, it knows nothing but love . . . and no space exists between the lovers to create the duality necessary to name something, for a sign or a signifier demands distinction. Pure love and true lovers thus disallow duality. The third reason builds on the second: there is not enough time to name God, for the perfectly detached person cannot turn away from her lover long enough; as she can only love, know, and be Love in the transparency of lovers, she cannot utter anything but Love. Finally, the soul that hovers in the love of lovers does not believe that God has any other name but love, since love contains all other names.[63]

What we see here is that, for Eckhart, even love ultimately dissolves into some kind of unicity.

Mystical Consciousness in Ordinary Life

When one reads mystical texts by such giants as John of the Cross or Teresa of Ávila, one finds quite a large taxonomy for prayer and mystical experiences. Teresa will discuss the "prayer of quiet" and its relationship to the "prayer of union," differences between active and passive contemplation, and so on. John will distinguish "imaginative visions" from "intellectual visions," "acquired contemplation" from "infused contemplation," and so on. Nothing like this is found in Eckhart's work. McGinn observes,

> For Eckhart, this continuous union with God is not an "experience" in any ordinary sense of the term—it is coming to realize and live out

[62] Cited in ibid., 188.

[63] Ibid., 193.

> of the ground of experience, or better, of consciousness. . . . Eckhart recognized that these forms of mystical consciousness [rapture, ecstasy, visions] did exist . . . but they did not pertain to the essence of union, and they might be harmful if they came to be seen as a necessary "way" to the goal, or confused with the goal itself.[64]

Paradoxically, Eckhart's mysticism expresses itself in very practical ways. Living in and through the divine *grunt*, in the freedom that has left the chains of any distinct ego to protect and advance, one lives not in isolation but in full communion with the created world, just as God does. For Eckhart, the radical detachment and deconstruction of the self, the merging into the divine ground will necessarily bear external fruits in an active life of loving service. In Eckhart's *Book of Divine Consolation*, he describes God as pure Love. God loves because of loving and works because of working. As he famously articulated in his Latin Sermon 40: authentic love lacks a *why*.[65] This kind of love is universal and makes no distinctions. The logic here is that if Christ took on universal human nature, and if we are fused to Christ and identified with him in union, then we must love all humans universally, loving without distinction.[66]

Eckhart scholars regularly note that he particularly emphasized ministering to those most in need. Richard Woods writes that "Eckhart was consistent in his ethical commitment to the primacy of mercy. . . . It is in our acts of mercy that we come to reveal our closest likeness to God. For, as Eckhart says in Sermon 39 . . . 'The just man is like God because God *is* justice.' True justice realizes itself in perfect friendship, an equality of persons that finds expression in works of mercy. "[67]

Final Thought

Is there a divine reality beyond the Trinity? Does the human being have something *essential* that is eternal and divine? Are we ultimately fused with the One in utter indistinction? Eckhart will regularly defend his mystical agenda philosophically by arguing such things as: God is indistinct from all reality, making him actually distinct (unique) from all reality; God's Triune

---

[64] McGinn, *Mystical Thought*, 149.

[65] Radler, "'In Love I am More God,'" 189.

[66] McGinn, *Mystical Thought*, 127.

[67] Richard Woods, *Meister Eckhart: Master of Mystics* (New York: Continuum, 2011), 91.

reality is God *as* God, but only in indistinct distinctions, which paradoxically make the divine *grunt* both indistinct and distinct; the human being is *formally* distinct from God but not in essence, or one is indistinct from God *only insofar* as one is just or one is the Son; and so on. He becomes a tortuous read in many places. If he has retained Christian orthodoxy, he has done so with the use of language games, sometimes fair and sometimes seemingly out of bounds. What seems clear is that he taught it was possible and even necessary to see that we are utterly one with God whose divine presence and life drive the human being in all its authenticity and truth. The call for humans is to recognize this oneness, and to return to the eternal ground of God that can be paradoxically understood as the only thing that really exists (as Being and Existence and beyond being and existence). And one achieves this recognition, this new consciousness, through radical deconstruction of both the self and God. Pervading that consciousness is perfect freedom, love, and union, particularly marked by compassionate action and an awareness of the intrinsic presence of the divine everywhere (and nowhere).

Mahayana and Eckhart in Dialogue

It is not the interest of this book to create a unified vision between Christianity and Buddhism. It is also not my interest to advance a pluralistic theology that imagines all or most religions are about the same thing. As I discussed in chapter 1, I recognize the postmodern, rightly considered axiom that no metanarratives are perfectly sustainable. And, I think that Mark Heim has an important insistence that we simply must let the religious other have its own voice, its own uniqueness, its own alterity. Still, one cannot help but look at the generally agreed-upon metaphysics of Mahayana and see stunning affinities with the thought of Meister Eckhart. These affinities are surely why Buddhist thinkers like D. T. Suzuki and Masao Abe have latched on to Eckhart so enthusiastically. Hee-Sung Keel notes that Eckhart bridges the dividing line between Asian religio-philosophical traditions and those of the West.

> One of the most amazing things about Eckhart's spiritual thought is the fact that it is remarkably free from the "dualistic" mode of thinking that has dominated Christian theology from antiquity down to the present day: the dualism of God and the world, the supernatural and the natural, grace and nature, the religious and the secular, this world and the other world, reason and revelation,

> as well as the dualism of spirit and matter, the soul and the body. True, such distinctions are not absent in Eckhart, but his thought is not built upon them; nor do they refer in him to two separate realms of reality.[68]

Jan van Bragt argues that "the brunt of the Buddhist onslaught of the idea of God . . . is directed against the 'objectification' and substantialization or 'reification' of the Transcendent . . . wherein the Transcendent is caught and set up in contrast with the human in an irreconcilable duality—which does not permit unification."[69] What we have seen in Eckhart is the virtual or complete elimination of any kind of dualism: God's ground and our ground are the same ground; the divine Sonship and our Sonship (insofar as we are sons) are the exact same Sonship. Compare the following two representative notions between Eckhart and Buddhism: "The eye in which I see God is the same eye in which God sees me" and "Enlightenment is the act of Buddha-nature seeing itself."[70]

A central aim of Buddhism, in all of its forms, is a deconstruction project of radical nonattachment. All things, beings, and persons lack any substantial or *essential* reality in themselves. This, too, is Eckhart's insistence. It is not that we ought to merely consider ourselves as "nothing," he asserts, but that we really are "pure nothing." His point is twofold. Absolute nonattachment radically dis-identifies the "I" from everything it might imagine as the essential self. There is only God. And, indeed, this is his second point: everything must return to its source, his *reditus* project, to recognize that the soul's only reality is that source. This kind of deconstruction, as we saw with John of the Cross, can feel like an annihilation of the self, but a fruitful one. Van Bragt writes,

> The element common to Buddhist and Christian contemplatives is the consciousness of an upheaval, a breakthrough, whereby something in the subject has to "give," to break, or to be annihilated. But this annihilation, painful as it may be at the moment, is not experienced as a loss or sacrifice but, on the contrary, as an immeasurable gain. What is broken or annihilated is . . . an obstacle or "cage."[71]

---

[68] Hee-Sung Keel, *Meister Eckhart: An Asian Perspective* (Louvain: Peeters, 2007), 295.

[69] Paul Mommaers and Jan van Bragt, *Mysticism: Buddhist and Christian: Encounters with Jan van Ruusbroec* (New York: Crossroad, 1995), 74.

[70] Keel, *Meister Eckhart*, 300.

[71] Mommaers and van Bragt, *Mysticism*, 95.

In both Mahayana and Eckhart, humans are grounded in an Absolute. Mahayana imagines this to be Buddha-nature or Suchness or Mind.[72] As Huang Po, the great ninth-century Zen master, asserts, "The real *substance of the universe* in this life: Mind and that *substance* do not differ one jot—that *substance* is Mind."[73] This is what is ultimately Real, and what conditions the possibility for enlightenment or full Buddhahood. What again is Buddha-nature or Suchness? Answering this becomes as elusive as the language games we found in Nagarjuna. As van Bragt notes regarding Buddhism, "The transcendence of the Absolute tends to become tenuous or ambiguous, and the Transcendent tends to lose all its contours."[74] This should not surprise us, as the Absolute cannot be objectified. It is *Shunyata*, emptiness that is even empty of emptiness, eternal and absolute, and knowable only in unknowability. Such depictions are strikingly similar to Eckhart's insistence on finding God beyond God. This is God in God's absolute *grunt*, as "pure nothingness" that is exactly the all. In short, for Buddhists, Buddha-nature grounds all beings and indwells as part of the ontology of all beings; for Eckhart, God grounds all beings and indwells as part of the ontology of all beings.

It strikes me also that both the image of the bodhisattva as well as other representatives of enlightenment act in the universe in the very same way as Eckhart suggests the one who has truly attained the divine *grunt*. In both cases the "saint" is deeply invested in the mundane world in a wholly transcendent way, one that is indiscriminately compassionate, one where mercy takes the forefront. McGinn refers to Eckhart's final spiritual posture in the world as a "mysticism of everyday life" with "down to earth practicality."[75] So, too, in Mahayana Buddhism, where the fantastical stories of magical deeds done by bodhisattvas are tempered with the day-to-day existence of one enlightened. Van Bragt observes, "Emptiness by itself is not the full expression of the true Buddhist ideal. It is a very important station on the Buddhist path, which must be gone through at all costs. However,

---

[72] Regarding Zen, John Blofeld writes, "Zen followers (who have much in common with mystics of other faiths) do not use the term 'God,' being wary of its dualistic and anthropomorphic implications. They prefer to talk of 'the Absolute' or 'the One Mind.'" See Translator's Introduction in *The Zen Teaching of Huang Po: On the Transmission of Mind*, trans. John Blofeld (New York: Grove Weidenfeld, 1958), 16, as cited in Mommaers and van Bragt, *Mysticism*, 71.

[73] Blofeld, *Zen Teaching of Huang Po*, 70, as cited in Mommaers and van Bragt, *Mysticism*, 190.

[74] Mommaers and van Bragt, *Mysticism*, 82.

[75] McGinn, *Mystical Thought*, 150, 157.

Buddhism does not stop there; it essentially goes a step further, by which it becomes more dialectical, complex, alive, and geared to everyday reality."[76]

Is Mahayana Theistic?

In discussing the debate between Western theists and atheists, Jan van Bragt notes "a polarization where both sides act as if they clearly knew that they were affirming or negating, as if they could tell you, at any given moment, precisely what 'God' is."[77] We've already noted above that what most Buddhists challenge is a "personal" God, a being distinct and outside of the universe. This is clearly what they seem to reject in Nirvana. And thus, both East and West have imagined Buddhism to be atheistic. In contrast, van Bragt argues that Buddhism "stands nearer to theism than atheism."[78] This is certainly the case in my mind. In reading commentaries on the sutras, both classical and modern, as well as a plethora of Mahayana literature, I cannot imagine Buddha-nature/Mind/Suchness, *as described by Buddhists*, as anything but an affirmation of theism. What else would one make of these terms that are also posited to be eternal, unchanging, the core of reality, the Ultimate, the Absolute? This certainly sounds like God.

If Buddhists insist that the Absolute *as* Absolute must be free from anthropomorphisms, conceptualizations, and objectifications, then they are insisting on exactly what the Christian mystical and philosophical traditions have been consistently insisting on as well.

Certainly classical theism could be a problem. David Tracy has argued that typical twentieth-century Thomism understood God's relationship to the world as conceptually external and while God's transcendence was affirmed, God's immanence was affirmed "in muted tones."[79] Tracy goes on to argue that "Insofar as classic theism is largely determined by categories of 'substance' rather than 'event' and 'relationality' (as it was and is), I believe there is no good philosophical defense."[80] This *kind* of theism is certainly not necessary, at least not in the Catholic tradition. In reflecting on Karl Rahner's career and its trajectories, Tracy observes,

---

[76] Mommaers and van Bragt, *Mysticism*, 131.

[77] Ibid., 70.

[78] Ibid., 71.

[79] David Tracy, "Kenosis, Shunyata, and Trinity: A Dialogue with Maseo Abe," in *The Emptying God: A Buddhist-Jewish-Christian Conversation*, ed. John Cobb and Christopher Ives (Maryknoll, NY: Orbis, 1990), 137.

[80] Ibid., 138–39.

> In his last several years, Rahner shifted mightily in his understanding of God: all theological thought became a "reduction to Mystery," which was clearly not identical to the intellectual "mysteries" of the neo-Scholastics. The more comprehensible God was, the more incomprehensible God became; indeed, even in the Beatific Vision, Rahner surmised, God would be more incomprehensible still—not Cartesianly clear as the neo-Scholastics hoped. This "mystagogical" turn in both Rahner and Lonergan (and Maréchal before them), like the "mystico-prophetic" turn of their Catholic successors (Metz, Schillebeeckx, Dupré, Gutiérrez, and many others—including myself) made "classical theism" either explicitly or more usually implicitly suspect as *the* Catholic understanding of God.[81]

Was then Eckhart a Buddhist in Dominican robes? Tracy is not convinced. He reminds us that Eckhart from start to finish was a "God-obsessed thinker."[82] We can also remember that, while radical unity was Eckhart's goal, it was a unity of love as well as knowledge. Lover and beloved merge, but there is indeed still love. There is *that* to be loved. Eckhart was a Christian. Certainly, he pushes us to the utter edge of language, concepts, and logic to point us to that which necessarily goes beyond, and he does so more radically than any other mystic in the Christian tradition. As McGinn concludes,

> No mystic in the history of Christianity was more daring and more detailed than Eckhart in the way in which he explored how true union with God must go beyond the mere uniting of two substances that remain potentially separable in order to attain total indistinction and substantial, or essential identity. . . . [But] we must remember that Eckhart's notion of indistinct union, like all of his thought was fundamentally dialectical, that is to say, union with God is indistinct in the ground, but we always maintain a distinction from God in our formal being as *ens hoc et hoc*. Even in the ultimate union of heaven, Eckhart insists, this distinction will remain.[83]

If Eckhart's mystical theology can remain within the bounds of Christian orthodoxy, and let us imagine that it can, then this suggests to me that

---

[81] Ibid., 138.

[82] Ibid., 148.

[83] McGinn, *Mystical Thought*, 148.

his theology could provide for Mahayana a way to consider its own religio-philosophical underpinnings to be theistic. They might believe in God after all! In my mind, the greatest distinction between an Eckhartian framework and a Mahayanan framework is the question of personal versus impersonal in their respective traditions. If Mahayana could legitimately be understood as theistic, it seems to have a take on the Absolute that is wholly impersonal. John Hick, in his *An Interpretation of Religion*, has argued that the Real (i.e., God) is both personal and impersonal and beyond both *as* the Real.[84] That Christian mysticism is personal (in some sense) and Buddhist mysticism is impersonal (in some sense) may be an answer to the distinction between Eckhart and Mahayana on this score. However, I have often wondered about this in Buddhism: *Why* is Buddha-nature (or Mind or Suchness) compassionate? Why would this characterize Buddha-nature as the Absolute? Kamalashila, whose stages of the bodhisattva path we noted above, says,

> He who wishes to gain omniscience [enlightenment] swiftly . . . should practice compassion from the very outset, for we know that compassion alone is the first cause of all the qualities of Buddhahood. . . . It is through compassion that the bodhisattva holds all the qualities of Buddhahood in the palm of his hand. . . . It is like life itself; only when there is life can the other faculties occur, and only when there is great compassion can the other qualities of a bodhisattva occur as well.[85]

In teaching Buddhism and its understanding that there is nonself, but all things are impersonal, my students often ask me questions such as, "What is being compassionate to what, and for what reason?" My short answer is that, while our aggregates are impersonal, their collectivity does indeed represent a sentient being who suffers. That is an incomplete answer. The real answer begs a deeper question: Why is the Absolute understood as compassion? Do Mahayana Buddhists think that "Buddha-nature *caritas est*"?

---

[84] John Hick, *An Interpretation of Religion: Human Responses to the Transcendent*, 2nd ed. (New Haven, CT: Yale University Press, 2004).

[85] Cited in Mommaers and van Bragt, *Mysticism*, 191.

Chapter 6

The Way of the Bodhisattva and the Spiritual Exercises

Shantideva (Eighth Century) and the *Bodhicaryavatara*

In the Indian medieval period, the preeminent scholarly institution was Nalanda in the northern state of Bihar, first established by King Shauraditya (c. 415–455), and later completed and expanded by a succession of Gupta kings. At Nalanda one could study Hindu and Buddhist philosophy, logic, grammar, medicine, art, and so on. It was not, per se, a Buddhist institution, and its royal benefactors were not Buddhists, but it was the greatest center for Buddhist learning for centuries, and even contained a large, thriving Buddhist monastery. Nalanda retained its intellectual grandeur in northern India until it was sacked by Muslim invaders in 1197. Among many of the great minds from Nalanda was Shantideva, an eighth-century monk and scholar whose *Bodhicaryavatara* is considered one of the most important Mahayana texts of the bodhisattva path. It also represents a robust defense of the Madhyamaka (Middle) school of Mahayana philosophy, which began with Nagarjuna and continued to develop under such greats as Aryadeva, Buddhapalita, Chandrakirti, and later Atisha, all of whom we met in chapters past. Finally, the *Bodhicaryavatara* is simply one of the most beautiful spiritual expressions of Mahayana Buddhism, and perhaps the premier spiritual text in Tibet.[1] *Bodhicaryavatara* could be translated "Undertaking the Way to Awakening," with *bodhi* meaning "awakening"; *carya* meaning "way to act," "path," or "training"; and *avatara* meaning "bringing out." The text

[1] Most of the *Bodhicaryavatara* was written in a form of poetry known as *anushtubh*, a simple two-line verse form of thirty-two syllables. Though it does not meet the standards of high Sanskrit *kavya* poetics, it does provide many of the kinds of rich metaphors and wordplays that *kavya* represents.

also has been given the title *Bodhisattvacharyavatara*, or "Undertaking the Way of the Bodhisattva." It is popularly known in the West as *The Way of the Bodhisattva.*

Little is truly known about Shantideva, though much has been written about him. According to several of his legends, he was born in southwestern India, the son of a royal chieftain. After his father's death, he abandoned his right to rule and sought training under a number of Buddhist masters. Shantideva eventually entered the monastery at Nalanda where he was said to have disappointed everyone. He seemed to spend his days aimlessly and often asleep, and was regarded by his peers as lazy. Unknown to them, he spent his nights in deep meditation practice and entered into realms where he could sit before and learn from the bodhisattva Manjushri. His brother monks, in an attempt to humiliate him, invited him to give a public recitation—"something new," they asked him. They erected a teaching-seat so high he would not have been able to ascend it, but with his magical powers he lowered the seat and began to recite the *Bodhicaryavatara*.[2] When he reached the penultimate portion (on wisdom), he ascended into the air and disappeared, although his voice could still be heard from the heavens. Other legendary material has him publicly countering the great Hindu yogi Shankaradeva, who with the support of the king demanded that if no Buddhists could erase a mandala that he could magically create in the sky, then they would be banned from the realm. Shantideva created a hurricane, which easily dispersed the mandala, and the king became a great public supporter of the Sangha.

Shantideva's legends are examples of a kind of typology in the Indian world. He seems to be lowly but is actually a great spiritual adept. He seems to be impotent but actually has great spiritual powers. All this gives his teaching authority, a reason to believe that it represents something transcendent. Most recessions of the *Bodhicaryavatara* have ten chapters: (1) Praising of *Bodhicitta*, (2) Confession of Sins, (3) Acceptance of *Bodhicitta*, (4) Perseverance in *Bodhicitta*, (5) Guarding Alertness, (6) Perfection of Patience, (7) Perfection of Endeavor, (8) Perfection of Meditation, (9)

---

[2] I will be normally following the Sanskrit recession that is found in the critical edition of the tenth-century commentary by Prajnakaramati and translation found in Shantideva, *The Bodhicaryavatara*, trans. Kate Crosby and Andrew Skilton (Oxford: Oxford University Press, 1995), and Shantideva, *Shantideva's Bodhicaryavatara* [with Original Sanskrit text and English translation], trans. Parmananda Sharma, 2 vols. (New Delhi: Aditya Prakashan, 1990). I will also augment these translations with Shantideva, *The Way of the Bodhisattva*, trans. Padmakara Translation Group (Boston: Shambhala, 2003).

Perfection of Wisdom, and (10) Dedication.[3] As we saw in chapter 5, most explications of bodhisattva training held ten stages or *bhumis*, and these tended to loosely follow the traditional ten perfections (*paramitas*), though ultimately Mahayana reduced them to six. While Shantideva does indeed have ten chapters, his outline more or less concentrates on the reduced six, with an extended presentation of *bodhicitta*.

As we saw in the last chapter, the bodhisattva path is an eons-long spiritual project toward complete Buddhahood. But it must begin somewhere, and Shantideva is clear that it begins with *bodhicitta* or enlightened mind. Recall that in Mahayana all have the Buddha-nature, which itself conditions the possibility for enlightenment. *Bodhicitta* in its absolute expression is that very Buddha-nature being itself. Yet it must become an active force in one's life. Tenzin Gyatso, the Fourteenth Dalai Lama, encourages generating the good will to seek enlightenment, and to do so out of compassion for others. Yet he also insists that this is not yet *bodhicitta*, but something of an aspiration for it.[4] Shantideva writes, "*Bodhicitta* in intention bears rich fruit for those still wandering in samsara. And yet a ceaseless stream of merit does not follow from it; for this will arise alone from active *bodhicitta*" (1.17).

Shantideva intends in his first chapter to drive home the importance of *bodhicitta*, the deep will for it, and ultimately the spontaneous expression of it in one's life. A human life is rare, and Shantideva asks, "If the advantage is neglected now, how will this meeting come again?" (1.4). Further, the stakes are high: "Except for perfect *bodhicitta*, there is nothing able to withstand the great and overwhelming strength of evil. . . . Only this will save" (1.6–7). D. T. Suzuki notes that when *bodhicitta* becomes an intense, spontaneous state of mind, one's whole consciousness changes. The fabricated desire now becomes utterly spontaneous, which "brings about a cataclysm in one's mental organization."[5] It is this new consciousness that makes one a bona fide bodhisattva.[6] "For when, with irreversible intent, the mind embraces *bodhicitta*, willing to set free the endless multitudes of beings, at that instant, from that moment on, a great and unremitting stream, a strength of

---

[3] (1) *Bodhicittanusamsa*, (2) *Papadeshana*, (3) *Bodhicittaparigrah*, (4) *bodhicittapramadah*, (5) *Samprajanyarakshanam*, (6) *Kshantiparamita*, (7) *Viryaparamita*, (8) *Dhyanaparamita*, (9) *prajnaparamita*, and (10) *Parinmana*.

[4] Tenzin Gyatso (Fourteenth Dalai Lama), *A Flash of Lightning in the Dark of Night: A Guide to the Bodhisattva's Way of Life*, trans. Padmakara Translation Group (Boston: Shambhala, 1994), 18.

[5] D. T. Suzuki, *Essays in Zen Buddhism* (London: Rider, 1950), 173, as cited in Francis Brassard, *The Concept of Bodhicitta in Shantideva's Bodhicaryavatara* (Delhi: Vasu, 2013), 20.

[6] Gyatso, *Flash of Lightning*, 12.

wholesome merit, even during sleep and inattention, rises equal to the vastness of the sky" (1.18–19).

If we can trust Prajnakaramati's commentary, chapters 2 (Confession of Sins) and 3 (Acceptance of *Bodhicitta*) were originally a single chapter.[7] Shantideva assumes that the reader has not yet attained deep-seated and spontaneous *bodhicitta*, and chapters 2 and 3 are aimed at its robust generation. Gyatso frames this chapter on confession as a form of the traditional Seven Branch Prayer for purifying oneself. This includes homage, offering, obeisance, and confession, the latter broken up into four powers (taking refuge, sincere regret for one's past unskillful acts, resolve to reform, and antidotes taken for reform).[8] More likely, this chapter represents the first half of that purification.[9] Shantideva begins, "In order to properly achieve this jewel of mind [*bodhicitta*], I offer worship to the Tathagatas, to the stainless jewel of the sacred Dharma and to the Sons of Buddhas, the oceans of excellence" (2.1). This is his homage. His offering is extraordinary, for he offers the entire world to them: "As many blossoms and fruits . . . as there are, as many jewels as there are . . . jewel-formed mountains, groves, incense, trees, lakes," and so on (2.2–5). Paradoxically, Shantideva declares that "I have no merit, I am completely destitute" (2.7). How then can he offer essentially all the good things of the entire world? Recall that, in Mahayana, all reality is interconnected or interdependent. There is no discrete separation in the chain of beings or the conditions that cause their arising. Gyatso reflects, "We all have a common responsibility for the world and are connected with everything in it. That is why we can make an offering of it."[10]

Finally, Shantideva announces his complete personal offering: "I give my entire self wholly to the Conquerors and to their sons. Take possession of me, sublime beings; out of devotion, I am your slave" (2.8). This is his transition to obeisance whereby he vows to serve, bathe, clothe, and so

---

[7] See Translators' Introduction, in Oxford text, xxxiv.

[8] Gyatso, *Flash of Lightning*, 21–27.

[9] Tobden describes the Seven Limbs as (1) prostrating to the buddhas and bodhisattvas, the antidote to pride; (2) making offerings, the antidote to greed; (3) confessing nonvirtues; (4) rejoicing in the positive karma created by ourselves and others, the antidote to jealousy; (5) requesting teachings; (6) requesting the masters do not abandon us; (7) dedicating the merit generated in the past, present, and future to the attainment of Buddhahood for the sake of all sentient beings. On this framing, chapter 2 represented the first three limbs and chapter 3 will represent the remaining four. See Geshe Yeshe Tobden, *Shantideva's Guide to Awakening: A Commentary on the Bodhicharyavatara*, trans. Manu Bazzano and Sarita Doveton, ed. Fiorella Rizzi (Boston: Wisdom Publications, 2017), 62–75.

[10] Gyatso, *Flash of Lightning*, 23.

forth all Buddhas and bodhisattvas, and to follow their previous examples of worship: "Just as Manjughosha [Manjushri] and others following him have worshiped the Conquerors, so I, too, worship the Tathagatas, who are Protectors, and their sons" (2.22). This leads him to go to the Buddha and Dharma for refuge (2.23), thereby beginning the above-mentioned four powers inherent in confession. Shantideva's confession is not a recitation of specific sins but something like realizing the state of existence for all beings, including himself. "By clinging to this transient life . . . I have acquired great evil" (2.43). He calls himself a "brute," a "doer of evil," and one "tormented by remorse." Chapter 2 moves from one terrifying image to another due to the karmic consequences of one's acts and the seemingly impossible situation one is in, only to show how one must take refuge in those beings who, like this future bodhisattva, will bring healing and escape. There is a "feverish horror which grips me, covered in my own uncontrolled excrement, as Death's terrifying messengers stand over me. . . . What saint will deliver me from this great fear? . . . Right now I go for refuge to the mighty Protectors of the world, who have undertaken the care of the world, the Conquerors who removed all fear" (2.45–48).

This is the posture that prepares one to truly attain *bodhicitta*. Notice that he does not ask any one of those "Conquerors" for forgiveness of his unnamed horrifying sins. Rather, those sins and the seemingly impossible karmic circumstance that he and the whole of sentient existence are imprisoned by shows him that the only way out is Buddhahood by the support of Buddhas and bodhisattvas before him. He must become like that! "Just as all the Buddhas of the past embraced the awakened attitude of mind, and in the precepts of the bodhisattvas, step by step abode and trained, just so, and for the benefit of beings, I will also have this attitude of mind, and in those precepts, step by step, I will abide and train myself" (3.23–24). Now he has bona fide *bodhicitta*, and the Buddhas before him praise it: "Today my life has given fruit. This human state has now been well assumed. Today I take my birth in Buddha's line, and have become the Buddha's child and heir" (3.26). Modern master, Geshe Yeshe Tobden, comments that now he is "a new bodhisattva."[11]

The whole of chapters 2–3 of the *Bodhicaryavatara* align impressively with the seven parts of the Supreme Worship (*anuttara-puja*), particularly found in the *Bhadracarya*, which circulated widely for many centuries before and after Shantideva. Shantideva himself recommends Supreme Worship in his other famous work, the *Shiksha Samuccaya* (Compendium of Texts).

---

[11] Tobden, *Shantideva's Guide to Awakening*, 75.

Crosby and Skilton note, "What then is the Supreme Worship, and what is its function? . . . [I]t is a ritual expressing the ideals of Mahayana Buddhism. More specifically it is concerned with furthering the central religious aspiration . . . namely the arising of the Awakening Mind."[12]

Recall from the last chapter that the first stage (*bhumi*) of the bodhisattva path is known as *joyful*. Chapter 3 of the *Bodhicaryavatara* begins, "With joy I celebrate the virtue that relieves all beings from the sorrows of the states of loss, and places those who languish in the realms of bliss. . . . The intention, ocean of great good, that seeks to place all beings in the state of bliss, and every action for the benefit of all: such is my delight and all my joy" (3.1–4). Now the bodhisattva path is not imagined to be merely arduous, but a great joy whereby service to all *is* the expression of Buddhahood. Some of the most moving verses in the whole of the *Bodhicaryavatara* come from this section whereby the emerging bodhisattva vows to become

> doctor, nurse, the medicine itself . . . For all sentient beings, poor and destitute, may I become a treasure ever plentiful. . . . And all my merits gained and to be gained, I give them all away withholding nothing. . . . Nirvana is attained by giving all, Nirvana the objective of my striving. Everything therefore must be abandoned, and it is best to give it to all others. (3.8–12)

This last verse should not be overlooked. Shantideva seeks Nirvana and is thereby willing to "abandon" all things, while also willing to give everything away in virtual eternal service:

> May I be a guard for those who are protectorless, a guide for those who journey on the road. For those who wish to go across the water, may I be a boat, a raft, a bridge. May I be an isle for those who yearn for landfall, and a lamp for those who long for light; for those who need a resting place, a bed; for all who need a servant, may I be their slave. (3.18–19)

There are another dozen verses in the same heroic and compassionate vein.

Chapter 4, *bodhicittapramada*, can be translated variously but reflects treating *bodhicitta* with the opposite of negligence. Shantideva begins, "The son of the Conqueror, who has grasped *bodhicitta* firmly, must never turn aside from it, but always strive to keep its discipline" (4.1). Like any heroic

---

[12] See translators' notes in Oxford edition, 11.

endeavor, it is still possible to lose one's momentum, and the gravity of this aspiration is indeed daunting. Shantideva recognizes that some vows are rashly made, but this one is not. It reflects aspirations of the Buddhas and has been thoroughly vetted. "So why should I now doubt and hesitate?" (4.3). Further, the stakes are great, not just for oneself, but for the whole world: "For if I bind myself with promises but fail to carry out my words in deed, then every being will have been betrayed. What destiny must lie in store for me?" (4.4). One must persevere no matter what. He again reminds the reader that a human birth is rare, that life is fleeting, and that slacking in resolve also betrays oneself (4.15, 16, 20, 23).

Shantideva calls for a kind of militant attitude, waging war on his own defilements; these are the enemies. Consider his own words: "This shall be my all-consuming passion; filled with rancor I will wage my war! Though this emotion seems to be defiled, it halts defilements and shall not be spurned. Better if I perish in the fire, better that my head be severed from my body than ever I should serve or reverence my mortal foes, defiled emotions" (4.43–44). In saying this, he does not exactly intend to support a kind of *righteous anger*. Rather, until the defilements or emotional attachments are completely eliminated, why not use one's karmic entanglement to be attached to the bodhisattva ideal? He ends with a clever Mahayana principle: the defilements themselves are empty anyway. So, if one is afraid of the great undertaking or overwhelmed by it, realize that "they are simple mirages, and so—take heart! Banish all your fear and strive to know their nature" (4.47). This is taken up fully in chapters 8 and 9 of the *Bodhicaryavatara*.

Bassard notes, "The distinction between fruitful and fruitless practice could be made on the basis of the type of mind adopted by the meditator, that is, by the one who is watching."[13] This is what Shantideva intends by his fifth chapter, "Guarding Awareness/Alertness." "Those who wish to keep a rule of life must guard their minds in perfect self-possession. Without this guard upon the mind, no discipline can ever be maintained" (5.1). All the defilements take to the mind unless it is guarded. He likens them to a rutting elephant and other hostile animals, or to ghosts, and so on. "By simple guarding of this mind alone, all these things are likewise bound" (5.5). As Gyatso has reflected, "All suffering in this life and others is created by the unsubdued mind. . . . Nothing is more important than guarding the mind."[14] This literally sums up Shantideva's fifth chapter. He reflects on extraordinary acts of generosity or daunting ascetical austerities, and

13 Bassard, *Concept of Bodhicitta*, 71.

14 Gyatso, *Flash of Lightning*, 41.

concludes that they are worthless without a guarded mind (5.16, 27). One has to scrutinize everything that enters or affects it, and give no quarter to unskillful mental states. In a series of verses, he reflects on these mental states, such as reactivity, inflated ego, contempt of others, and so on. He ends each verse with "I remain like a block of wood" (5.48–53), that is, I will not engage them.

Chapters 6 and 7 of the *Bodhicaryavatara* reflect two of the traditional six Mahayana perfections, patience and endeavor. The brunt of chapter 6 deals with patience in a threefold way: enduring suffering or pain (6.11–21), patience as a reflection on the teaching (6.22–32), and patience in light of injuries from others (6.33–75). The larger framework for it all is anger, how one can cope with it and how one can avoid it. Shantideva calls it "my enemy" that "has no other function but to kill me" (6.8). Gyatso suggests that "the main obstacles to the development of *bodhicitta* is desire toward harm, resentment, and anger."[15] This is surely reflected in the *Bodhicarya-vatara*, and Shantideva argues for a radical change in perspective. The first has to do with understanding the very nature of all phenomena, which arise because of causes and conditions affecting it. If, then, the actions of people are determined by this network of causes, how can one really blame any individual for the consequences? There is no sentient being that has an independent self-will uninfluenced by these outside causes. So, while sentient beings do have levels of volition, Shantideva wants us to focus on the causes that affect both their actions and volitions. Most strikingly, however, he also argues from the law of karma that his past actions have actually conditioned the evil that has come back to him via the person harming me. "Previously, I too caused just such pain to living beings. Therefore this is just what I deserve" (6.42). One's karmic responsibility gets even graver: "Those who harm me come against me, summoned by *my* evil karma. But they will be the ones who go to hell, and so it is myself who bring *their* ruin. . . . Therefore I am *their* tormentor!" (6.47–49).

Thich Nhat Hanh, in reflecting on the perfection of patience, suggests something quite insightful. He sees this perfection as really about enlarging one's heart and mind. It "is the capacity to receive, embrace, and transform."[16] For Thich Nhat Hanh, only when our hearts and minds are loving and spacious can we engage pain, hatred, and fear in a transformative way. Shantideva takes it even further, reminding us that life's challenges help us to develop on the bodhisattva path: "Therefore, since he helps me on the

---

[15] Ibid., 57.

[16] Thich Nhat Hanh, *The Heart of the Buddha's Teaching* (New York: Harmony, 1998), 198.

path to Awakening, I should long for an enemy like a treasure discovered in the home, acquired without effort" (6.107).

As patience is the antidote to anger, chapter 7's perfection of endeavor is the antidote for laziness. Shantideva spends much of this chapter on mental states typically regarded as unskillful, such as desire, delight, and pride. Here, the term he uses for desire is *chanda*, not *trshna*, which is craving or thirst. *Chanda* becomes the very source for endeavor. One surely desires spiritual development, Buddhahood, and the release of suffering in the world. Delight or pleasure (*rati*) can be an attachment, but it can also reflect experiencing a harmonious and flourishing mind and heart. Pride (*mana*) can be an ego-attachment, and typically is. Shantideva distinguishes negative pride from self-confidence, something one positively has to have in order to progress. "For I must conquer everything. Nothing should conquer me. This pride should be wedded to me, for I am a son of the lionlike Conqueror. . . . They are truly the heroes, who bear their pride to victory over the enemy pride; who, slaying the enemy pride though he is ubiquitous, readily present the fruit of their victory to the people" (6.59).

As we saw in Buddhaghosa, Buddhist spiritual development can be characterized in three ways: morality, meditation, and insight. And as noted, all three imply each other. The last two of the six Mahayana *paramitas*, meditation and insight, represent Shantideva's next two chapters. Shantideva's focus is in his insistence on the imperative for solitude and freedom from distraction, that is, the monastic life. Further, he advocates at length for the cultivation of a kind of disgust for the body and its unremitting search for gratification, what Buddhaghosa called *ten meditations on foulness*. In this sense, we see a relatively truncated presentation of the many kinds of mental absorption exercises available. What is most interesting in this chapter is his meditation of *equalizing self and others*. "At first one should meditate intently on the equality of oneself and others as follows: 'All equally experience suffering and happiness. I should look after them as I do myself'" (8.90).

Why should you care if others suffer? Shantideva seems to want to prove that this is simply the most rational thing to do. He compares the collection of sentient beings to limbs of a body that are really "undivided in its nature to suffer and be happy" (8.91). He also argues that "I should dispel the suffering of others because it is suffering like my own suffering" (8.94). "I and other beings in wanting happiness are equal and alike . . . in fleeing suffering, are equal and alike. What difference is there to distinguish us?" (8.95–96). In anticipating the question of why I would not naturally care for myself and my future more than that of others, Shantideva responds that our future lives are not really the same "me." Thus, to be concerned for my future life is to be concerned for some "other" person. Why then not be concerned for the contemporary other (8.97–98)? And then to the question of some kind of continuum of consciousness from one life to the next, he replies that such things are not real. "The person who experiences suffering does not exist" (8.101). This is presumably because all things are empty, the ultimate truth.

Since the time of Nagarjuna, Mahayana has distinguished between conventional or relative truth (*samvriti*) and absolute truth (*paramartha*). *Paramartha* is the transconceptual, nondual realization of emptiness, while *samvriti* refers to empirical existence. Shantideva has effectively jumped from one level of discourse to another. Is this a legitimate move? Paul Williams, in an extended critique of Shantideva's argument, cries foul. "Even if there are no true Selves, there are everyday transactional distinctions. A conventional person is the owner of the pain. If I can distinguish at all between myself and you, then I can give priority to myself even if that is held to be selfish. The 'ought' of unselfishness simply does not follow the 'is' of *anatman* (non-self). Why should I not be selfish [or at least give priority to my own condition]? This cannot be answered by the perspective of no Self."[17]

I believe the only real answer that Shantideva might ultimately give is what we saw in chapter 5 of this volume: that the very nature of Ultimate Reality is compassion. And the only way to be authentic to one's own nature—one's Buddha-nature—is thus to be compassionate, universally and indiscriminately. Shantideva distills his presentation in several verses:

> All the joy the world contains has come through wishing happiness for others. All the misery the world contains has come through wanting pleasure for oneself. Is there need for lengthy explanation? Childish beings look out for themselves, while Buddhas labor for the good of others. See the difference that divides them? If I do not give away my happiness for others' pain, Enlightenment will never be attained, and even in samsara, joy will fly from me. . . . If this "I" is not relinquished wholly, sorrow likewise cannot be avoided. . . . To free myself from harm and others from their sufferings, let me give myself away, and cherish others as I love myself. (8.129–36)

It is simply the nature of things.

Shantideva begins his section on the perfection of wisdom (insight) thus: "All these branches of the Doctrine the Powerful Lord [Buddha]

---

[17] Paul Williams, *Studies in the Philosophy of the Bodhicaryavatara: Altruism and Reality* (Delhi: Motilal Banarsidass, 2000), 111.

expounded for the sake of wisdom. Therefore they must generate wisdom who wish to have an end to suffering" (9.1). In his wisdom chapter, Shantideva recognizes the distinction between conventional and absolute truth, and spends essentially the entire chapter defending the Madhyamika school's belief that absolute truth or complete *prajna* is experiencing emptiness (*shunyata*) at the core of all things as well as Suchness (*tathata*)—the suprarational, nonconceptual, nondual realization of the way things really are. The whole purpose of Madhyamika is to silence the restless, questing intellect of all fabrications for this realization. As Gyatso writes, "The final stage of the bodhisattva is combining insight into emptiness—the ultimate nature of reality—with universal compassion."[18] The entire chapter is devoted to showing how the Madhyamika school has this correct and why competing schools do not. Thus, he will refute the non-Mahayanists, the Mind-only school, the Samkya theory of self, the Nyana understanding of self, and so on, all to establish that there is only really *shunyata* at the bottom of all experience.

"By the good that is mine from considering the *Bodhicaryavatara*, may all people adorn the path to Awakening. Through my merit may all those who in any of the directions suffering distress in body or mind find oceans of happiness and delight" (10.1–2). Shantideva's final chapter, "Dedication," acts as a conclusion that is strikingly similar to chapter 3, yet there is a significant difference in the kind of self-offering. In his first chapter, Shantideva writes, "*Bodhicitta*, the awakening mind, in brief is said to have two aspects: First, aspiring, *bodhicitta in intention*; then, *active bodhicitta*, practical engagement" (1.15). As noted above, what Shantideva means by intention is really something extraordinary. It is far more than a volitional commitment, as it also contains a spontaneous and decisive mental state, a decided change in consciousness. Once this has taken hold, one truly enters the bodhisattva path and has become "the Buddha's child and heir" (3.26). Now in this final chapter of the *Bodhicaryavatara* one has literally become an *active bodhisattva*. The vows of this final chapter represent a "dedication in wisdom unstained."[19] These vows, while also including the vow to provide sustenance to all in need, and so on, now include profound powers: "Throughout the spheres and reaches of the world, in hellish states wherever

---

[18] Tenzin Gyatso (Fourteenth Dalai Lama), *Practicing Wisdom: The Perfection of Shantideva's Bodhisattva Way*, trans. Thupten Jinpa (Boston: Wisdom Publications, 2005), 15.

[19] Kunzang Pelden, *The Nectar of Manjushri's Speech: A Detailed Commentary on Shantideva's Way of the Bodhisattva*, trans. Padmakara Translation Group (Boston: Shambhala, 2010), 394.

they may be, may beings fettered there, tormented, taste the bliss and peace of Sukhavatii [Amitabha's Pure Land]. May those caught in the freezing ice be warmed. And from the massing clouds of bodhisattvas' prayers may torrent rain in boundless streams to cool those burning in infernal fires" (10.4–5). Now, with the bodhisattva path successfully tread, one has the power to act as a radical advocate, healer, and guide.

Ignatius of Loyola and the Spiritual Exercises

In contrast to the little we know historically of Shantideva, we know a great deal about Ignatius of Loyola, his life and personal experiences—thanks to the historical period in which he lived, his extant letters, and both his autobiography and spiritual diary.[20] Ignatius (1491–1556) was born to a noble family in the Basque town of Loyola in what is today northern Spain. He spent much of his early life as a soldier striving to promote himself in the royal court. He took up arms for the Duke of Najera in 1509, and for over ten years was a successful soldier. But in 1521, while storming the fortress of Pamplona, a cannonball shattered his leg. He returned to his family's estate in Loyola to convalesce. Prior to his injury and convalescence he had been inspired by many chivalrous stories of romantic glory. During his recovery he only had religious literature to read, such as the Gospels and lives of the saints. These, too, kindled within him a like kind of enthusiasm. He noticed, however, that the tales of chivalry and heroism that had energized and inspired him also quickly left him dry and dissatisfied. But when he read the lives of the saints, he not only felt inspired in the moment, he also experienced a prolonged satisfaction and inner joy. Ludolph of Saxony's *The Life of Christ*, a commentary on the Gospels that borrowed deeply from the church fathers, proved particularly important to Ignatius's spiritual development. He discovered within himself a desire to be like Christ and emulate the heroic lives of the saints.

In 1522, the recovered Ignatius made a pilgrimage to a Benedictine abbey in Montserrat, Spain. There he dropped "his sword and dagger at our Lady's altar in the church."[21] In his autobiography, *A Pilgrim's Journey*, Ignatius describes the change from "having a vain and overpowering desire

[20] Some of the following introductory material is also found in my *Christian Spirituality: Lived Experience in the Life of the Church* (Winona, MN: Anselm Academic, 2015), 175–79.

[21] Ignatius of Loyola, *A Pilgrim's Journey: The Autobiography of Ignatius of Loyola*, trans. and commentary Joseph Tylenda (Collegeville, MN: Michael Glazier, 1991), no. 17.

to gain renown" to feeling "loathsomeness for all his past life."[22] He left the abbey as a poor pilgrim and went to live in a cave in Manresa where he prayed many hours a day. Ignatius describes his year at Manresa as filled with mystical experiences of the Trinity, the way God created the world, the divinity and humanity of Christ, the presence of Christ in the Eucharist, and a particularly intriguing experience along the Cardoner River about a mile from Manresa:

> As he [self-reference] sat there the eyes of his understanding were opened and though he saw no visions he understood and perceived many things, numerous spiritual things as well as matters touching faith and learning, and this was with an elucidation so bright that all these things seemed new to him. He cannot expound in detail what he then understood, for they were many things, but he can state that he received such a lucidity in understanding that during the course of his entire life—now having passed his sixty-second year—if he were to gather all the helps he received from God and everything he knew, and add them together, he does not think they would add up to all that he received on that occasion.[23]

Tylenda notes, "So vivid and so powerful were these interior illuminations that Ignatius said he could not doubt their truthfulness and that he was even willing to give his life for them."[24]

Manresa was a decisive moment in his life where he reconsidered what it meant to follow Christ. Previously, he had viewed Christ as a model to be imitated. In addition to this, he now saw Christ as the one sent by the Father to win all humanity to salvation, and to call others to follow him in that single pursuit.[25] It was also at Manresa where Ignatius began formulating the Spiritual Exercises, a monthlong retreat that stands at the heart of his spiritual path. Ignatius briefly traveled to the Holy Land, only to be rebuffed as a begging nuisance and ordered by the Catholic Church authorities back to Europe. He decided that, in order to help others, he needed a theological education, which he began at the University of Alcala. He continued his

---

[22] Ibid., nos. 1, 10.

[23] Ibid., no. 30.

[24] Ibid., no. 37. Later, his interior life was so animated by divine grace that he writes, in 1547, perhaps in contrast to his autobiography, that "what he received at Manresa . . . was little compared to what he was receiving then." See "General Introduction," in *Ignatius of Loyola: The Spiritual Exercises and Selected Works*, ed. George Ganss (New York: Paulist, 1991), 31.

[25] "General Introduction," in *Ignatius of Loyola*, 32.

studies in Paris, where he met several students who also desired to live exclusively in the service of God and the church. They would ultimately migrate to Rome and form the religious order the Society of Jesus, or the Jesuits.

The Spiritual Exercises as a Path

The Spiritual Exercises is a silent retreat designed to help in making an "election" or decision, or confirming on a deep level a decision one has already made. It serves as a systematic way to come to a deep spiritual conversion. In the retreat director's manual, Ignatius explains,

> By the term *spiritual exercises* is meant every method of examination of conscience, of meditation, of contemplation, of vocal and mental prayer, and of other spiritual activities . . . every way of preparing and disposing the soul to rid itself of all inordinate attachments, and, after their removal, of seeking and finding the will of God in the disposition of our life for the salvation of our soul.[26]

Ignatius begins the exercises with the *First Principle and Foundation*: One is "created to praise, reverence, and serve God our Lord, and by this means to save his soul." This is the foundation. He continues, "The other things on the face of the earth are created for one to help them in attaining the end for which he is created. . . . Consequently, as far as we are concerned, we should not prefer health to sickness, riches to poverty, honor to dishonor, a long life to a short life. The same holds for all other things. Our one choice should be what is more conducive to the end for which we were created."[27]

Week One

The Exercises are divided into four periods, each lasting roughly one week. The entire Exercises follow the foundation that persons are created to praise and serve God. Everything in the world, then, is only valuable insofar as it supports this end. The first week commences with the meditation on the absolute love of God in creating human beings for the august end of

---

[26] *The Spiritual Exercises of St. Ignatius*, trans. Louis Puhl (Chicago: University of Loyola Press, 1951), no. 1. All citations are exact, except for my substituting inclusive language.

[27] Ibid., no. 23.

living in union with God eternally. Once the soul clearly understands this, the rest of the week focuses on sin (universal and personal) and how the world and one's own life have resisted this divine plan. By the end of the week, one ought to see one's sins clearly and be repulsed by them as well as realize that one is loved and saved by Christ even as a sinner.

Week Two

As the purpose of the first week is to bring souls to a deep conviction of their personal sinfulness and God's overwhelming grace, the purpose of the second week consists of eliciting a response to the question: Do you want to follow Christ? Week two's meditations help the soul to identify with the life of Christ and his ministry. One moves from meditations on the incarnation to his ministry and glorious entry into Jerusalem. Week one highlights personal impotence, while week two is about experiencing the liberating call of Jesus to be part of his universal saving project.

As a preparation for the second week, Ignatius has the retreatant meditate on the Call of the Earthly King. Here one imagines a king addressing his subjects with the following offer: "It is my will to conquer all the lands of the infidel." The king promises to fight side by side with one under the arduous conditions of war, with the promise of victory and a share in that victory." In this culture of knightly chivalry, it would seem impossible to say no to such a call. Then, of course, the a fortiori meditation following is that Christ now is the real king and wishes much more. "It is my will to conquer the whole world and all my enemies [Satan and sin], and thus to enter into the glory of my Father." Who could say no? One prays,

> Eternal Lord of all things, in the presence of Thy infinite goodness, and of Thy glorious mother, and of all the saints of Thy heavenly court, this is the offering of myself which I make with Thy favor and help. I protest that is it my earnest desire and my deliberate choice, provided only it is for Thy greater service and praise, to imitate Thee in bearing all wrongs and all abuse and all poverty, both actual and spiritual, should Thy most holy majesty deign to choose and admit me to such a state and way of life.[28]

In beginning the formal work of week two, Ignatius provides something of the rationale of the week; then, presuming the retreatant has

---

[28] Ibid., nos. 92–98.

taken up the Call of the King, "This is to ask for what I desire. Here it is to ask for an intimate knowledge of our Lord, who has become human for me, that I may love him more and follow him more closely."[29] Later in the second week, "A Meditation on the Two Standards" has the retreatant consider that both Christ and Lucifer call the soul to themselves. Lucifer inspires horror and terror and summons his demons to destroy the world. They tempt with riches and the empty honors that go with the sin of pride. Christ, on the other hand, sends his followers throughout the world to serve the saving gospel. He attracts his followers with spiritual poverty, that is, humility. We must clearly choose Christ. Throughout the second week, the retreatant gets to know Christ, his values, and his ministry. This, Ignatius thought, is the Christ one must desire with all one's heart and serve with all one's strength.

Retreatants also ask for the grace to decide *how* to follow Christ. Other meditations include Three Classes: those who rid themselves modestly of attachments, those who rid themselves of attachments so as to desire God above all things, and those who rid themselves of attachments such that they seek only God's will. Of course, one ought to seek the third option. Another meditation is on the Three Kinds of Humility: one that would never consent to a mortal sin; one that is indifferent to poverty or riches, honor or dishonor, and so forth, and is committed to avoiding even venial sins; and one with the positive desire for poverty and dishonor so as to fully resemble the poor and disdained Savior of the world. Here one begs the Lord for the grace of the third kind of humility.

Week Three

The third week of the Exercises is meant to confirm the decision (election) by considering the consequences of such a choice. This consists of a meditation on the passion of Christ and an identification with Jesus, who suffers with and for the brokenness of the world. One meditates on every part of Jesus's final week in Jerusalem, including the Last Supper, his agony in the garden, his trials with the Sanhedrin and Pontius Pilate, and his crucifixion. The point here is that the decision to follow Christ and share in his victory must also be a decision to do so in and through the Passion. This is the cost of discipleship. While daunting, the cross becomes a meeting place of God's power, witness to the gospel, and deep forgiveness.

---

[29] Ibid., no. 104.

Week Four

In the third week, retreatants elect to join Christ through everything. They have fallen deeply in love with him, become convinced of his message and ministry, and are prepared to embrace a discipleship that includes a paschal movement of dying to themselves for his sake. Now, during the fourth week, they meditate on his resurrected victory and share the glory of conquering evil. The retreatants experience Jesus alive, having surpassed all, and feel empowered to live in Jesus's unrestricted presence in the world. The mission and service of the gospel must be grounded in a lived experience of his victory.

During this final part of the Exercises, Ignatius has the retreatant enter into the Contemplation to Attain the Love of God. He reminds us that "love ought to manifest itself in deeds rather than in words." One meditates on standing before God and his angels and saints ("who intercede for me"), and then is enjoined to "ask for what I desire: an intimate knowledge of the many blessings received, that filled with gratitude for all, I may in all things love and serve the divine majesty. . . . I will make this offering of myself":

> Take, Lord, and receive all my liberty, my memory, my understanding, and my entire will, all that I have and possess. Thou has given all to me. To Thee, O Lord, I return it. All is Thine, dispose of it wholly according to Thy will. Give me Thy love and Thy grace, for this is sufficient for me.[30]

Making Sense of Ignatius and the Exercises

One ought not to imagine that after this comparatively short period of retreat one has become a full-fledged saint or has no ambivalence about the cost of discipleship. The Exercises represent a start, a rightly ordered aspiration for sainthood. The Exercises and all of Ignatian spirituality also collectively represent a particular kind of sainthood. The sainthood of John of the Cross is one of an elite monastic virtuoso whose life is highly contemplative and typically cloistered. One need not be a monk, of course, but it certainly helps a great deal. Ignatius's spirituality is an active one. As William James notes, "Saint Ignatius was a mystic, but his mysticism made him assuredly one of the most powerfully practical human engines that ever

[30] Ibid., nos. 230–34.

lived."[31] His discipleship and mysticism were geared to action. His spirituality strives quite consciously and systematically to discover God's presence in the day-to-day. It tries to *find God in all things* and to learn to become a *contemplative in action*, two key Ignatian principles.

The ways for doing this skillfully have to do with principles of *discernment of spirits* and the regular *consciousness examen*, both of which are introduced in the Spiritual Exercises.[32] Without losing ourselves in the details of how Ignatius understood discernment of spirits, he was confident that, upon scrutiny, one would perceive the movements of the Holy Spirit in one's life. One could also assess one's cooperation with those divine movements. Where was my openness to God, my generosity and self-offering? Where was my resistance to God, my fear or inordinate attachment? In order to discover this, he recommended a daily examination of consciousness where in prayer one reviewed the past events of the day and, with the aid of God's grace, confronted any lack of full engagement with God. Ignatius's contemporaries report that he practiced an examination of consciousness not just daily but hourly.[33] His goal was to be constantly in contact with his own consciousness and its unremitting commitment to service and to become increasingly sensitive to movements of the Holy Spirit guiding him.

One of the most important insights in Ignatius's discernment of spirits is that when one's will is rightly ordered, it can be trusted to be also God's will. God's will and the soul's will ought to be the same will. Karl Rahner understood God's grace—God's ongoing, active, saving presence in the soul—as a *supernatural existential*. As an *existential*, it represents a fundamental, necessary reality of the human condition. As *supernatural*, it represents something that is of God. God is always present, always speaking to the soul, always drawing it to himself and driving it toward the loving service of others. God's ongoing presence in the soul becomes the condition of possibility for the soul to experience itself. Reflecting on Ignatius and his extraordinary experiences of God, Rahner writes that "the awakening of such an experience with the divine is actually not an infusion of something not previously present in the person, but the explicit coming into one's own and the free acceptance of the human disposition that is always present."[34]

---

[31] Cited in Harvey Egan, *Ignatius Loyola: The Mystic* (Wilmington, DE: Michael Glazier, 1987), 135.

[32] See nos. 313–336 and 43, respectively.

[33] Egan, *Ignatius Loyola*, 63.

[34] Karl Rahner, *Ignatius of Loyola Speaks*, trans. Annemarie Kidder (South Bend, IN: St. Augustine's Press, 2013), 14.

Shantideva and Ignatius in Dialogue

What might we imagine in placing these two spiritual paths together? Of course, they have both similarities and differences, and these can be highlighted. Doing so has its own assets, but perhaps we can learn something about the very nature of the hero's journey, for this is what both of them fundamentally are. As we have seen in this chapter and the one preceding it, the bodhisattva path is more than daunting. To those versions of Mahayana where it is still possible to attain arhatship or the level of a *pratyekabuddha*, the bodhisattva vow seems particularly extraordinary, since it is unnecessary to attain enlightenment. According to Kamalashila's *Bhavanakrama* (*Stages of Meditation*), one could attain arhatship at the fourth of ten stages of development. Thus, perfect Buddhahood for the sake of all sentient beings becomes extremely heroic, particularly as this would involve eons of additional rebirths. For those versions of Mahayana where these other enlightenment experiences do not obtain, we can still appreciate the overwhelming task on which the bodhisattva-to-be embarks.

Ignatius is a hero as well. One of the more interesting historical facts in the formation of the early Jesuits is that in 1552 Jerónimo Nadal traveled to all the Jesuit houses in Europe to propagate the order's revised constitution among the many newly formed Jesuit communities. Nadal found that many of the early Jesuits did not quite know what it meant to be a Jesuit. Nadal used Ignatius's autobiography as their model. As I noted in an earlier publication,

> This is who the Jesuits would become: they were to be more "Ignatiuses," who could discover God in the context of service. Among other things, Ignatius's autobiography describes a soul who has learned how to discern disordered desires, and so reject them, and has discovered how to encounter God in daily life. . . . For Ignatian spirituality, being radically open to God's call, whatever it might be, requires cultivating a spacious, open heart and mind. Ignatius's autobiography focuses on helping souls and adopting the life of a pilgrim.[35]

Both paths or spiritualities crisscross each other in interesting ways. On the one hand, Ignatius seemed only focused on God's will with no strictly necessary regard for anyone else. Shantideva's path is wholly obsessed with others around him. Shantideva wishes to be balm for the sick, treasure for the destitute, protector, lamp, doctor, nurse, and medicine itself (3.8–19). On

---

[35] Feldmeier, *Christian Spirituality*, 176.

the other hand, Ignatius saw his service to Christ as wholly and completely one of doing God's work on earth. Service of souls dominates the Ignatian way. Interestingly enough, it is Shantideva who sees his help for all sentient beings as embracing monastic withdrawal and not active service. Direct aid comes somewhat late into the developing bodhisattva. In contrast, Ignatius sees his experience of God in the context of service. This is what *contemplation in action* is all about.

In both paths, Shantideva and Ignatius seek their own salvation. Nirvana is, in a sense, Shantideva's sole interest. It is "the object of my striving" (3.12). Personal salvation also dominates Ignatius, as we saw in his principle and foundation: "One is created to praise, reverence, and serve God our Lord, and by this means to save his soul" (no. 23). For both of them, however, personal salvation implicated the whole world and a universal salvation project. There is not one without complete engagement with the other.

Another creative tension we find in both spiritualities is the extraordinary witness of great humility and even some sense of impotence along with a strong sense of self-authorization. Shantideva recognizes, as we have seen, that this is a rare life and not one to be squandered. "This will be my all-consuming passion. . . . I will wage war. . . . I will bind my mind. . . . I will remain a block of wood [against unskillful thoughts]. . . . For I must conquer everything" (4.43; 5.48ff.; 6.59). Ignatius also has a great sense of self-authorization. The principle and foundation is designed that one may "save his [own] soul" (no. 23). The Call of the King challenges him: "Whoever wishes to join me in this enterprise must be willing to labor with me" (no. 95) and so "this is the offering of myself which I make . . . to imitate Thee" (no. 98).

In both Ignatius and Shantideva we see such inner confidence and resolve in a creative tension with utter humility, and the need for—may we say it—grace. As noted above, Shantideva imagines that he has little to nothing to offer in and of himself. Without the spontaneous arising of *bodhicitta*, which is itself Buddha-nature awakened, "I have no merit, I am completely destitute" (2.7). Without "perfect *bodhicitta*, there is nothing able to withstand the great and overwhelming strength of evil. . . . Only this will save" (1.6–7). This recognition, that he is a sinner and inextricably caught in samsara, is exactly what makes him take refuge in the Buddhas. He realizes that the Buddhas are not just images of perfection or inspiring models, and he expects their necessary support. He vows to worship and serve the Buddhas and bodhisattvas, and he recognizes that it is *they* who will deliver him from his fears and become his protectors (2.8, 45–48). Ignatius, too, rather than characterizing the path as a works-righteousness Pelagianism, constantly has to rely on God's grace. We know from his autobiography that his life was dominated by God's grace, and we see this dominance in the Exercises. Every spiritual advancement depends on God's grace; every exercise begs for the graces, principally to experience true knowledge of oneself in the first week, to identify with Christ in the second, to gain the strength and resolve to accept the cost of discipleship in the third, and to experience the joy of sharing in Christ's victory in the fourth week. There is grace at every turn.

This creative tension between confidence and humility or between self-authorization and a recognition of one's lowliness and neediness is not really a paradox. It can be understood in two ways. The first is that both understand their very makeup as potential for empowerment. For Shantideva this is Buddha-nature, and for Ignatius this is being made in the image and likeness of God. For Shantideva, the very nature of the universe is compassion expressed; he is being who he is when empowered by *bodhicitta*. For Ignatius, his well-formed will and God's will are the same will. Ignatius is only fully human—expressing his truest nature—when aligned with God. The second way we might look at this is something of a study of the saints. When one reviews the lives of the saints in Catholicism, one sees an interesting combination of confidence and humility. When there is no arrogance or ego to advance, they experience themselves as empowered by God to do great things.

Recognizing that all good only comes from God in no way implies that one's self-authorization gets eradicated. Rather, God and the soul form a holy synergy. The synergy for Shantideva is that of universal Buddha-nature and his own experience of *bodhicitta*. It gives him a new consciousness, a new way of seeing things. Ignatius experienced this new consciousness in Manresa. The "eyes of his understanding were opened and . . . he understood and perceived many things, numerous spiritual things as well as matters touching on faith and learning, and this was with an elucidation so bright that all these things seemed new to him."[36]

The road to holiness is long and hard. Both of our spiritual heroes demand constant effort, constant vigilance, and unqualified self-awareness. Both regularly reflect on the cost of discipleship. Shantideva characterizes it as innumerable lifetimes of inner and outer work. Ignatius will identify it as taking on the passion of Christ in utter selflessness and humility. And both are empowered at the end. Shantideva is now ready to bring tastes of Amitabha's Pure Land bliss to those in hell states as Buddha's heir. Ignatius is able to "drop his sword and dagger" and take up the King's call for a new war, one that seeks

---

[36] Ignatius, *Pilgrim's Journey*, no. 30.

to walk with Christ into the heart of sin so that all who came from Christ in creation can now return back to him purified in his blood.

One could imagine a comparison of these two paths and the spiritualities that undergird them in other ways. A Christian could certainly learn from Shantideva strategies on how to consider annoying or even malicious persons in our life. We might realize that, given our sins, we deserve persecution. Or we might recognize the fact that human freedom is never an expression of an unadulterated free will. There really are conditions and causes outside of us that affect how we engage life. Likewise, perhaps a Buddhist could learn from Ignatius how poverty, humility, and even persecution can actually energize one's spiritual life in surprising ways.

This particular comparison may tell us something else. I suggest that one could extrapolate the similarities in both paths—paths that have very different assumptions about the way the universe works or how the human being is made up—to see something potentially more universal. Humans have the potential to do great things and become great beings. They cannot do it on their own, nor can they solely depend on what is outside of their will. Rather, they must create a synergy between the Absolute and the individual. This synergy sets up the conditions for working the path from start to finish. It will necessarily be a path that demands nothing less than everything and requires deep acknowledgment of one's sins, weaknesses, and history. It will necessarily be a path that requires skillful ways to obtain self-knowledge and skillful ways to keep constant vigilance of the movements in one's heart and mind. And above all, it will necessarily be a path where the Absolute Transcendent axis is unified and interpreted through the mundane axis of wholesome, healing service to the world. Both axes have to be present at the same time and all the time.

Chapter 7

Zen Mind/Christian Mind

Introducing Zen

Buddhism was introduced into China by the end of the first century CE, but it was at best only marginally successful. The Buddhist Indian values, such as solitary meditation, celibacy, monasticism, and renunciation of social class, ran counter to the Chinese Confucian culture. This is not to suggest that Buddhism in China did not have some popular and even royal support—it did. Nonetheless, it did not take off until the arrival of the missionary Bodhidharma in the sixth century. According to ancient tradition, Bodhidharma was the son of an Indian prince and the twenty-eighth patriarch in a direct line of transmission from the Buddha. Bodhidharma is a legendary figure, and this term ought to be taken in both its typical usages: he is a heroic figure whose influence in creating Zen[1] cannot be overstated. He is also a figure of legends, as little reliable historical information is known about him.[2]

One famous tradition has him traveling to China in 527 where he met the emperor, a devout Buddhist. The emperor said to him, "Since I came to the throne, I have built countless temples, copied countless sutras, and given supplies to countless monks. Is there any merit in this?" Bodhidharma replied, "There is no merit whatsoever." Then the emperor asked, "What, then, is true merit?" He replied, "True merit consists in the subtle comprehension of pure wisdom, whose substance is silent and void."[3] After his audience with the emperor, he crossed the Yangtze River and found a mountain cave where he remained seated in meditation for nine years until his

---

1 Also see *Ch'an* in Chinese.

2 Bodhidharma may also simply be a composite figure and not exactly historical at all! See Karl Olson, *The Different Paths of Buddhism: A Narrative-Historical Introduction* (New Brunswick, NJ: Rutgers University Press, 2005), 225.

3 Cited in John Wu, *The Golden Age of Zen* (New York: Image Books, 1996), 34–35.

legs wasted away. Another legend offers a riff on his nine-year meditation: At one point in those nine years he fell asleep. To ward off another failure in practice he cut off his eyelids so he could not fall asleep again. However, tea leaves grew to replace them. Thus began the practice of drinking tea in order to sustain mental alertness. One hopeful disciple, Hui-k'o, tried to get his attention during this period and was fully ignored by Bodhidharma. To show his earnestness, Hui-k'o cut off his arm at the elbow and presented it to Bodhidharma. Bodhidharma, impressed by this, took him on as a student and transmitted the Dharma to him. What is important about this story, which hopefully is exaggerated, is the importance of the teacher-disciple relationship and the establishment of dharma transmission from master to disciple.

One of the most important Mahayana sutras is the *Lankavatara Sutra*, composed originally in Sanskrit and imagined to be the Buddha's teaching while on a short visit to Sri Lanka. Probably written in the fifth century, it became enormously important to Zen. According to tradition, Bodhidharma gave Hui-k'o a Chinese copy of it and told him everything he needed to know was in it. The *Lankavatara* teaches that enlightenment is realized by doing away with all duality and rising above all distinctions. Further, it taught that the mind is inherently pure and, in fact, already enlightened. The challenge then is to realize this ever-present pure consciousness (Buddha-nature), which is also the absolute truth of all things. As we have already seen, Mahayana teaches that there is no objectifiable reality. This is not new. What might be new is the insistence that ultimately reality is simply the flow of reality revealing Buddha-nature. This being the case, the *Lankavatara Sutra* emphasizes the importance on just seeing this, on unmasking through meditation the fallacy of making any distinctions. A text attributed to Bodhidharma expresses the core insight of Zen:

> *A special transmission outside the scriptures,*
> *Not founded upon words or letters;*
> *By pointing directly to one's mind;*
> *It lets one see into one's own true nature,*
> *And thus attain Buddhahood.*[4]

One Japanese text, attributed to Bodhidharma though probably written a couple of centuries later, expresses the core of Zen:

---

[4] Cited in Heinrich Dumoulin, *Zen Buddhism: A History,* vol. 1, *India and China,* trans. James Heisig and Paul Knitter (New York: Macmillan, 1999), 85.

> If you wish to seek the Buddha, you ought to see into your own Nature; for this Nature is the Buddha himself. If you have not seen into your own Nature, what is the use of thinking of the Buddha, reciting the Sutras, observing a fast, or keeping the precepts? By thinking of the Buddha, your cause [meritorious deed] may bear fruit; by reciting the Sutras your intelligence may grow brighter; by keeping the precepts you may be born in the heavens; by practicing charity you may be rewarded abundantly; but as to seeking the Buddha, you are far away from him. . . . The Buddha is your own Mind.[5]

The great Zen scholar D. T. Suzuki summarizes it crisply: "This [spiritual] Nature is the Mind, and the Mind is the Buddha, and the Buddha is the Way, and the Way is Zen. . . . Zen is to see directly into one's original Nature."[6]

A further conceptual development came through Fa-tsang (643–712), the foremost protagonist of the Hua-yen school in China. As we have seen from the Buddha on, all phenomena exist only through causes and conditions outside of themselves. Further, we noted in the last chapter that Shantideva imagined all sentient beings as limbs of a body. For Shantideva, what made sentient beings indistinguishable was their suffering and wanting to be happy. Fa-tsang advanced this dramatically by teaching that all sentiency interpenetrated, that causes and conditions forming the possibility of phenomenal existence create a kind of web of sentiency where nothing is left out. Touch any part of that web, and the whole web is affected. Thus, all phenomena exist collectively as a kind of singular reality. Carl Olsen describes it thus: "Since each individual thing embraces everything else that is embraced by every one of those individual things, all phenomena are manifestations of the universal principle: everything in the cosmos is interconnected."[7]

What are we to make of these developments? Succinctly, in Zen, the interpenetrating, ever-changing universe is, at its core, Buddha-nature always expressing itself. And to distinguish oneself from others, or even other things, is to create a subject-object duality, to live in delusion. In the *Platform Sutra of the Sixth Patriarch*, the story is given on how Hui-neng became the sixth Zen patriarch (Bodhidharma being the first). Hung-jen (601–674), the fifth patriarch, intended to name his successor by a writing

[5] D. T. Suzuki, *Essays in Zen Buddhism: First Series* (New York: Grove Press, 1949), 233–34.

[6] Ibid., 234–35.

[7] Olson, *Different Paths of Buddhism*, 227.

contest on the nature of the practice. Shen-hsiu, the presumed heir apparent, wrote the following:

The body is the Bodhi tree.
The mind is like a clear mirror.
At all times we must strive to polish it,
And must not let dust collect.

The seemingly lowly monk Hui-neng wrote a response:

Bodhi originally has no tree,
The mirror has no stand.
Buddha-nature is always clean and pure;
Where is there room for dust?

The mind is the Bodhi tree.
The body is the mirror stand.
The mirror is originally clean and pure.
Where can it be stained by dust?[8]

What one sees in Shen-hsiu's poem, though beautiful and wise, is a fundamental dualism still present. The body and mind are characterized as holy and need to be constantly attended to in order to retain purity. In short, they are in contrast to the rest of reality. Hui-neng challenges any dualism, any separation among things. The challenge, as Hui-neng saw it, is not to keep the mind or body unstained; it is to realize that there is no separation or radical distinction in anything. Bodhi (enlightenment) is not a tree but *mind* as the very nature of everything in a co-arising universe.[9]

Another way to consider this issue of nonduality and how to skillfully live it comes from Master Ch'ing-yuan:

> Thirty years ago, before I began to study Zen, I said, "Mountains are mountains, waters are waters." After I got insight into the truth of Zen through the instruction of a good master, I said, "Mountains are not mountains, waters are not waters." But now, having attained

[8] Philip Yampolsky, trans. *The Platform Sutra of the Sixth Patriarch* (New York: Columbia University Press, 1967), 130–32.

[9] See my own take on this in Peter Feldmeier, *Encounters in Faith: Christianity in Interreligious Dialogue* (Winona, MN: Anselm Academic, 2011), 176–77.

> the abode of final rest [enlightenment], I said, "Mountains are really mountains, waters are really waters." Do you think that these three understandings are the same or different?[10]

In this first stage of consciousness we have a conventional understanding that differentiates. Rational minds make distinctions. There is the mountain, and there is the stream. A deeper penetration—second stage—reveals that the conventional understanding is really a mental construct, where in fact reality is the ever-flowing, interpenetrating universe. Objectifying or rarifying phenomena in the world or of the self are overcome, and the seemingly clear distinctions between oneself and all else dissolve in the context of interrelatedness. With no duality, where everything is recognized as empty, then reality itself reveals Buddha-nature. There is no exterior or eternal reference of assessment, but only the interpenetrating flow of all reality. The third stage of realization is to see how emptiness reveals itself in form. Here there can be a kind of affirmation of things in the context of their relativity. The truly awakened self experiences the fullness of Dharma in the wonder of mountains and streams. Here one does not revert to the initial perspective but knows absolute truth in the context of conventional truth, the ultimate dimension in the context of the relative dimension. Buddha-nature is ever revealing and expressing itself.

Zen characterizes enlightenment as *Ordinary Mind* or "nothing special," since enlightenment is posed here as just being fully nondualistically present. Consider the following well-known story: A disciple asks his master how he disciplined himself in the truth. He replied, "When I am hungry I eat; when tired I sleep." The disciple observed, "Everybody does this." "No," he replied, because when they eat they do not just eat but are thinking of various other things, thereby allowing themselves to be disturbed; when they sleep, they do not sleep, but dream of a thousand and one things. This is why they are not like myself." Another widely told Zen story goes back to the time of the Buddha.[11] In this narrative the Buddha had gathered his disciples around him to teach them. Instead of speaking, however, he merely held up a lotus flower. Some were waiting for him to speak after this, thinking that patient attention was part of the lesson. Others imagined that the lotus flower itself was the sermon. The lotus had regularly been used in the Indian culture as

---

[10] Cited in Masao Abe, *Zen and Western Thought* (Honolulu: University of Hawaii Press, 1985), 4.

[11] Walpola Rahula, *Zen and the Taming of the Bull: Towards the Definition of Buddhist Thought* (London: Gordon Fraser, 1978), 19.

a metaphor. It arises out of muddy waters, but its texture is such that none of the slime or mud sticks to it. Thus, the enlightened person remains pure in the midst of the world. It turns out that the Buddha neither intended to speak nor was he using the lotus as a symbol for anything. Only one monk, Mahakashyapa, understood the teaching, and in doing so was enlightened. What did Mahakashyapa see or understand? The flower did not represent anything. It is what it is, and he simply saw it wholly, completely, and nondualistically.

The great Theravada scholar Walpola Rahula has commented on these Zen examples, but without being much impressed. He reflects that these simply represent what the *Satipatthana Sutra* (Four Foundations of Mindfulness) calls *sampajana-pabba* or "mindfulness with clear comprehension."[12] What Rahula might be missing is that these are not merely cases of full mindfulness, as challenging as that can be, but rather expressions of nondual participation in Buddha-nature. The great Zen master Dogen Zenji reflects, "To study the Buddha Way is to study the self. To study the self is to forget the self. To forget the self is to be actualized by myriad things. When actualized by myriad things, your body and mind as well as the bodies and minds of others drop away. No trace of enlightenment remains, and this no-trace continues endlessly."[13]

What we see here takes us beyond what we have seen in Nagarjuna or Shantideva. "No trace of enlightenment remains, and this no-trace continues endlessly." Why would no trace of enlightenment remaining be a good thing? For Dogen, enlightenment is already there, already realized. To imagine enlightenment as if it were something other than the endlessly continuous flow of reality—as if it *could* have a trace—is to misunderstand its very nature. As Master Shido Munan once put it, "Enlightenment is the Buddha's greatest enemy."[14] Dogen:

> Now, when you trace the source of the Way, you find that it is universal and absolute. It is unnecessary to distinguish between "practice" and "enlightenment." The supreme teaching is free, so why study the means to attain it? The Way is, needless to say, very far from delusion. Why, then, be concerned about eliminating the latter? The Way is completely present where you are, so of what use is practice or enlightenment? However, if there is the slightest

---

[12] Ibid., 18–19.

[13] Cited in Stephen Addis, *Zen Sourcebook: Traditional Documents from China, Korea, and Japan* (Indianapolis: Hackett Publishing, 2008), 152.

[14] Cited in Feldmeier, *Encounters in Faith*, 176.

> difference in the beginning between you and the Way, the result will be greater separation than between heaven and earth. If the slightest dualistic thinking arises, you will lose your Buddha mind.[15]

Satori

During the eighth century, Chinese Zen masters arrived in Japan, but Zen failed to flourish in Japanese soil until the Japanese master Myoan Eisai (1141–1215) returned from his second trip to China. There he was exposed to and transformed by the southern school of Zen known as Rinzai Zen, based on the Lin-chi school. Rinzai is the Japanese rendering of Lin-chi. Lin-chi is famous for the axiom "When you meet the Buddha, kill the Buddha." His fuller teaching was, "When you meet the Buddha, kill the Buddha; when you meet a Patriarch, kill a Patriarch. Only then will you obtain absolute emancipation from any attachment."[16] Lin-chi made shouting and even violence a standard pedagogical tool during his career. His whole point, and the aim of the southern school, was to provoke a sudden enlightenment or *satori* experience.[17] As Suzuki asserts succinctly: "Satori *is* enlightenment."[18]

Satori marks Zen dramatically from what we have seen in other forms of Buddhism so far. Heretofore, traditional Buddhism imagined that enlightenment would be a many-eons-long project of innumerable lifetimes. It was an ongoing progress of developing the perfections and penetrating deeper levels of meditative absorption and wisdom. As Suzuki notes, "Zen ignores all these, and boldly declares that when one sees into the inmost nature of one's being, one instantly becomes a Buddha."[19] Suzuki writes,

> Practically, satori means the unfolding of a new world hitherto unperceived in the confusion of a dualistically trained mind. . . . The world for those who have gained satori is no more the old world as it used to be. . . . The opening of satori is the remaking of life itself.

---

[15] Cited in Addis, *Zen Sourcebook*, 141–42.

[16] Cited in Donald Lopez, "Introduction," in *Religions of Tibet in Practice*, ed. Donald Lopez (Princeton, NJ: Princeton University Press, 1997), 4–5.

[17] Julia Ching, "The Encounter of Ch'an with Confucianism," in *Buddhist Spirituality II: Later China, Korea, Japan and the Modern World*, ed. Takeuchi Yoshinori (New York: Crossroad, 1999), 46.

[18] D. T. Suzuki, *Essays in Zen Buddhism* (London: Rider & Co., 1973), 266 (emphasis mine).

[19] Ibid., 363.

> When it is genuine—for there are many simulacra of it—its effects on one's moral and spiritual life are revolutionary. . . . The birth of a new man is really cataclysmic.[20]

While Suzuki recognizes that there are different levels to satori experiences, a "gradation in satori as to its intensity,"[21] nonetheless, the satori experience cannot be overstated. Suzuki again:

> Without the attainment of satori no one can enter into the mystery of Zen. It is a new birth, religiously and morally the revaluation of one's relationship with the world; the world now appears to be dressed in a different garment, which covers up all the ugliness of dualism. Satori is the *raison d'etre* of Zen, and without which Zen is no Zen. Therefore every contrivance (*upaya* [skillful means]), disciplinary or doctrinal, is directed toward the attainment of satori.[22]

Traditional stories of satori or sudden enlightenment experiences fill the annals of Zen literature, and they have a typical pattern: a deeply earnest monastic strives diligently in the practice for years. Something confounds him (these stories are typically male) and obsesses him for years until a sudden breakthrough comes. Walpola Rahula notes, "Although the attainment of awakening or enlightenment or emancipation, related to all these Theravada or Zen stories, seems to be 'sudden,' it is, in fact, not really so. . . . The so-called 'sudden awakening' occurs only after a long and hard discipline, training, striving, and practice."[23]

One famous story is that of Kyogen in the early ninth century. Kyogen's master, Hyakujo, had died, and Kyogen went to visit another senior disciple of the master named Yisan. After meeting and talking for a long while, Yisan commended Kyogen's intelligence and learning but also recognized that he was not enlightened. So he asked him, "Let me have your view as to the reason of birth-and-death; that is, as to your own being before your parents gave birth to you." Kyogen simply had no reply and left the monastery. He built a hut near a cemetery and lived as a hermit for years, obsessed with the question about his own being before his birth. One day, while sweeping

---

[20] Ibid., 230–31.

[21] Ibid., 246.

[22] Ibid., 261.

[23] Rahula, *Zen and the Taming of the Bull*, 23.

the path outside his hermitage, he heard the vibration of a pebble rubbing against his broom, and he instantly experienced satori, enlightenment.[24]

Other stories are more dramatic, particularly to modern ears, as they describe masters beating and berating disciples in order to "push the right button" to create satori. One famous story has the master Chu-ti pointing his finger at a disciple time and time again, but the disciple failed to understand. Finally, the master took a knife and cut off his disciple's finger. The wounded disciple ran out of the meditation hall screaming. Chu-ti followed him and then called out his name. When the disciple looked back, Chu-ti smiled and raised his finger. His unnamed disciple instantly became enlightened.[25]

The Pressure Cooker of *Koans*[26]

Koan is a word that means "public document" and refers to a saying or riddle intended to throw disciples out of their conventional way of thinking and into a satori experience. We might look at two famous koans from the tradition as exemplars. The first is this: Two hands clap, and there is a sound. What is the sound of one hand? The second: A disciple asks, "Does a dog have a Buddha-nature?" The master answers "*mu* [no]." The disciple responds, "But what do you mean by this?" And the master replies, "That is what a dog would say if you asked it."

On the surface, these questions or brief dialogues appear meaningless. A single hand does not clap, nor may one dialogue with a dog. Is there a right answer? There are, in fact, exemplary responses or "traditional answers" (*kenjo*) to many koans that are preserved in the tradition. Yet the master is hardly looking for the "right" answer. The only point in any answer is evidence that one has grasped the state of mind expressed by the koan itself. This would be some kind of state of mind that transcends linear thinking.

Consider the question of a dog having a Buddha-nature. The master's response could indeed have a number of possible interpretations. One is that *mu*, which means no, simply means "no" to the question. Yet it is certainly a Zen dogma that all sentient beings have a Buddha-nature. So, how could

---

24 Suzuki, *Essays in Zen Buddhism*, 242–43.

25 David Lorenzen, "Early Evidence for Tantric Religion," in *The Roots of Tantra*, ed. Katherine Anne Harper and Robert Brown (Albany: State University of New York Press, 2002), 29.

26 See my treatment of this in Feldmeier, *Encounters in Faith*, 179–81.

the answer be no? Perhaps the master is trying to shock the disciple out of a speculative framework, or insisting that the very question seems to rarify Buddha-nature, a particularly big problem. Perhaps the master was asserting that, since all is empty (*shunyata*), the dog does not have anything. Perhaps the master is refusing to acknowledge the dog is a discrete being able to be distinguished and rarified from an interpenetrating co-arising universe. Perhaps the master was making a joke. The original koan is Chinese where the master says *wu* (no). One way that dogs bark is by making a sound much like *wu* (dogs certainly cannot make an *ef* sound in *woof*). Thus, by telling the disciple to look at and listen to a dog being its natural self by barking, he could experience the dog expressing its Buddha-nature. The master could have meant any, some, or none of these. Confounding his disciple from a linear perspective is essential in koans.

The key to koans is to attempt to reach the state of mind of the master posing the koan. The master is not seeking a "thoughtful" response but is using the *koan* to take the disciple out of conventional considerations. The point is to force the disciple's psyche into another kind of paradigm, and in so doing to force a profound experience. Masters wanted their students to use their minds in order to transcend their minds.

The great master Hakuin (1683–1768), who invented the koan of the one hand clapping, had himself undergone the koan of *mu*. He describes his experience in his book titled *Orategama*:

> When I was twenty-four years old I stayed at the Yegan Monastery of Echigo. I assiduously applied myself to it [the *mu* Koan]. I did not sleep days and nights, forgot both eating and lying down, when quite abruptly a great mental fixation took place. I felt as if freezing in an ice-field extending thousands of miles, and within myself there was a sense of utmost transparency. There was no going forward, no slipping backward; I was like an idiot, like an imbecile, and there was nothing but "Joshu's Mu." Though I attended the lectures by the master, they sounded like a discussion going on somewhere in a distant hall, many yards away. Sometimes my sensation was that of one flying in the air. Several days passed in this state, when one evening a temple-bell struck, which upset the whole thing. It was like smashing an ice-basin, or pulling down a house made of jade. I suddenly awoke again and I found that I myself was Ganto [famous ninth-century master] the old master, and that all through the shifting changes of time not a bit [of my personality] was lost. Whatever doubts and indecisions I had before were completely dissolved like a piece of thawing ice. I called out loudly:

> "How wondrous! How wondrous! There is no birth-and-death from which one has to escape, nor is there any supreme knowledge (Bodhi) after which one has to strive."[27]

The master Bukko (1226–1286) describes working on Joshu's *mu* nonstop for six years:

> "Mu" became so inseparably attached to me that I could not get away from it even while asleep. This whole universe seemed to be nothing but "Mu" itself. . . . All of a sudden the sound of striking the board in front of the head monk's room reached my ear, which at once revealed to me the *original man* in full . . . I laughed loudly, "Oh, how great is the Dharmakaya! . . . My eyes, my mind, are they not the Dharmakaya itself? . . . Today even in every pore of my skin there lie all the Buddha-lands in the ten quarters."[28]

According to Zen, and indeed all of Mahayana, the great problem for the mind is its habitual dualistic thinking, one that creates subject-object oppositional engagement with reality, including one's own self. We could imagine ourselves perhaps trying to tackle the koan of the sound of one hand clapping. Working with the koan day and night with particular intensity during formal meditation periods (*zazen*), we might imagine ourselves living inside the koan. Could we imagine the possibility whereby the koan and oneself become singular, and where oppositional thinking dissolves? The two hands have become one in our very experience, and thus no difference exists between the sound of two hands and the sound of one hand.

Here are some other famous koans:

- What is your original face before your parents were born?
- If you meet the Buddha, kill him.
- *Master:* I don't like to hear the word "Buddha." *Disciple:* Do you help people or not? *Master:* Buddha! Buddha!
- *Disciple:* Who is the Buddha? *Master:* Three pounds of flax.
- *Disciple:* When not a thought is stirring in one's mind, is there any error here? *Master:* As much as Mount Sumeru.
- *Disciple:* What is the meaning of the first patriarch's visit to China? *Master:* The cypress tree in the front yard.
- *Disciple:* What are honest words? *Master:* Eat an iron stick!

---

[27] Cited in Suzuki, *Essays in Zen Buddhism*, 254–55.

[28] Ibid., 256–57.

What would be the right answer to bring to the master? Surely many responses could be legitimate. The master is not looking for any answer per se, but for indication that the disciple's mind is opening to its own Buddha-nature. The great fifteenth-century master Koin Jokin wrote,

> Apply yourself wholeheartedly to the task of holding on to your *koan*, never letting it go off the center of your consciousness, whether you are sitting or lying, walking or standing still. . . . The time will most assuredly come to you when it is absolutely impossible for you to go on with your inquiry, as if you had come to the very foundation of a stream and were blocked by the mountains all around. This is the time when the tree together with the entwining wisteria breaks down, that is, when the distinction of subject and object is utterly obliterated, when the inquiring and inquired are fused into the one perfect identity. Awakening from this identification, there takes place a rare *satori* that brings peace to all your inquiries and searchings.[29]

What Is Zen Enlightenment?

As noted above, Suzuki makes two claims that are, I believe, representative of Rinzai Zen. The first is that no longer is the enlightenment project an eons-long process of spiritual development, but could happen the instant a wholly dramatic satori experience happens. As he claimed, satori *is* enlightenment. Of course, we saw that such instantaneous enlightenment experiences are not without deep and long practice, but they are believed to be attainable in this lifetime, and even in a few years of intensive practice, as was the case of Master Bukko. Bukko began his practice of the koan *mu* in his late teens and was enlightened six years later.

In the Theravada tradition, once one experienced at the core the dynamics of dependent origination and utterly saw that there was no self, all clinging and craving was eliminated, along with all future karma formations. This realization takes many lifetimes. For Nagarjuna, Nirvana or enlightenment represented seeing nonduality as well as the nonsubstantiality of all phenomena (*dharmas*). This was still imagined to be daunting and also not easily realizable in this one lifetime. Such is the case all the more with Shantideva, whose commitment to the perfections and compassionate activity was unendurably long. Full Buddhahood was an innumerable set of lifetimes

[29] Cited in D. T. Suzuki, *The Essentials of Zen Buddhism*, ed. Bernard Phillips (Westport: CT: Greenwood Press, 1962), 313.

as a project. None of this is the case in Rinzai Zen, or probably the Soto Zen that Dogen taught. Is it, comparatively, really that easy?

The second claim Suzuki makes is that once one is enlightened, one's moral life is utterly reconceived; satori brings a moral "revolution."[30] There is no question that a Zen master would be highly skilled in focus, mindfulness, self-discipline, stability, confidence, and loyalty. These are part of the Zen culture and necessary prerequisites for deep practice. On the other hand, deep Zen practice, at least as it has traditionally been framed, need not be all that concerned about the world at large or relations outside of the monastery.

There is in the Zen tradition literature known as Transmission of the Lamp, where biographies of great Zen virtuosos are told, including of course their enlightenment stories. We have seen highlights of some examples in this chapter. What is striking in the literature is that virtually none of the stories explicitly describes the cultivation or heroic expressions of compassion, justice, generosity, or even empathy.[31] In 2003 and 2005, Brian Victoria published two books, *Zen War Stories* and *Zen at War*, respectively, that shook the Buddhist community.[32] Here, Victoria documents how Zen masters became willing participants in Japanese imperialist expansion in the 1930s and 1940s. It is not simply that Zen masters were unaware or merely tolerated the government's aggression, in perhaps the same way European or American Christian monastics tolerated or at least were fundamentally silent about unethical violence pursued by their own governments. Rather, masters took an active role in recruiting and training young men to serve.

Victoria asks how it could be conceivable that highly regarded Zen masters could witness, without challenge, "what were clearly war atrocities committed against Chinese civilians, young and old, without having confronted the moral implications of . . . this mindless brutality."[33] Some Buddhists responded to Victoria that these clearly were not authentically enlightened Zen masters. Such a response, however, ignores the "sheer numbers of authenticated Zen masters whose actions in the war fit this pattern."[34]

---

30 Suzuki, *Essays in Zen Buddhism*, 231.

31 Dale Wright, *What Is Buddhist Enlightenment?* (Oxford: Oxford University Press, 2016), 95.

32 See Brian Victoria, *Zen War Stories* (London: Routledge/Curzon, 2003), and *Zen at War* (New York: Rowman & Littlefield, 2005). I was led to Victoria's material by Wright and am relying on Wright's description.

33 Cited in Wright, *What Is Buddhist Enlightenment?*, 92–93.

34 Ibid., 93.

One sees this problem in the West as well. The scandal of Zen teachers in the United States involved in sexual relations with students has been widely documented and does not need to be analyzed here. But I would like to allow for three examples that may highlight the problem. The most recent is the scandal of Sogyal Rinpoche, who founded an international network of over one hundred Buddhist centers in twenty-three counties. He is the famous author of *The Tibetan Book of Living and Dying*. Sogyal Rinpoche, a monk and widely respected lama, has been credibly accused by almost a dozen of his closest students of sexual, physical, and emotional abuse, as well as criticized for living lavishly on donations of supporters. On July 20, 2017, the Buddhist publication *Lion's Roar* published an article with excerpts from a letter written to him by eight members of Rigpa, one of his most important Sanghas, where he acted as its direct spiritual leader. This letter details his abuse over a many-year period. The letter also details how Sogyal Rinpoche carefully crafted and managed his public profile as a compassionate and wise lama. On August 11, 2017, Sogyal resigned from Rigpa.

My second example is John Tarrant, an Australian psychotherapist and noted *roshi*. I have personally been inspired by Tarrant's writings since reading his insightful book *The Light inside the Dark*. I regularly assign my students his book on Zen koans titled *Bring Me the Rhinoceros*. But Tarrant is a controversial figure. He has been publicly criticized for training methods that are abusive, and he had a number of sexual relationships with his students over the years as their *roshi*. So controversial was Tarrant in Australia that several Buddhist organizations there publicly criticized him and called for his removal. Tarrant now resides in California, where he heads the Pacific Zen Institute. Tarrant received his dharma transmission from the widely respected *roshi* Robert Aitken and was for nine years Aitken's designated dharma heir.

Finally, as someone who grew up in Minneapolis and taught for many years in St. Paul, I had come to have a great respect for Dainin Katagiri Roshi, who died in 1990. Katagiri was one of the most important Zen masters who brought Soto Zen from Japan to America in the twentieth century. Katagiri lived and died a highly revered Zen master, with countless students and priests who started their own Dharma centers in the Twin Cities. I had never heard of a single challenge to Katagiri's authority or authenticity as a *roshi*. Years after his death, one of his students casually mentioned having had a sexual relationship with him, which she characterized as a happy one. The leadership of the Sangha, the Minnesota Zen Center, was shocked and began an investigation, only to find out that he had engaged in several sexual relationships with female students, though all were secretive and he was a married man. His former student, Natalie Goldberg, describes her own wounding upon learning about his affairs in her thoughtful memoir *The Great Failure: My Unexpected Path to Truth*.

What ought one to make of these accounts? They differ from each other in important ways. We might think of Sogyal Rinpoche as perhaps something of a charlatan. He used his position to manipulate students and enrich himself. John Tarrant's partners appear not to have thought of themselves manipulated, but with a PhD in psychology it should have been obvious to him that he was in a power position regarding them and that their freedom was compromised. Further, the very fact that he had sexual relations with members of his own religious community obviously had a corrosive effect on his immediate Sangha and Zen communities that knew about it. They were scandalized. Finally, Katagiri's relationships, even where some of his partners experienced them in positive ways, were secretive and simply adulterous.

The great issue for me is that in all three cases the protagonist was believed by credible traditions and other leaders in those traditions to be enlightened. Were they simply not, now that the evidence betrays them, or were they indeed enlightened in a Zen sort of way, but not wholly morally transformed? I believe the answer is the latter. Let us recall Suzuki's striking claim noted above: "When one sees into the inmost nature of one's being, one instantly becomes a Buddha."[35] This is difficult to believe.

Zen spirituality, like all spiritualities, exists in a culture, a paradigm. This is one of the great insights of postmodernity: no metanarratives allowed. As traditionally posed, Zen enlightenment imagines itself as a kind of metanarrative, a nondual engagement of reality *as it really is*. I believe that this is naïve. Zen enlightenment looks like the various traditions and lineages that its representatives are trained in, and such training has limitations. I think enlightenment is really a moving target, as it depends on the setting, culture, and specific training that provide its conditions of possibility. In the monastic context, Zen enlightenment would depend on prior education, certain forms of socialization, customs, and specific training valued by that monastic community.[36] If this is true, then there is no "pure experience," as Suzuki claims.

My final reflection is to appeal to two realities I think essential to respect when addressing religion or any other noble human endeavor. The first is that the mind is very complex. I have known many religious persons who have excelled in impressive ways along their respective spiritual paths,

---

35 Suzuki, *Essays in Zen Buddhism*, 363.

36 Wright, *What Is Buddhist Enlightenment?*, 158.

but who have significant blind spots as well as significantly undeveloped parts of their psyche. This is true of me and anyone reading this book. The second reality, related to the first, is that we simply must respect human finitude. We can and we must have ideals, but we must also remember that they are aspirations yet to be achieved, aspirations located in a certain kind of paradigm of what looks like human flourishing. Further, as Dale Wright has observed, "No matter how much we improve, we can always catch glimpses of greater levels of excellence beyond where we are right now."[37]

A more holistic approach has taken hold of Zen in the West through the Engaged Buddhism movement over the past generation.[38] Sallie King refers to its intersection with major forms of social activism as a "new Buddhism."[39] In 1993, the Network for Western Buddhist Teachers published an "Open Letter" that articulates this new sensitivity. The letter's first point is excellently telling:

> Our first responsibility as Buddhists is to work towards creating a better world for all forms of life. The promotion of Buddhism as a religion is a secondary concern. Kindness and compassion, the furthering of peace and harmony, as well as tolerance and respect for other religions, should be the three guiding principles of our actions.[40]

A Christian Reflection

In forming a dialogue or response to the material above, I think it might be best to consider the last part first, which was something of a critique of Zen enlightenment as it has traditionally been framed. My greatest critique above had to do with questioning whether Zen enlightenment was a "full" enlightenment—that is, was the whole person enlightened, a new Buddha, as Suzuki seems to argue? It seems not. Further, as we looked at the Transmission of the Lamp material, we saw that the heroes of these narratives looked a great deal like their culture, time, and lineage. This shouldn't surprise us.

Sandra Schneiders, a foremost scholar in Christian spirituality, has written widely on scholarly method in spirituality. Schneiders sees the

---

[37] Ibid., 132–33.

[38] For an overview of the movement, see Christopher Quest, ed., *Engaged Buddhism in the West* (Boston: Wisdom Publications, 2000).

[39] Sallie King, "Contemporary Buddhist Spirituality and Social Activism," in *Buddhist Spirituality II*, 455.

[40] "An Open Letter from the Network for Western Buddhist Teachers," *Turning Wheel: Journal of the Buddhist Peace Fellowship* (Summer 1993): 40, as cited in ibid., 455.

academic project fundamentally in three processes.[41] The first is descriptive. The scholar addresses a text, school of spirituality, or historical figure by creating a "thick" description of the historical location, ecclesiological setting, claims, values, and religious experience being advanced in one's subject. The second stage is that of critical analysis. Here one addresses theological criticism, issues that affect the spirituality under study, biases in the church or culture that affect its explication and practice, and so on. The point here is that one simply cannot embrace a given spiritual expression as though it were not affected by its historical location. Consider, for example, how persecutions affected the apostolic church and may have overemphasized some aspects of Christian spirituality at the cost of ignoring other aspects. Or consider how Neoplatonism affected the patristic church's understanding of the role of sexuality. Schneiders's third step then is constructive. Here the scholar seeks, with all due attention to the first two steps, how a given historical spirituality might be authentically appropriated in one's current time and culture.

These aspects of scholarly pursuit are rather obvious to those in the field, but become less obvious when these same scholars look at other religious traditions. We might look romantically and whimsically at Master Chu-ti's conditioning of the enlightenment of his disciple by cutting off his finger. Perhaps we might ask how many other disciples had lost a finger without becoming enlightened. Is there a downside to the kind of absolute loyalty and obedience given to one's master? It is this kind of loyalty and obedience that may very well have created Zen tyrants historically and allowed for modern Zen masters to take liberties with their students.

The Christian tradition has the same need for this analytical/critical agenda, as Schneiders shows. For example, we would do well to consider whether it was or is a good spiritual practice to follow Ignatius of Loyola's teaching on absolute solicitude to the institutional church. In his Spiritual Exercises, Ignatius adds at the end a number of rules for discernment, scruples, giving alms, and so on. Among them are "Rules for Thinking with the Church." Ignatius writes,

> We must put aside all judgment of our own, and keep in mind ever ready and prompt to obey in all things the true Spouse of Christ our Lord, our holy Mother, the hierarchical Church. [#353] . . . We must praise all the commandments of the Church, and be on

---

[41] See, for example, "A Hermeneutical Approach to the Study of Christian Spirituality," in *Minding the Spirit: The Study of Christian Spirituality*, ed. Elizabeth Dreyer and Mark Burrows (Baltimore. MD: Johns Hopkins University Press, 2005), 49–60.

> the alert to find reasons to defend them, and by no means in order to criticize them. [#361] . . . If we wish to proceed securely in all things, we must hold fast to the following principle: What seems to me white, I will believe black if the hierarchical church so defines. For I must be convinced that in Christ our Lord, the bridegroom, and in His spouse the Church, only one Spirit holds sway, which governs and rules for the salvation of souls. For it is by the same Spirit and Lord who gave the Ten Commandments that our holy Mother Church is ruled and governed. [#365][42]

Are these dicta pious aids that lead us to greater spiritual depth and pastoral responsiveness, or are they deluded cultlike qualities that can be critiqued? As is well known, the Catholic Church has changed its policies and formal teachings on various issues, from slavery to sexual relations to the status of non-Christians, all because of respectful theological challenge. What certainly seemed pious to Ignatius in the sixteenth century looks far less sanguine under historical scrutiny. In another text, I suggested qualities of religious groups that were dangerous or cultlike. These included issues of control, creating a *we-versus-them* culture, authoritarian power structure, lack of transparency, and so on.[43] Through the ages and into our own historical period, the Catholic Church has indeed displayed these dynamics. It is simply not impious, but rather courageous, to respectfully address these dynamics and their magisterial fallout. Failure to do so when the evidence reveals a significant problem strikes me as a moral, ecclesial, and spiritual failure.

The Koan of Christ

According to all the Gospels, Jesus said something like this, and perhaps often: "For those who want to save their life will lose it, and those who lose their life for my sake will save it" (Lk 9:24).[44] Obviously, if one were to take this literally, one might say to oneself, "Since I *ultimately* want to save my life, I will *lose* it and thus *save* it." But this cannot work, for it would violate the first half of Jesus's paradox. "But if I stopped caring about my life and am ready and willing to lose it for Christ's sake, then why would I care about whether it will be saved or not?" Thus, we have confounded the second

---

[42] Ignatius of Loyola, *Spiritual Exercises*, nos. 352–70.

[43] Feldmeier, *Encounters in Faith*, 252.

[44] See also Mt 10:39; Mk 8:35; Lk 14:26; Jn 12:25.

part. His paradox works like a koan because one cannot get out of it or solve it logically. John's Gospel ramps up the intensity of the paradox by representing Jesus's divinity as most clearly revealed in his offering of himself on the cross. Here power and weakness collapse into each other. It is on the cross, in his humiliation and death, where he will draw all to himself (Jn 12:32), and where he expresses his absolute glory (Jn 17:1), and even most clearly can be known by the Old Testament's divine self-designation, *I AM* (Jn 8:28). His true glory is his emptiness.

This paradox of simultaneous emptiness and fullness, of glory and humiliation, of realizing one's true nature and destiny only in the context of a profound spiritual death is everywhere in the tradition. Bonaventure writes, "For by transcending yourself and all things, by the immeasurable and absolute ecstasy of pure mind, leaving behind all things, and freed from all things, you will ascend to the super-essential ray of darkness."[45] Only by leaving everything does one find everything. We saw this dynamic in John of the Cross, where "the path of Mount Carmel, the perfect spirit: nothing, nothing, nothing, nothing, nothing, nothing, and even on the Mount, nothing." Even union is characterized as nothing one can point to or claim; union is "nothing." Yet God seems to cohere so radically that one cannot draw the line between oneself and God; emptiness is divinization, and the Absolute (God) and the relative (human) become a single act of love and expression of truth.[46]

What we see here is that one is only *something* when one is *nothing*. Any attempt to be *something* is an advancement of the ego and the very thing that will keep one from union with God. But if you want union with God, then you have to stop wanting *any-thing*. How can you want something (union) and then attain it when you want *no-thing*? This is the paradox. The truth of this Christian paradox, like those in Zen koans, can only be experienced when one has let go of linear logic, and at a certain point all conventional conceptuality.

Is There a Christian Satori?

The Christian tradition certainly has no satori experience as characterized by the Zen tradition. Zen satori is the full realization of nondual reality, and this simply has little parallel in Christianity. But the Christian tradition

[45] Bonaventure, *Bonaventure: The Soul's Journey into God; Tree of Life; The Life of St. Francis*, trans. Ewert Cousins (Mahwah: NJ: Paulist Press, 1978), 115.

[46] See *Spiritual Canticle* 22.3; *Living Flame* 2.33–34; 3.6, 10, 24–25; 4.14.

does have dramatic spiritual experiences that radically change the soul, and often these are conditioned by a long road of spiritual practice or intense engagement with the spiritual life.

As noted in the last chapter, Ignatius of Loyola had numerous dramatic spiritual experiences, many of which were mystical encounters in the form of visions and locutions. The singular experience of his life was mystical, but had no exact content. It was during his year living in a cave at Manresa. Already, he notes in his autobiography, God had revealed himself profoundly. He had visions of Jesus and visions of Mary. None of these would approach the profundity he had while at the bank of the Cardoner River. As already noted,

> As he sat there the eyes of his understanding were opened and though he saw no visions he understood and perceived many things, numerous spiritual things as well as matters touching faith and learning, and this was with an elucidation so bright that all these things seemed new to him. He cannot expound in detail what he then understood, for they were many things, but he can state that he received such a lucidity in understanding that during the course of his entire life—now having passed his sixty-second year—if he were to gather all the helps he received from God and everything he knew, and add them together, he does not think they would add up to all that he received on that occasion.[47]

Karl Rahner describes this experience as "architectonic," as one that "transformed Ignatius into another man" with a different intellect, a man who had encountered God "in such nearness and grace as is impossible to confound or mistake."[48] As Harvey Egan interprets it, "The Cardoner experience altered radically the way Ignatius viewed all reality. His particular mystical horizon was born."[49]

In a less dramatic fashion the modern mystic Thomas Merton describes his own turn. In his *Conjectures of a Guilty Bystander*, Merton relates an experience also noted in his personal journal:

> Yesterday, in Louisville, at the corner of 4th and Walnut, I suddenly realized that I loved all the people and that none of them were or could be totally alien to me. As if waking from a dream—the dream

[47] Ignatius of Loyola, *Pilgrim's Journey*, no. 30.

[48] Rahner, *Ignatius Speaks*, 11.

[49] Egan, *Ignatius of Loyola*, 44.

> of my separateness, of the "special" vocation to be different. My vocation does not really make me different from the rest of men or put me in a special category except artificially, juridically. I am still a member of the human race, and what more glorious destiny is there for man, since the Word was made flesh and became, too, a member of the Human Race! Thank God! Thank God! I am only another member of the human race, like all the rest of them. I have the immense joy of being a man. As if the sorrows of our condition could really matter, once we begin to realize who and what we are—as if we could ever begin to realize it on earth.[50]

At this point in his life, Merton had been a monk for almost twenty years. He had leadership positions in his monastery and was an internationally famous spiritual writer. He obviously had enormous spiritual depth and insight into the human condition. And yet his experience on Fourth and Walnut changed his life. This moment in Louisville happened in the middle of an ordinary day, when Merton was running errands for the monastery. But something snapped or dramatically revealed itself. From this time on, Merton's writings reveal something one does not see as clearly or as regularly in his earlier works, but dominates his later years as a thinker, writer, and spiritual person. God and God's love interpenetrate everything and are the foundation for everything. This is not a new theological insight for him. Rather it becomes an expression of his new consciousness. In his small book *Spiritual Direction and Meditation* he sums up the kind of unity that already exists among people and in God: "The very identification which we seek . . . is therefore a *conscious realization of the union that is already effected between our souls and by God by grace*."[51] Regarding prayer, he writes that "we discover what we already have. . . . We already have everything but we don't know it and don't experience it. . . . All we need is to experience what we already possess."[52]

The greatest problem in experiencing this divine core is the delusion of what Merton called the "false self," the sense of one's identity separate and independent from God. Ultimately, for Merton, the contemplative life consists of dismantling this false self and entering into the very communion

---

[50] Thomas Merton, *The Intimate Merton: His Life from His Journals*, ed. Patrick Hart and Jonathan Montaldo (New York: HarperSanFrancisco: 1999), 124.

[51] Thomas Merton, *Spiritual Direction and Meditation* (Collegeville, MN: Liturgical Press, 1960), 45 (emphasis in original).

[52] As cited in Patrick Hart, ed., *Thomas Merton, Monk: A Monastic Tribute* (New York: Sheed & Ward, 1974), 79.

that already exists. "What happens is that the separate identity that is *you* apparently disappears and nothing seems to be left but a pure freedom indistinguishable from the infinite Freedom, love identified with Love. . . . He is the *I* who acts there. He is the one Who loves and knows and rejoices."[53] I believe that these insights come directly from Merton's *enlightening* moment at Fourth and Walnut.

My final example is that of Augustine's conversion in Milan. In his *Confessions* Augustine describes a long search for truth. He had been *converted* to seeking truth as a young man after having read Cicero's *Hortensius* (now lost). This led him briefly to become a "hearer" in the Manichean religion, which seemed initially to answer the difficult problem of the intractability of sin. Ultimately, the tenets of Manicheanism failed to satisfy him intellectually. Upon moving to Milan he became fascinated with an intellectualized version of Christian faith that did finally answer his questions. Under the guidance of St. Ambrose and tutelage of the priest Simplicianus, he accepted the truth of the faith. But he still could not convert. As Boulven Madec notes, his conversion was not limited simply to the decision to be baptized, it "was also a commitment to a life of asceticism and contemplation."[54] Taking the faith seriously meant for Augustine that he had to renounce any interest in indulging his body or ego; everything about him had to be directed to the glory of God and aligned with the will of God, with no room for any other desires. For Augustine, the question of whether to be modestly interested in wealth, fame, or anything else was tantamount to missing the profound depth of a real conversion. There was no middle ground.[55] Augustine describes the fight he had with disordered desires:

> Vain trifles and triviality of the emptyheaded, my old loves, held me back. They tugged at the garment of my flesh and whispered: "Are you getting rid of us?" . . . I hesitated to detach myself, to be rid of them, to make the leap to where I was being called. Meanwhile the overwhelming force of habit was saying to me: "Do you think

---

[53] Thomas Merton, *New Seeds of Contemplation* (New York: New Directions, 1961), 283, 287.

[54] Boulven Madec, "Preface," in *Augustine of Hippo: Selected Writings* (New York: Paulist Press, 1984), xiii.

[55] In describing the happy life, Augustine concludes, "This, therefore, is the complete satisfaction of souls, that is, the happy life: to know precisely and perfectly Him through whom you are let into the truth, the nature of the truth you enjoy, and the bond that connects you with the Supreme Measure." See *The Happy Life*, no. 35, in *Augustine of Hippo*, 193.

> you can live without them?" I blushed with embarrassment because I was still listening to the mutters of those vanities, and racked by hesitations I remained undecided.[56]

Augustine's moment of conversion is well known. He was weeping bitterly at this personal trial when he heard a child's voice chanting, "Pick up and read, pick up and read." He took this to be a divine command, went to where he had a copy of St. Paul's epistles, and opened it up. His eyes lit on Romans 13:13–14. Augustine writes,

> "Not in riots and drunken parties, not in eroticism and indecencies, not in strife and rivalry, but put on the Lord Jesus Christ and make no provision for the flesh in its lusts." I neither wished nor needed to read further. At once, with the last words of this sentence, it was as if a light of relief from all anxiety flooded into my heart. All the shadows of doubt were dispelled. . . . The effect of your converting me to your self was that I did not now seek a wife and had no ambition for success in the world. . . . You *changed my grief into joy* [Ps 29:12].[57]

It was an immediate and (dare we say it) complete conversion.

In all three of these examples, we find earnest, deeply spiritual persons. Ignatius had been profoundly changed the year before his Cardoner experience and was living a focused, prayerful, and ascetical life. He had already had mystical experiences and intense engagements with spiritual consolations and desolations. But something indelibly marked this moment for him that changed him radically. As noted, Merton had been a monk for almost twenty years before his experience in Louisville. His earlier writings suggest also that he had mystical experiences, and he was widely regarded as having great spiritual depth and insight. The Fourth and Walnut experience did not emerge out of a vacuum and certainly was the fruit of long periods of prayer and solitude. And yet his realization, his enlightening experience, came dramatically. We can say the same for Augustine. He had been intensely searching for over ten years before his conversion. Further, in his *Confessions* he notes other mystical experiences he had before his conversion. This is his most dramatic:

---

[56] Augustine of Hippo, *Confessions*, trans. Henry Chadwick (Oxford: Oxford University Press, 1986), 152.

[57] Ibid., 152–54.

> With you as my guide I entered into my innermost citadel. . . . I entered and with my soul's eye, such as it was, saw above that same eye of my soul the immutable light higher than my mind . . . It transcended my mind. . . . It was superior because it made me, and I was inferior because I was made by it. The person who knows the truth knows it, and he who knows it knows eternity. Love knows it. . . . When I first came to know you, you raised me up to make me see that what I saw is Being. . . . I trembled with love and awe. And I heard as it were your voice from on high: "I am the food of the fully grown; grow and you will feed on me. And you will not change me into you like food your flesh eats, but you will be changed into me."[58]

Augustine's conversion was not out of the blue but represented a long and deeply penetrating engagement with the spiritual life. As Henry Chadwick notes, "The conversion was no sudden flash, but the culminating of many months of painful gestation. He himself was later to compare the process of conversion to pregnancy."[59]

Like Zen satori experiences, these enlightenment experiences were prefaced by deep and intense spiritual practice. They were not conditioned by a master who had "pushed the button" at just the right time but by God's grace intervening in their lives. Nonetheless, some kind of button was pushed, and they saw or experienced something that served to inform the rest of their lives. They were not saints at that moment, but as I have argued above, I do not think that Zen satori experiences make their recipients fully enlightened or that they are now Buddhas. Is *full enlightenment*—that is, fully integrated throughout every part of one's psyche—even humanly possible? I am convinced that conversion or radical realization, like all things human, has to be integrated, and the spiritual life has to continue to be cultivated in every aspect of one's life for one to be fully holy or enlightened. But in both Buddhist and Christian experiences, those who had them could no longer unsee what they had seen or forget what they now knew to be true.

My Own Satori

Anyone who knows me well also knows that I am hardly a saint and certainly that there are aspects of my spiritual life that need far greater deepening and integration. Yet I believe I have also had a Christian/satori

---

[58] Ibid., 123–24.

[59] Ibid., 26.

experience, actually two of them. Surely many readers of this book have also had them. My first satori was when I was in my late twenties and making the Ignatian Exercises. I was at the end of the first week, the week when one comes face-to-face with one's own sinfulness, seeking the grace of "shame and confusion." I received this grace in spades! I came to see most clearly, among other things, that part of my psyche was constantly assessing myself. In prayer, for example, part of my mind was praying and another part was observing and assessing my praying: *Peter's such a good boy, look at him praying so earnestly.* I simply could not get away from my own ego advancement. It was agonizing to see this clearly.

As I had repeated many of the Exercises several times and was no longer gaining the fruit of them, I suggested to my retreat director that I thought I was ready to move on to the second week. He told me to stay in the first week for one more day, and he gave me an exercise that was certainly not in Ignatius's plan. I was to imagine what I would want as an epitaph on my gravestone, that is, who was I or whom did I aim to be? He shared with me what his was, which by now I have forgotten, though I was inspired by it at the time. For the next twenty-four hours I obsessed over this assignment, not only during the five formal hourlong periods of meditation but really constantly. I came up with a number of possibilities, each of which I considered and ultimately rejected. It was terribly frustrating, and all I could think of was "nothing." I could think of nothing good, nothing authentic. Nothing.

The next evening, while doing my formal meditation in the chapel of the Jesuit Novitiate in St. Paul, I sat looking at the wall behind the altar. I imagined my grave and the headstone. I strove to imagine what could be written on that headstone as I rotted in the grave under it. At that moment I saw (or imagined) a large yellow orb above and to the left of the grave. This was Jesus Christ to me. And I saw (or imagined) my soul rise from the grave and become drawn into and fully absorbed by that yellow orb. Jesus was everything and I was nothing; everything about myself was subsumed into him. And then I realized, "Nothing, I'm nothing!" I loudly laughed with a realization of freedom I had never before experienced. "I'm nothing. I knew it!"

In no way did this experience feel denigrating. Quite the opposite, it felt like supreme freedom. There was no ego to protect, no ego to advance: "I'm nothing." I was giddy, and it was all I could do to remain in the chapel for the rest of my appointed hour. This nothingness that is me, this insight, has dominated my spiritual life ever since.

My second satori experience is as follows: I was studying for an STL degree at Weston School of Theology in Cambridge, Massachusetts, in the late

1980s and early 1990s. I was around thirty years old. My two years at Weston were among my best in life. They were also years of great interior drama for me. My first year was filled with spiritual consolations that at times overwhelmed me. In contrast, my second year was dominated by a dark night of the soul, albeit in no way like the depths we see in John of the Cross. During this second year I believe I have never experienced the depth of compassion and generosity as I had then, and this suggested to me that God was very active in my life, though in an absolutely hidden way. So hidden was the divine that I taunted Jesus by renaming him "Mr. Stone Face"!

My daily practice included going to Mass at noon at Weston, and then I would eat lunch. I walked into the chapel, where I discovered Mass was going to be presided over by certainly the worse liturgical presider among the Jesuit community. I would have left but was spotted coming in and thus was stuck for a Mass I would have wanted to avoid. After Mass, I was walking up the street to Harvard Square to buy a sandwich. For about five minutes I experienced the entire block as interpenetrated by the Divine. Though my literal vision was sharp and I saw clearly the bricks, windows, sidewalk, and people, still everything was infused with and animated by the radiant presence of God. I do not recall whether I ate lunch that day, and the rest of the day was something of a blur. I had been completely taken out of myself. By the next day I was back in the dark night.

I cannot unsee or unknow what I saw and realized during these experiences. No one imagines me a saint; I certainly know I'm not. Still, in both cases, a switch flipped, and I know what I know.

Chapter 8

Zen Oxherding Pictures and the Stages of Faith

In the last chapter, we saw a number of accounts of Zen enlightenment taking the model of a period of intense practice over years culminating in a kind of pressure-cooker struggle and releasing itself into a satori explosion. Above all, it was a profound experience of insight into the nondual nature of all reality and the realization of Buddha-nature underlying all conditioned things. Enlightenment happened in an instant, even as that moment was conditioned by years of practice. It can be conceived of in another way, however, one with typical progressive stages along a well-trodden path. Suzuki, an advocate of sudden satori, also concedes that "so long as our relative minds are made to comprehend one thing after another by degrees and succession and not all at once and simultaneously, it is impossible *not* to speak of some kind of progress."[1]

Suzuki notes that Zen attainments can also be understood as gradations and variations. He highlights this with the example of the seventh patriarch Nangaku, who had six accomplished disciples, each of whose attainments were different from each other and even different in depth. Nangaku compared his disciples with different parts of his body:

> You all have testified to my body, but each has grasped a part of it. The one who has my eyebrows is the master of manners; the second, who has my eyes, knows how to look around; the third, who has my ears, understands how to listen to reasoning; the fourth, who has my nose, is well versed in the act of breathing; the fifth, who has

[1] D. T. Suzuki, *Essays in Zen Buddhism* (London: Rider & Co., 1973), 363 (emphasis added).

> my tongue, is a great arguer; and finally, the one who has my mind knows the past and the present.[2]

Suzuki again: "This gradation was impossible if 'seeing into one's nature' alone was considered. . . . It is, however, no contradiction of the principle of satori . . . to say that in fact there is a progressive realization in seeing, leading one deeper and deeper into the truth of Zen."[3] The great modern Korean master Kusan references his own history as involving three different satori experiences, each leading him deeper into the truth of Zen.[4]

Chinese Zen masters developed a series of pictures and verses that highlighted the kind of progression ultimately leading to a full realization of Buddha-nature; these are the famed "Oxherding Pictures." The idea of herding an ox as a metaphor for spiritual practice goes back to some of the earliest centuries of Buddhism as well as early Chinese culture. One early Pali commentary of the *Satipattana Sutra* reads,

> This bhikkhu's mind, which was for a long time scattered among such objects as visible forms does not like to enter into the path of a subject of meditation, but runs only into a wrong path like a chariot yoked to an untamed bull. Just as a herdsman, who desires to break in an untamed calf . . . would remove it from the cow, and having fixed a big post on the side would tie the calf to it with a rope . . . in this same way, this bhikkhu, who desires to tame the villainous mind . . . should tie it to the post of the object of the presence of mindfulness by the rope of mindfulness.[5]

In China, one finds ox paintings as early as the eighth century CE, as the ox has traditionally been one of the animals most intimately associated with humanity. Clay images of an ox were even used in the Welcoming Spring Ceremony "in order to dispel the ether of the cold."[6] In the Southern Song dynasty (960–1279), oxherding pictures were part of a larger body of pastoral images, such as fishermen and woodcutters. They represented something of a Confucian eremitism, whereby the Confucian scholar who

---

[2] Ibid., 365.

[3] Ibid.

[4] Martine Batchelor, "The Ten Oxherding Pictures," *Tricycle: The Buddhist Review* 9, no. 3 (2000): 41.

[5] Cited in Walpola Rahula, *Zen and the Taming of the Bull: Towards the Definition of Buddhist Thought* (London: Gordon Fraser, 1978), 15.

[6] Scarlett Ju-Yu Jang, "Oxherding Paining in the Sung Dynasty," *Artibus Asiae* 52, no. 1 (1992): 54–55.

has discharged his public duty enters the rural life of withdrawal in order to pursue deeper self-cultivation. During the twelfth century, Ch'an (Chinese Zen) masters began creating a series of pictures to illustrate poems or songs of oxherding.

Versions of oxherding are many, including as few as five pictures (stages) and as many as twelve. Some represent stages of the ox progressively changing from black to white to disappearing, while others focus on the oxherder's transformation. Historically, two sets of oxherding diagrams proved most enduring, one by Puming (eleventh century) and the other by Kuo'an Shiyuan (twelfth century).[7] Kuo'an's pictures and verses found a modest audience in China but became widely known and studied in Japan during the early decades of the Kamakura period (1185–1333).[8] There is still a twelfth-century scroll extant that has ten paintings, Kuo'an's verses, and a brief commentary by his disciple Ciyuan. I rely here principally on this document as translated by Sakamoto.[9] In Kuo'an's presentation, the oxherder is the practitioner, the inner self or "I" who seeks one's original home of intrinsic enlightenment or Buddha-nature. The ox is more complicated, sometimes representing the raging mind that needs to be tamed, and at other times Buddha-nature itself. Ultimately, what we see is that "the ox is not really an ox, the person is not really a person. As the dualistic distinction between the two vanishes, they revert to one."[10]

No spiritual path is clean or strictly linear, and the ten oxherding pictures are not meant to suggest this. Every aspirant will come with her own karmic conditions as well as her own spiritual, mental, and emotional predilections. Further, we might imagine that Zen progression as framed here something more like a spiral than a straight line (particularly in the early stages), whereby one works through different aspects of the path, always returning to deepen what was discovered in earlier stages even as one progresses along the path.

Mindful of these provisos, let us consider Zen development through the oxherding pictures. This particular investigation will be both an exposition of the Zen path itself as well as a kind of commentary that I hope will be useful for Christian readers in their own spiritual practice.

---

[7] Sheng-Yen (with Dan Stevenson), *Hoofprint of the Ox: Principles of the Chan Buddhist Path as Taught by a Modern Chinese Master* (Oxford: Oxford University Press, 2002), 382–83.

[8] Stephanie Wada, "Introduction," in *The Oxherder: A Zen Parable Illustrated*, trans. Gen Sakamoto (New York: George Braziller, 2002), 16.

[9] Ibid.

[10] Sheng-Yen, *Hoofprint of the Ox*, 387.

The Oxherding Pictures: A Zen and Christian Commentary

I. Searching for the Ox[11]

One aimlessly pushes the grasses aside in search.
The rivers are wide, the mountains far away,
And the path becomes longer.
Exhausted and dispirited,
One hears only the late autumn cicadas
Shrilling in the maple woods.[12]

[11] The following pictures are in the public domain. They are believed to have been created by the fifteenth-century Rinzai master Tensho Shubun (1414–1463). Tradition has it that they are copies of Kuo'an Shiyuan's paintings, though I believe this is doubtful, given the extant scroll we now have. (Retrieved from Wikimedia Commons, these pictures are photographs of images located at the Museum of Shokoku-ji Temple in Kyoto, Japan.)

[12] The following poems by Shiyuan and commentaries by Ciyuan come from *The*

The path of Zen begins, like all authentic spiritual paths, with facing the reality that something is seriously wrong or missing in our lives. Christians may recognize their own sinfulness and real need for divine forgiveness and reconciliation. This is what I think St. Paul intended in the beginning of Romans with a denunciations of Gentiles and then Jews, culminating in the universal claim, "All have sinned and fall short of the glory of God" (Rom 3:23). This bad news, that we are sinners, becomes good news only when we realize the truth about ourselves and place ourselves at God's mercy through faith (Rom 3:24–28). To be found/saved, first you have to know that you are lost/condemned.

I imagine that most modern souls are not haunted by their sinfulness so much as the ennui of a mediocre life, one without great meaning or purpose. There's something more, something else, and the first step is realizing that there *is* something out there to seek, something that will guarantee value in who one is. The search cannot begin until the problem is faced directly: I am lost, I need more. If the more is little other than better adjustment in the world—a healthier version of the *pathology of normalcy*—there are therapists and life coaches we could use. But if the more is really seeking one's true self, one's deepest identity, then both Christianity and Buddhism demand searching for what is Absolute. The mystic Simone Weil reflects,

> When we force ourselves to fix the gaze, not only of our eyes but of our souls, upon a school exercise in which we have failed through sheer stupidity, a sense of our own mediocrity is borne in upon us with irresistible evidence. If we can arrive at knowing this truth with all our souls we shall be well established on the right foundation.[13]

In Zen, we are already enlightened in the sense that we have or are Buddha-nature and the mind is inherently luminous. But we do not know this yet by experience. We begin by recognizing that the way our mind operates is reactive, deluded, and filled with greed, anger, and ignorance. We think with the big "I," and there is a great sense of separateness from oneself and from the rest of the world. The ox, here representing enlightenment, has to be sought; it is somewhere *out* there.

Oxherder: A Zen Parable Illustrated. Besides Wada's introductory material, the book contains no pagination and thus will not be cited further.

[13] Simone Weil, *Waiting for God* (New York: Harper & Row, 1992), 103, 109, as cited in Robert Kennedy, *Zen Gifts to Christians* (New York: Continuum, 2004), 14.

II. Seeing the Footprints of the Ox

By the water, and under the trees,
There are numerous traces.
Fragrant grasses grow thickly,
Did you see the ox?
Even in the depths of the distant mountain forest,
How could the upturned nostrils of the ox be concealed?

The second step on the path is to actually do something about our dissatisfaction. Engaging a competent teacher or spiritual director is crucial; engaging a trusted path is paramount. During my doctoral studies, I recall that at my comprehensive exams defense one of my examiners asked me if I thought one could be holy without engaging formally in a religious tradition. My answer, after a long pause, was, "Yes, but I haven't run into anyone who is holy who is not robustly involved in a tradition." In Zen, this stage represents someone who has decidedly engaged both teacher and tradition, particularly the practice of *zazen*, where the power of one's mind can begin to unravel the constant internal dialogue.

This stage has two very different possible challenges. The first is that it could be a kind of honeymoon period, where one becomes highly elated in the newfound practice. This is particularly true in the West, where Zen is still somewhat exotic. There can be a kind of romanticizing of the practice, which can result in imagining great breakthroughs when one has really just started. A second possible problem is that practice can be erratic. Like any discipline, we are bound to become disheartened with difficulties and can be easily frustrated.

John of the Cross describes both conditions in *beginners*, those Christians who have yet to really engage the contemplative life. He writes,

> The soul finds its joy, therefore, in spending lengthy periods at prayer. . . . Its penances are pleasures; its fasts happiness; and the sacraments and spiritual conversations are its consolations. . . . [But, he warns], they conduct themselves in a very weak and imperfect manner. Since their motivation in their spiritual works and exercises is the consolation and satisfaction they experience in them, and since they have not been conditioned by the arduous struggle of practicing virtue, they possess many faults and imperfections. . . . [S]ince these persons have not had time to acquire those firm habits their work must of necessity be feeble, like weak children.[14]

He will go on to describe spiritualized versions of the seven deadly sins, including spiritual pride, avarice for religious experiences, anger at judging themselves, and sloth given their lack of discipline.[15] St. John also characterizes persons in this stage as having the tendency to quickly move from one practice to another, always trying to experience something new and immediately emotionally rewarding.[16]

So the challenge is to gently and lovingly stay the course. With the cultivation of a spacious heart and mind and with the practice of stilling the mind, we begin to get a glimpse of what we are looking for. Kuo'an ends his poem, "How could the upturned nostrils of the ox be concealed?" What he means, I think, is that to find traces of the ox, of your true self, you ought to have confidence that you are on the right track. Buddha-nature is there, and you are beginning to see how you might find it. But as yet, one's experience is all too provisional.

---

14 *Dark Night* I.1.3.

15 *Dark Night* I.2–7.

16 *Dark Night* I.3.1.

III. Seeing the Ox

A bush warbler sings upon a branch,
Warm sun, soft breezes, green willows on the bank.
Nowhere can the ox escape to hide.
But those majestic horns are difficult to draw.

Kuo'an's disciple Ciyuan describes the second stage as "Not having entered the gate as yet." In this third stage one has now truly "entered the gate." Modern master Sheng-yen describes the authentic seeing of the ox, that is, seeing into one's true nature as "having opened one eye." The initial glimpse is not very deep, but it is a watershed moment and, Sheng-yen believes, "the beginning of genuine Ch'an [Zen] practice."[17] But it is only the beginning. Some Mahayana sutras describe as many as sixteen different levels of insight into *shunyata* or emptiness.[18] The oxherder has caught a glimpse of "seeing one's nature" for the first time, but it is only yet a glimpse.

[17] Sheng-Yen, *Hoofprint of the Ox*, 394–95.
[18] Ibid., 392.

In a like manner, John of the Cross will describe one's initiation into contemplative prayer as one whereby the soul experiences interior strength and energy. "Its fruit is quiet, delicate, solitary, satisfying, and peaceful, and far removed from all the other gratifications of beginners, which are very palpable and sensory."[19]

The oxherder is overjoyed at seeing the ox for the first time. Now practice is no longer abstract, no longer looking for something about which we really do not have any concrete notion. Now, one engages in something one experiences directly. The ox cannot escape now. The oxherder has attained a level of *prajna* or wisdom. Thus he is informed by the bush warbler singing, the warm sun and soft breeze, the willows along the river. Ciyuan writes, "If one's eyes are wide open, one sees it [*prajna*] clearly, not as something else."

IV. Catching the Ox

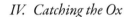

[19] *Dark Night* I.9.6–7.

With all my energy, I seize the ox.
His will is strong, and his power inexhaustible,
He cannot be tamed easily.
Sometimes he charges to the high plateau,
And there he stays, deep in the mist.

Finding the ox, experiencing one's true nature, seeing nonduality for the first time, is a daunting experience that requires sound guidance and disciplined practice. But this is nothing compared to catching and taming the ox. Kuo'an's poem makes it clear: "His will is strong and his power inexhaustible." Martine Batchelor says it quite simply: "There are many obstacles: restlessness, sleepiness, daydreaming, etc. We have to realize that for the last twenty, thirty years we have cultivated many habits which promoted distractions, and when we meditate we go against all these habits. It is going to take some time before we dissolve these tendencies."[20] These are the dispositions of the mind and defilements (*vasana*) that need to be purified through ongoing practice. Ciyuan's gloss on his master's words: "His mind is still stubborn, and his wild nature remains. If I wish him tamed, I must whip him." In Kuo'an's progression, "catching the ox" is not simply finally getting a rope around it. It will include "whipping it"—that is, taming it or putting it under control.

Now the ox represents both Buddha-nature and the unruly mind at the same time. Under the rubric of training or discipline, it ought to be understood as the latter. Suzuki notes, "The cow [mind] is hard to keep under control. She constantly longs for sweet graces. The wild nature is still unruly, and refuses to be broken in. If he wishes to have her completely in subjection, he ought to use the whip freely."[21] Resistance is typical to any ongoing search for real spiritual depth. Janet Ruffing notes this in her own experience with spiritual directees: "No one whom I have accompanied through the transition from discursive prayer into contemplative prayer has failed to resist some aspect of this development; all persisted in returning to forms of prayer that no longer supported or even worked until she or he had grown accustomed to this new experience in prayer."[22]

Another problem with getting hold of the ox or realizing our Buddha-nature is that it is necessarily a floating target. One cannot say, "That's it," or "It looks like that." All is impermanent and empty. Buddha-nature is not the supernatural substratum of life to be distinguished from the world of

[20] Batchelor, "Ten Oxherding Pictures," 35.

[21] Suzuki, *Essays in Zen Buddhism*, 373.

[22] Janet Ruffing, *Spiritual Direction: Beyond the Beginnings* (New York: Paulist Press, 2000), 41.

shunyata. It carries a different kind of reference. So the challenge in catching the ox is not holding firm to some kind of supernatural vision of reality, but something more mysterious, something that can only be realized in *shunyata*. Dogen notes,

> Our body is not really ours. Our life is easily changed by life and circumstances never remaining static. Countless things pass, and we will never see them again. Our mind is also continually changing. Some people wonder, "If this is true, on what can we rely?" But others who have the resolve seek enlightenment, due to this constant flux to deepen their enlightenment.[23]

V. Herding the Ox

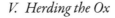

[23] Cited in Kennedy, *Zen Gifts to Christians*, 50.

One does not let go of the whip or the rope,
Afraid it will stray and choose the dusty mist.
A well-tended ox becomes gentle,
And even with no rope will follow people by himself.

Kuo'an seems to have two opposed ideas here. At first, he commends one not to "let go of the whip or rope." We see this from the picture. The oxherder has both whip in one hand and the ox's reins firmly held by the other. Ciyuan reflects this in his accompanying commentary: "Pull tightly on the nose-rope and do not hesitate." Along with the previous stage, this one requires great discipline. Modern *roshi* John Daido Loori notes that without constant practice, we "shape our practice to fit our egocentric notions and preferences. Such a self-styled spiritual path is one of the most sticky and difficult places to extricate ourselves from."[24]

You can see this in every practice. One gains a number of authentic spiritual experiences and now imagines oneself as some version of *holy*. Ongoing practice can sometimes serve to strengthen the ego by gratifying one's sense of oneself at that place. It may not be a place of sin or a place whereby one loses a real sense of God, but it would certainly be a place where the soul stalls. In many ways, the spiritual life is an ongoing deconstruction project, as we have seen in earlier chapters. You can stop deconstructing at any time, but what a tragedy.

Kuo'an finishes his poetic description with what appears to be a contrast to his first two lines. Here, instead of seeming to fear letting go of the whip, fearing the ox will stray, he says that the "ox becomes gentle, and even with no rope will follow." How so? As one progresses in Zen, practice changes. While one still has to stay alert, the mind has become far more subdued. Gradually, the ox (mind) gets tamed. Sheng-yen notes that "the ox readily responds to command, so there is no struggle like before. Not much effort but attentive practice continues though now even subtler."[25]

If we were to compare this to the practice of Christian contemplation, it would be similar to what Teresa of Ávila understands to be access to God's infused graces or *four degrees of prayer*. She uses the image of watering a garden:

> You may draw water from a well (which is a lot of work). Or you may get it by means of a water wheel and aqueducts. . . . The method

[24] John Daido Loori, *Riding the Ox Home*, ed. Konrad Ryushin Marchaj (Boston: Shambhala, 2002), 40.

[25] Sheng-Yen, *Hoofprint of the Ox*, 400.

> involves less work than the other, and you get more water. Or it may flow from a river or a stream. (The garden is watered much better by this means because the ground is more fully soaked, and there is no need to water so frequently—and much less work by the gardener.) Or the water may be provided by a great deal of rain. (For the Lord waters the garden without any work on our part—and this way is incomparably better than all the others mentioned.)[26]

While attentive and keeping watch over oneself, the graces come. Or in the sense of Zen progression, realization comes without great work in wrestling with an unruly mind. It has been pacified, and the ox follows without much restraint.

VI. Riding the Ox and Returning Home

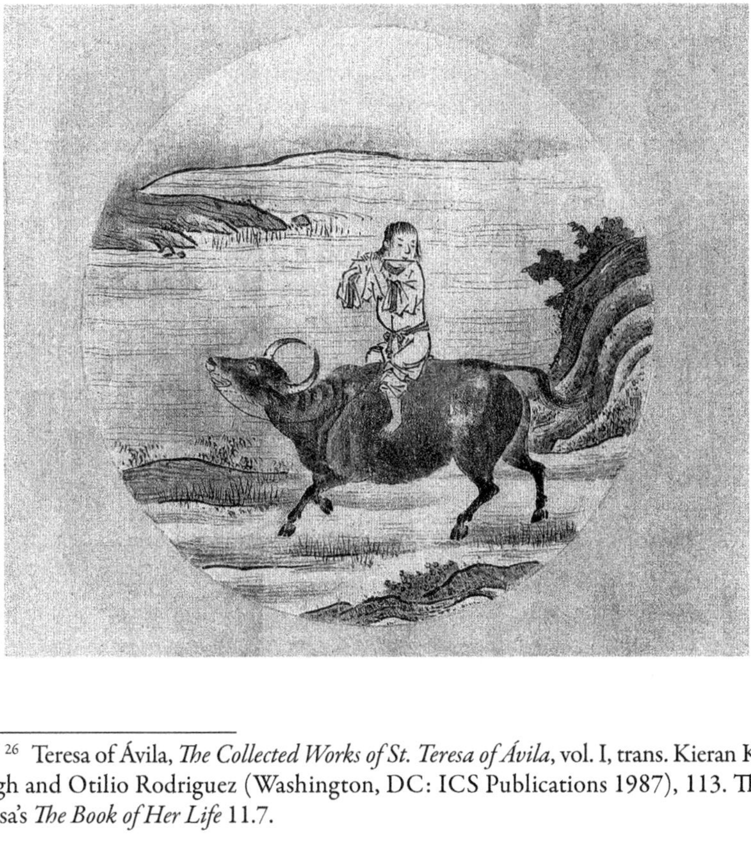

[26] Teresa of Ávila, *The Collected Works of St. Teresa of Ávila*, vol. I, trans. Kieran Kavanaugh and Otilio Rodriguez (Washington, DC: ICS Publications 1987), 113. This is Teresa's *The Book of Her Life* 11.7.

Riding the bull, I leisurely wander toward home.
Exotic flute melodies echo through sunset clouds,
Each beat and each time indescribably profound.
No words are needed for those who understand music.

The premise to the oxherding pictures is that the aspirant is wholly engaged in Zen Buddhism. In other words, he has taken the precepts and is morally dedicated to a wholesome life. It also means that he has developed both *samadhi*, or deep levels of concentration, as well as insight into emptiness and impermanence. Sheng-yen says that "to reclaim and fully actualize one's Buddha-nature is to *return home*."[27] The oxherder has not yet returned home but is on the way. And how so? Here Kuo'an describes it as a leisurely wander. The challenges of previous stages and the intense struggle for mindfulness, mental balance, perseverance, and so on have ended by bearing fruit in simply living, in living freely. Certainly, practice is still necessary, as one is still on the way. But it is now something like effortless practice. The modern master Yamada Mumon reflects, "When the struggle in the mind has subsided, the person of no-mind rides the ox of no-mind home. There is nothing to be bothered about and nothing about which to feel constrained.... Wherever you go, you feel no reserve."[28]

Consider how issues of pride, confidence, humility, and shame are often addressed. Pride is not one end of the continuum where shame is at the other. Both are expressions of the same narcissism. Confidence is not the opposite of humility. And there is no golden mean we need to attempt for a *balanced* psyche here. In studying Christian saints and Buddhist masters, I have seen the same dynamic: both represent witnesses of confidence while also being selfless and humble.

Imagine a life where there is no ego to preserve, none to advance. All affectations, even the most subtle, are gone. Imagine a life of spontaneous creativity, a childlike joy in simply being. This is the oxherder's life now happily playing his flute while riding on the back of the ox. Kuo'an suggests that not only is this a joyful play, it is also a profound play. One expresses Buddha-nature (to a degree) and it feels both simple and profound at the same time. Even the most ordinary life is now an expression of deep art. Further, as one continues to progress in the practice, one finds that the three afflictions of the conditioned mind—greed, anger, and ignorance—are

[27] Sheng-Yen, *Hoofprint of the Ox*, 403.

[28] Yamada Mumon, *Lectures on the Ten Oxherding Pictures*, trans. Victor Sogen Hori (Honolulu: University of Hawaii Press, 2004), 64.

being transformed into compassion, wisdom, and enlightenment. Emptiness and form are engaged lightly, playfully, and profoundly.[29]

VII. The Ox Forgotten, the Man Remains

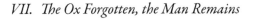

Riding on the ox, he has come home.
There is no ox there, and he is at ease.
Although the sun is high, he is still dreamy,
The whip and rope abandoned in the thatched hut.

As we have seen, the ox throughout these pictures has tended to change references. Here the ox can be understood variously in the same picture. In one sense the ox is the Dharma or even the practice of Zen. Once home, the

[29] Loori, *Riding the Ox Home*, 46.

oxherder no longer needs to rely on the Dharma or practice. These collectively represent the raft that has safely taken him home. Why cling to the ox now? Master Mumon says that this picture represents satori or enlightenment.[30] Once enlightened, we get a better sense of Bodhidharma's claim: "A special transmission outside the scriptures, not founded upon words or letters. By pointing directly to one's mind, it lets one see into one's own true nature, and thus attain Buddhahood."[31]

The ox can also represent here one's sense of "self" that has now disappeared, and there is even more radical freedom than what we saw in the last picture. In Master Keizan's *Denkoroku*, or Transmission of the Lamp collection, he offers an account by the twenty-first patriarch Vasubandhu, whose words I will relate in verse:

I do not seek the Way, yet I am not confused.
I do not venerate the Buddhas, yet I am not conceited.
I do not meditate for long periods of time, yet I am not lazy.
I do not restrict myself to just one meal a day,
yet I am not attached to food.
I do not know what is enough, yet I am not covetous.
When the mind seeks nothing, this is called the way.[32]

Finally, the ox can represent satori itself. If, indeed, the ox and this stage represent enlightenment, could we then say that the path is complete? Mumon warns, "Even satori can be clung to. . . . This is what is meant by the phrase, 'fettered by the Buddha, fettered by the Dharma.'"[33] Consider the earlier discussion of the bodhisattva Manjushri. Why was he not now a Buddha? The paradox there is that Manjushri realizes in the context of emptiness that there is no full Buddhahood, and in realizing this he has in fact attained full Buddhahood. The same dynamic goes here. As Mumon continues, "Where there is no attaining satori, that is satori. You have to forget the ox."[34] In enlightenment, there simply cannot be any dualism. The ox has to go as the herder and the ox are one.

---

[30] Mumon, *Lectures on the Ten Oxherding Pictures*, 71.

[31] Cited in Heinrich Dumoulin, *Zen Buddhism: A History: India and China*, trans. James Heisig and Paul Knitter (New York: Macmillan, 1999), 85.

[32] Keizan, *The Record of Transmitting the Light: Zen Master Keizan's Denkoroku*, trans. Francis Cook (Los Angeles: Center Publications, 1991), 110.

[33] Mumon, *Lectures on the Ten Oxherding Pictures*, 72.

[34] Ibid.

VIII. The Ox and the Man, Both Forgotten

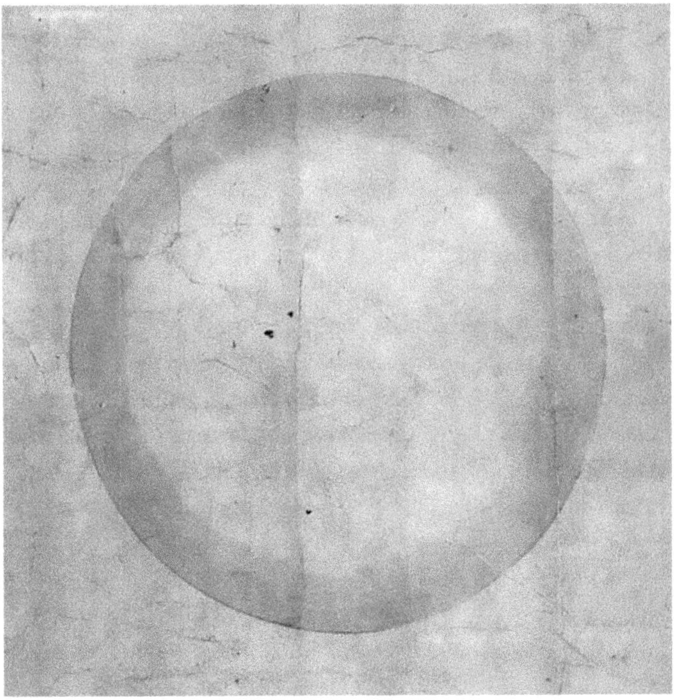

Whip, rope, man, and ox,
All are nonexistent.
The blue sky being vast,
No message can be heard,
Just as the snowflake cannot last
In the flaming red furnace.
After this state, one can join the ancient teachers.

As we have seen in chapters past, everything is interconnected and everything is *shunyata*, a kind of emptiness that is also full of Suchness (*tathata*). Neither the oxherder nor the ox are discretely real, and ultimately they must disappear into a circle of oneness. In the seventh picture, the ox had disappeared only to leave the herder in repose. Now there is no person to repose.[35] To *identify* with Buddha-nature is to identify with *no thing*, but rather to be a living instantiation of form and emptiness. Recall from the last chapter how Master Ch'ing-yuan described his practice. Initially, mountains were mountains, waters were waters. He then realized that mountains were not

[35] Sheng-Yen, *Hoofprint of the Ox*, 407.

mountains and waters were not waters.[36] That is to say, one realizes that dualistic designations are only designations without rarified, discrete identities. Only when one realizes this can Buddha-nature actualize fully. Kuo'an begins his poem, "Whip, rope, man, and ox, all are nonexistent." Kuo'an's disciple Ciyuan comments beautifully, "All confusion fallen away, the enlightened mind is not there. . . . Not lingering in either reality, one cannot be seen."

Many masters warn about this stage. Since it represents a complete knowledge of *shunyata*, and because Buddha-nature is revealed, one can remain here. Sheng-yen says that Buddhism's aim is not to simply disappear into the reality of *shunyata*. The path has yet to be completed. Loori Roshi will describe the danger of stalling in this stage as dwelling aloof and not realizing that enlightenment is not complete.

If we were to make any parallels with what we've seen in our Buddhist-Christian encounter, it would certainly be that of Meister Eckhart. Ultimately one sees God's ground as one's own ground, where to find God is to "take leave of God" so as to enter the primordial *grunt* (ground) where God and the soul are a "pure unity."[37] Everything following must come from nonduality or it is simply not a complete realization.

IX. Return to the Fundamentals, Back to the Source

[36] See Maseo Abe, *Zen and Western Thought* (Honolulu: University of Hawaii Press, 1985), 4.

[37] Bernard McGinn, *The Harvest of Mysticism in Medieval Germany* (New York: Crossroad, 2005), 179, 137.

In returning to the fundamentals and going back to the source,
I had to work so hard.
Perhaps it would be better to be blind and deaf.
Being in the hut, I do not see what is outside.
The river flowing tranquilly,
The flower simply being red.

The eighth stage automatically leads into the ninth. In the previous picture the oxherder experienced the depths of *shunyata*, of emptiness and impermanence. Now the world of phenomenal existence is reaffirmed. Now *mountains are really mountains, waters really waters.* As we saw in the last chapter, this is no reversion to the first perspective, but rather the affirmation of things in the context of their relativity. One sees the absolute truth in the context of the relative. Master Mumon notes that you end up where you started, but now see it all for the first time as an expression of Buddha-nature, of Suchness (*tathata*).[38] One sees it, much like Mahakashyapa saw the lotus the Buddha held up. In this verse, Kuo'an describes how hard it was to get to where he was going. Was it worth it? "The river flowing tranquilly, the flower simply being red." Indeed, now one experiences the luxuriant hills; bamboo and blossoms reappear. The oxherder, who is not in the picture, now has the wisdom that illuminates everything in wonder.

Master Sheng-yen describes this experience as "Things are just as they are . . . Forgetting self entirely and affirming the spontaneous function of the world without imposing any boundary."[39] Zen seems to affirm that the world, just as it is, is perfect. This is a strange paradox, since the world is one of tooth and claw, of racism and genocide, of environmental degradation. These are not somehow ignored or pretended away. Rather, underlying all the beauty and ugliness of the universe is Buddha-nature, Suchness. The oxherder now experiences that. Master Mumon says that you see true reality.[40] I am reminded of the ending of T. S. Eliot's famous poem *Little Gidding*:

And the end of all our exploring
Will be to arrive where we started
And know the place for the first time.
Through the unknown, remembered gate
When the last of earth left to discover

[38] Mumon, *Lectures on the Ten Oxherding Pictures*, 90.
[39] Sheng-Yen, *Hoofprint of the Ox*, 411.
[40] Mumon, *Lectures on the Ten Oxherding Pictures*, 90.

Is that which was the beginning;
At the source of the longest river
The voice of the hidden waterfall
And the children in the apple-tree
Not known, because not looked for
But heard, half-hearted, in the stillness
Between two waves of the sea.
Quick now, here, now, always—
A condition of complete simplicity
(Costing not less than everything)
And all shall be well and
All manner of thing shall be well
When the tongues of flame are in-folded
Into the crowned knot of fire
And the fire and the rose are one.[41]

X. Entering the City with Hands Hanging Down

[41] T. S. Eliot, *The Four Quartets* (New York: Harcourt Brace Javanovich, 1971), 59.

He enters the city barefoot, with chest exposed.
Covered in dust and ashes, smiling broadly,
No need for the magic powers of the gods and immortals,
Just let the dead tree bloom again.

In analyzing the Zen oxherding pictures, particularly from the point of view of Nagarjuna's philosophy, Steve Odin sees pictures one through seven as representing a kind of self that is affirmed, one still imagined independent. The eighth picture represents the full-on experience of *shunyata*, whereby all is nullified and emptied. Pictures nine and ten then represent a confluence of the two where authentic personhood is now achieved and social community is now robustly engaged, knowing emptiness at its core. "All phenomena, once negated are now affirmed as they are in true Suchness at the standpoint of absolute nothingness."[42]

This is the fully realized and actualized saint in the oxherding path. Our protagonist is no longer an oxherder, but a wandering and hidden saint. In the picture, he is an unkempt vagabond, giving something to a beggar. In Kuo'an's poetic description, he enters the city and engages the populace, "covered in dust and ashes, smiling broadly." Suzuki characterizes him, "He is found in the company of wine-bibbers and butchers; he and they are all converted into Buddhas."[43] Even if they do not realize their Buddha-nature, *he* does. And, engaging in the world whose absolute reality is Buddha-nature, he brings forth healing in whatever he touches. "No need for the magic powers of the gods and immortals, just let the dead tree bloom again," Kuo'an writes.

Loori identifies this stage now as "nirmanakaya, the physical body and the teachings of the Buddha manifesting in the world for the benefit of others."[44] But he expresses this in utter ordinariness, simply by being present. "He displays no trace of enlightenment. There is no stink of holiness or arrogance about him. This is Deshan [ninth-century master] who bends with the wind; Deshan with no agenda."[45]

There is a story of the tenth-century wanderer named Hotei Osho, who always dressed in an old robe and wandered around with a big bag, a straw mat, and a staff. Whenever he was tired, he would simply lie down wherever he was. If he was given something he put it into his bag and later dispersed it to the poor children of the town. He spent most of his days mingling with

---

[42] Steve Odin, "The Middle Way of Emptiness in Modern Japanese Philosophy and the Zen Oxherding Pictures," *Eastern Buddhist* 23, no. 1 (1990): 40–43.

[43] Suzuki, *Essays in Zen Buddhism*, 376.

[44] Loori, *Riding the Ox Home*, 68.

[45] Ibid., 75.

common people and laughing a great deal. The day he was to die, he seated himself on a great rock just beyond the deck of a temple and composed the following poem:

Maitreya, the true Maitreya;
Embodied in myriad selves;
Time and again he reveals himself,
Yet no one at the time knows.

After his death there were reported sightings of him from time to time, and people concluded that he must have been an incarnation of Maitreya, the future Buddha to come. This made him an important figure, and many temples in China have a large statue of Hotei enshrined in front of the Buddha Hall.[46]

I want to end this with a personal story. In 1996, the Monastic Interreligious Dialogue group sponsored their first Gethsemani Encounter, a weeklong conference at Merton's historical monastery outside of Louisville. One of the participants I got to know during that week was Zenkei Blanche Hartman, the co-abbot of the San Francisco Zen Center. During lunch on our last day, I asked Blanche to give me a teaching. She demurred that she did not have any great wisdom to offer, and we ended up talking seemingly casually until I had a realization that dramatically affected my interior life for the next two years. A button was pushed, or something hidden emerged. How did she do that? The conversation ended this way: I said to her, "You know, Blanche, you are so ordinary, such an obvious nothing." Blanche hugged me. She said, "Thank you for such gracious words, for this is my life's goal."

Christian Progress through Spiritual Stages

As we have seen in previous chapters, the Christian tradition sees the end-game of the spiritual life as some form of union with God. This union represents the divinization (*theosis*) of the soul whereby the soul lives the life of God even as it remains a created being. Surely, this is no easy process, and the tradition has, like the Zen oxherding pictures, versions of stages of spiritual development. Let us simply survey the array of different depictions.

---

[46] Mumon, *Lectures on the Ten Oxherding Pictures*, 96–97.

The Eastern Orthodox tradition is highly influenced by the works of Evagrius Ponticus, a crucial voice of the initial monastic expression. The five Evagrian texts that we have follow a progressive development in spiritual maturity as well as prayer.[47] They are the *Praktikos*, *Gnosticos*, *Kephalaia Gnostica*, *Chapters on Prayer*, and *Letter to Melania*. With each text a different level of spiritual progress is described and analyzed. One finds at each level different virtues to cultivate, ways of interpreting spiritual experiences and temptations, what to look out for at each given level, and so on. So important was going through the necessary stages that Evagrius believed one should not even have access to texts that were beyond one's given stage.[48] In the *Philokalia*, Orthodoxy's collection of classical spiritual texts, we also find progressive strategies in the *eight stages of prayer* and the *eight stages of the spiritual life*.[49] In both presentations, only the last stage involves the kind of contemplation we saw in John of the Cross.[50] Such stages are important to respect, and if one is not deeply grounded in the interior life, high stages simply would not produce spiritual fruit[51] and could even be dangerous to the soul.[52]

One sees the same concerns in John Climacus's *The Ladder of Divine Ascent*, which provides thirty steps of the spiritual ladder. While not strictly linear, it is only in the last stages where one is purified enough to engage in infused contemplation. The twenty-sixth step of the ladder is critical because it describes the ability to discern spirits—that is, that spiritual capacity to distinguish the true good from the apparent good, and grace from its counterfeits. Climacus writes,

> Among beginners, discernment is real self-knowledge; among those midway along the road to perfection, it is a spiritual capacity to distinguish unfailingly between what is truly good and what in nature is opposed to the good; among the perfect, it is a knowledge resulting from divine illumination, which with its lamp can light up

---

[47] I am relying here on the work of Jeremy Driscoll, *Spiritual Progress: Studies in the Spirituality of Late Antiquity and Early Monasticism* (Rome: Studia Anselmiana, 1994).

[48] Evagrius's *Ad Monachos* describes the whole path, beginning with asceticism and ending with possibilities of contemplative union with God. See Driscoll, *Spiritual Progress*, *passim*, and Irenee Hausherr, *Penthos: The Doctrine of Compunction in the Christian East*, trans. Anselm Hufstader (Kalamazoo, MI: Cistercian Publications, 1982), 72.

[49] See *Philokalia*, trans. and ed. G. Palmer et al. (London: Faber & Faber, 1979 [vol. 1]; 1981 [vol. 2]; 1984 [vol. 3]; 1995 [vol. 4]).

[50] Ibid., 3:108–43.

[51] Ibid., 2:63, 107, 125, 157, 219, 222, 360.

[52] Ibid., 4:65, 268–69.

> what is dark in others. To put the matter generally, discernment is—and is recognized to be—a solid understanding of the will of God in all times, in all places, in all things; and it is found only among those who are pure of heart, in body, and in speech.[53]

The West has a plethora of presentations of stages in spiritual progress. John Cassian describes it in his ninth and tenth conferences on prayer with the *prayer of repentance* for beginners, the *prayer of renunciation* for those traveling the path earnestly, the *prayer of intercession* for those developing greater compassion for others, and finally the *prayer of thanksgiving*, which he understands to be infused, divinizing contemplation. This he describes as "a powerful and wordless pouring forth of prayer to God, which the spirit with groanings that cannot be uttered, sends up though not conscious of its content."[54] Cassian warns, "We shall be utterly unable to attain to the more sublime forms of prayer . . . if our mind has not been slowly and gradually brought forward through the series of those intercessions [earlier forms of prayer]."[55]

Other examples include Bernard of Clairvaux's treatment on the Song of Songs, where each step of spiritual progress represents different levels of our knowledge of and relationship to Christ; Catherine of Siena's degrees of purification through the metaphor of spiritual tears; Jan van Ruusbroec's *Seven Steps on the Ladder of Spiritual Love*; Walter Hilton's stages of active and passive prayer in his *Scale of Perfection*; and Richard of St. Victor's twelve stages of spiritual progress in *The Twelve Patriarchs*.

One of the most well-known descriptions of the spiritual path comes from the sixteenth-century Carmelite saint Teresa of Ávila and her *Interior Castle*.[56] Here the castle principally represents the soul, which contains a series of concentric levels, each with many rooms, with God dwelling in the center. For Teresa, the spiritual journey is one of self-discovery and divine intimacy as one progressively moves deeper into the recesses of the soul. There are seven levels or *dwelling places*.

The first dwelling place is that of self-knowledge. Teresa challenges her readers to face their absorption in worldly affairs and pursuit of trivial

---

[53] John Climacus, *The Ladder of Spiritual Ascent*, trans. Colm Luibheid and Norman Russell (New York: Paulist Press, 1982), 229.

[54] John Cassian, *The Conferences*, trans. Boniface Ramsey (New York: Paulist Press, 1997), 345–46.

[55] Ibid., 339.

[56] I am using *The Collected Works of St. Teresa of Ávila*, vol. 2, trans. Kieran Kavanaugh and Otilio Rodriguez (Washington, DC: ICS Publications, 1980).

comforts. All these represent a kind of false self of egoism with dangerous temptations to mortal sin. Here one recognizes the peril the soul is in and fears that predicament. The first step in the spiritual life, she assures, is genuine repentance and a conscious decision to embrace the spiritual path seriously.

The second dwelling place represents those souls who are engaged in spiritual practices but are not sufficiently resolute. The central issue is the quality of the will: Do I really want a holy life, and am I willing to pursue it with all the challenges that this may demand? What souls need now is simply effort. Habits of sin and spiritual lethargy are difficult to overcome. Teresa believes that at this stage one ought to seek God through meditations, from the beauty of creation to the inspiration that come through meditating on scripture, listening to inspiring sermons, and so on. Souls will receive something of the divine presence, though it will always be indirect. Because souls will fail often in their diligence, she recommends both great vigilance as well as patience and gentleness with oneself. In essence, she recommends: Forgive yourself for failing, but jump right back in.

The third dwelling place depicts souls whose spiritual progress has really grown. They now habitually avoid venial sins and are committed to prayer and a holy lifestyle. As habits change, these souls now find that prayer and virtue come much easier. Teresa recognizes that there may be times of spiritual aridity during this stage, and she believes that this principally comes from the soul's lack of ardor. With a habitual practice of prayer and service to others, she believes that most of this aridity will dissipate.

Up until this point, every experience of God has been mediated through the created world. God's grace is authentically experienced through wholesome relationships, the beauty of creation, inspiring sermons, spiritual conversations, and so on. Experience of God in prayer has been mediated through the subjectivity of one's consciousness, in what she calls *mental prayer*. The fourth dwelling place is one of transition from mental prayer to the *prayer of recollection*. The first three dwelling places prepare for this. Now inner silence replaces the kinds of prayer that focused on words and images. Now the soul advances more by simply being present and silent before God. From this posture in prayer, Teresa says one could even experience the *prayer of quiet*, by which the soul might experience God far more directly. Here God enlarges the heart.

Teresa frames the fifth dwelling place as by far the largest and as having the most rooms. She believed that most of the cloistered sisters in her community attained this dwelling place. Here God interacts with the soul quite directly, and the prayers of recollection and quiet would be typical. As we have seen earlier, since God transcends conceptuality, the soul seeking more direct knowledge of God has to do the same. It is in this dwelling place that Teresa introduces the *prayer of union*, a profound experience that overwhelms the soul in love.

While in the fifth dwelling place, the soul has fallen in love with God on a deep level; here, Teresa insists that they have yet to "betroth" themselves to each other. The sixth dwelling place is the stage of spiritual betrothal. Here the soul can experience great heights of spiritual rapture as well as the kind of dark night of the soul that John of the Cross describes. Teresa recounts one experience of ecstasy that is captured in Lorenzo Bernini's sculpture called *The Ecstasy of Teresa*, which sits in the Church of Santa Maria della Vittoria in Rome:

> I saw close to me toward my left side an angel in bodily form . . . saw in his hands a large golden dart and at the end of the iron tip there appeared to be a little fire. It seemed to me that the angel plunged the dart several times into my heart and that it reached deep within me. When he drew it out, I thought he was carrying off with him the deepest part of me; and he left me all on fire with great love of God. The pain was so great that it made me moan, and the sweetness this greatest pain caused me was so superabundant that there is no desire capable of taking it away; nor is the soul content with less than God. . . . It seems the Lord carries the soul away and places it in ecstasy.[57]

The sixth dwelling place, like John of the Cross's dark night of the soul, can be also extraordinarily dry as the soul is stretched to love God for God's sake.

Teresa's seventh dwelling place is what she calls *mystical marriage*, whereby the soul exists in full divinizing union with God. Teresa says that while the "lower part" of the soul continues to engage the world normally, the "spiritual part" of the soul experiences herself in perpetual union with God. There are no more raptures here, as they represented something of a defect, which is to say that experiences of union before the seventh dwelling place overwhelmed the soul. Now union is the soul's norm. A final note about this stage is that Teresa describes the soul in union as having extraordinary energy to serve God in other people. One does not stay on some mystical heights divorced from the world, but engages it through the compassionate love of God.

[57] Teresa, *Autobiography*, 29.13–14. I am utilizing *The Collected Works of St. Teresa of Ávila*, vol. 1 (revised), trans. Kieran Kavanaugh and Otilio Rodriguez (Washington, DC: ICS Publications, 1987).

Comparing Paths

One could make some broad parallels between Teresa's seven stages of spiritual development and the Zen oxherding pictures. Both begin with a stark look at oneself and one's woeful spiritual condition. Early stages in both demand practices, moral and spiritual, that are hard at first but become progressively easier and more aligned to the spiritual person one is becoming. Both recognize that early experiences, as authentic as they may be, are really just glimpses of the absolute and little more. In both, the stakes become increasingly higher, and progress is more tentative. As we saw, there are many temptations to stall on the oxherding path. Teresa also notes that the vast majority of the sisters in her convent, while achieving some degree of infused contemplation (fifth mansion), rarely go further. As we saw in John of the Cross's deconstruction of the self, Teresa has something of the same in her sixth mansion. It is here that the soul endures long periods of spiritual aridity so as to strip it of all narcissism. Surely there are parallels in Buddhism, itself requiring the deconstruction of self and world. As noted above, Olsen saw the first seven pictures depicting versions of the self, and only in the eighth is a full-blown *shunyata* experienced. Finally, we might say that in both, to become completely united to the Absolute, be that Buddha-nature or God, is to become utterly humble, selfless, and free. Further, the Zen saint and the Christian saint ultimately understand that embodying compassion and wisdom in their life has everything to do with loving service to others.

None of these insights requires much genius, and all are rather obvious and typical of any authentic path. We might also recognize that they are, in fact, different paths. The oxherder is trying to find his true nature and trying to experience the interpenetrating emptiness and Suchness of all things. The Christian saint is trying to find God and be radically divinized by union with God. This is a very personal God, who is love. God is not really imaged as Buddha-nature in ways that Zen would easily recognize or ought to.

I think perhaps one of the most important insights we might receive from our modest comparison at the end of this chapter is that there are indeed venerable paths that are available, paths that masters of our religious traditions have trodden and recognize as capable of providing the conditions of possibility for radical transformations of consciousness. Here one moves from experiencing great separateness from oneself and from the spiritual foundation of the world into an active and unitive participation with that foundation. These transformations make one literally a different person, one who sees what no one else sees and engages the world in profoundly authentic and compassionate ways.

Can a Christian Be a Roshi?

If they are truly different, what ought we to make of those Christians who have attempted and perhaps succeeded in pursuing both robustly? Forty years ago, widely respected Jesuit missionary priests—such as William Johnston, Hugo Enomiya-Lassalle, and Heinrich Dumoulin—were commending Zen insights and meditational practices for Christians. More recently, Christian leaders such as Father Robert Kennedy, Father Willigis Jäger, Lutheran pastor Gundula Meyer, and Catholic theologian Ruben Habito have been officially designated as a *roshi* or Zen master in respected Zen lineages. They argue that a successful unity can be achieved between Zen and Christianity. While not collapsing differences, they argue that Zen does not conflict with Christianity and can be wholly embraced while also wholly embracing the Christian faith. So it is possible, they argue, for both cross-referencing similarities and allowing the traditions to complement each other—all this without compromising Christianity or undermining the true nature of Zen.

Some of the claims one encounters in such projects strike me as somewhat contrived or at least overstated. Kennedy, for example, simply states that Christian faith is nondualistic, thus wholly aligning with what is sought in Zen.[58] This extraordinary claim requires a detailed argument. Kennedy also sees that many religions seek transformation into the absolute.[59] This is, of course, true, but he fails to demonstrate how the absolute in Zen works with or is the same as the absolute in Christianity. Is Buddhist nonself the same as dying unto Christ?[60] A case would have to be made metaphysically. Kennedy also imagines that Zen is not "a religion at all, but a way of seeing life that can enhance any religious faith."[61] It certainly appears to be a religion, with rites, doctrine (of some kind), its own moral system, and specific paths to reach its ultimate end. If it is true that Zen is not a religion, then, again, a case would have to be robustly made.

We have already noted many similarities in classical Buddhist and Christian paths, such as the deconstruction of the self as an independent and separate, rarified object. And we saw that God qua God ought not to be objectified in Christianity, just as Buddhism sees as necessary regarding everything from phenomenal reality to Buddha-nature. We also noted in earlier chapters questions for Mahayana Buddhism on the issue of abso-

[58] Kennedy, *Zen Gifts to Christians*, 70.

[59] Ibid., 103.

[60] Ibid.

[61] Robert Kennedy, *Zen Spirit, Christian Spirit* (New York: Continuum, 2004), 14.

lute compassion as intrinsic to Buddha-nature. This universal metaphysical substructure to all reality sounds theistic. If this is the case, then perhaps Mahayana aligns with Christianity *because* it is another form of theism.

Ruben Habito's work is more focused on arguing for the interconnectedness of sentiency itself and the ubiquitous presence of God interpenetrating all reality. Sin, for Habito, is conditioned on our sense of separation from this truth. Having lost (or never having found) our intrinsic interconnectedness makes us addicted to attachments and to treating ourselves, the world, and even God as objects to exploit as they are imagined to orbit our narcissistic sun. It is a "cosmic woundedness."[62] For Habito, Zen becomes the kind of praxis that awakens both wisdom and compassion. It helps us to break out of these egoistic chains and "plunges us into the heart of the world."[63]

Kennedy, Habito, and works such as Johnston's *Christian Zen* succeed best when they help us make connections and show us how the practice of Zen can legitimately support a Christian life. The metaphysics is far more problematic, and I have not encountered a sustained argument that convincingly shows they can be robustly aligned. I would like to end, however, with a wonderful comment by Father Robert Kennedy Roshi:

> Yamada Roshi [his master] told me several times that he did not want to make me a Buddhist, but rather he wanted to empty me in imitation of "Christ your Lord" who emptied himself, poured himself out, and clung to nothing. Whenever Yamada Roshi instructed me in this way, I thought that this Buddhist might make a Christian of me yet![64]

---

62 Rubin Habito, *Healing Breath: Zen for Christians and Buddhists in a Wounded World* (Somerville, MA: Wisdom Publications, 2004), 4–17.

63 Ibid., 52.

64 Kennedy, *Zen Spirit, Christian Spirit*, 14.

Chapter 9

The Heart of Buddhist Experience, Pure Land, and Christian Theology

Lives of Faith and Grace: How Far apart Are We?

One of the great supposed contrasts between Buddhism and Christianity lies in the dominance of faith and grace in Christianity and its absence in Buddhism. In the New Testament alone, we find the term faith (*pistis*) used over 250 times and grace (*charis*) well over 100. In Romans, Paul understands justification as both an expression of grace—"justified by his grace as a gift" (3:24)—and response by the believer who is "justified by faith" (3:28). For Paul, grace and faith are intrinsically united in being aligned with and united to God. The *Catechism of the Catholic Church* (*CCC*) describes faith as our "response to God," who brings "superabundant light" to our search for "ultimate meaning" (*CCC* 26). Salvation ultimately starts and ends with God's grace who moves the heart and converts it to God (*CCC* 153). "Grace is first and foremost the gift of the Spirit who justifies and sanctifies us" (*CCC* 2003). It has been common to imagine that Protestants understand justification depending solely on faith, while Catholics understand justification as a combination of faith and works. This is simply a mischaracterization. As clarified in the Lutheran-Catholic *Joint Declaration on the Doctrine of Justification*, "All persons depend completely on the saving grace of God for their salvation," and "when Catholics say that persons *cooperate* in preparing for and accepting justification by consenting to God's action, they see such personal consent as itself an effect of grace."[1]

[1] *Joint Declaration on the Doctrine of Justification*, the Lutheran World Federation and the Catholic Church, 19–20.

We might compare this utter reliance on God's grace as a striking contrast to one of the Buddha's final exhortations: "Bhikkhus, dwell with yourselves as an island, with yourselves as a refuge; with the Dharma as an island, with the Dharma as a refuge, with no other refuge."[2] Thus relying on the teaching (Dharma), it appears to be all about one's own practice and determination.

Pope John Paul II, in assessing such a divergence in religious approaches writes, "It needs to be said right away that the doctrines of salvation in Buddhism and Christianity are opposed."[3] Characterizing Buddhism, he continues,

> Both the Buddhist tradition and the methods deriving from it have an almost exclusively *negative soteriology*. The "enlightenment" experienced by Buddha comes down to the conviction that the world is bad, that it is the source of evil and of suffering for man. To liberate oneself from this evil, one must free oneself from this world, necessitating a break with the ties that join us to external reality. . . . The more we are liberated from these ties, the more we become indifferent to what is in the world, and the more we are freed from suffering, from the evil that has its source in the world. Do we draw near to God in this way? . . . Buddhism is in large measure an "*atheistic*" *system*. We [Buddhists] do not free ourselves from evil through the good which comes from God; we liberate ourselves only through detachment from the world, which is bad. . . . To *save oneself* means, above all, to free oneself from evil by becoming *indifferent to the world, which is the source of evil.* This is the culmination of the spiritual process.[4]

Given the material we have already reviewed in this book, it should be obvious that John Paul's depiction of Buddhism is problematic. First, of course, there is no "Buddhism" to depict. While one can appreciate that the pope intended only a generalization, Buddhism is simply far too varied to generalize on the very points he makes. One could, of course, generalize on the Four Noble Truths or the Eightfold Path. All of Buddhism also shares some sense of nonself and impermanence. Further, it is broadly accepted in Buddhism that the primary problem in the human condition is craving or thirst and that a

---

[2] *Majjhima Nikaya* III.91.7.

[3] John Paul II, *Crossing the Threshold of Hope*, trans. Jenny McPhee and Martha McPhee (New York: Knopf, 1994), 85.

[4] Ibid., 85–86, emphasis in original.

conditioned mind suffers from anger, greed, and ignorance. But Buddhism's supposed *atheism*, rejection of the world as evil, and *negative soteriology* do not accurately depict Buddhism, even in the Theravada tradition.

Recall that, while the Buddha commended his disciples to themselves and the Dharma, Buddhism never lost the three refuges: Buddha, Dharma, Sangha. We saw that taking refuge in the Buddha constituted not merely inspiration in his witness, but literal refuge. How is the Buddha accessible in the Theravada tradition? This is complicated and not easy to answer. We already know that early Buddhists affirmed Buddha-fields (*buddha-kshestra*) where the Buddha continued in some manner to be a *natha*, or protector.

We also saw in chapter 2 that the Buddha was cagey about the nature of Nirvana and particularly about final-Nirvana. "The Tathagata is liberated from reckoning. . . . He is profound, immeasurable, unfathomable like the ocean. The term 'reappears' does not apply, the term 'does not reappear' does not apply, the term 'both reappears and does not reappear' does not apply, the term 'neither reappears nor does not reappear' does not apply."[5] Further, we saw in chapter 3 that Buddhaghosa assures us Nirvana is a real reference. It certainly does not mean extinction, nor is it merely an indication that one has stopped clinging or craving. Nirvana is real, but it is a *parammattha-sacca*, an ultimate truth that cannot be conceptualized. What the Buddha pointed to and the path he gave led to *reality-beyond-the-world* (*lokuttara-dharma*), something ultimately transcendent and transcendental.

Another factor to consider in this discussion is just how one attains Nirvana. In no way do I want to rehash material from chapters 2 and 3. Rather I want to point out that *one cannot save oneself.* Because Nirvana is an actual referent, and because Nirvana is beyond the world, that is, beyond karma formations, it cannot be *caused*. As John Ross Carter writes,

> In the Theravada vision, one does not save or liberate oneself. There is no enduring substantial self that could *do* the saving, or releasing, or bring about liberation in the first place. . . . In the *magga*/path, there is the "discarding of defilement," which happens because the other factor necessary for it now takes place, namely, contact with the *reality-beyond-the-world*. But this contact is not a production in one's being, but an encounter firsthand.[6]

---

[5] *Majjhima Nikaya* 72.20.

[6] John Ross Carter, *In the Company of Friends: Exploring Faith and Understanding with Buddhists and Christians* (Albany: State University of New York Press: 2012), 126, 129.

Carter goes on to describe the "change of lineage" process in the Theravada school or becoming a "stream enterer." Here attainment of Nirvana is close at hand. Still, any attempt to cause Nirvana as "self-centered calculations would represent defiling *sankharas* [conditioned phenomena] that would, in the nature of the case, merely continue giving rise to the presence of defilements."[7] What the aspirant can do is avail oneself to Nirvana, when purified Nirvana arises.

Saddha means "faith" in the sense of entrusting oneself, or placing one's heart on something. This faith is crucial in all of Buddhism. As the noted Burmese scholar Ven. Pannyanada writes, "*Saddha* [faith] is an indispensable factor governing all spiritual growth; it is called the seed from which is born the tree that bears the fruit of deliverance. [Of the] five factors of spiritual powers and seven faculties, the primary factor is *saddha*. It, if accurately cultivated, conditions the development of the rest."[8] Essentially, what the aspirant must do is live the life of faith, entrusting herself to the process and ultimately entrusting herself to Nirvana, that transcendent, absolute Ultimate.

We have already seen that there is an Absolute in Mahayana. There is, Nagarjuna taught, a Suchness (*tathata*) that alone lies outside of delusion. His synonyms, as we saw, include the *Inexpressible*, the *realm of non-discrimination*, the *Unconditioned*, *Nirvana*, *Buddhahood*, *Wisdom*, and *Enlightenment*. As Mahayana develops, we discover innumerable Buddha-fields with innumerable Buddhas and bodhisattvas whose sole existence is devoted to compassionate service to all sentient beings. Those beings who serve their Buddha-fields transcend time, space, and any given instantiation they may have at any particular moment. What they express is Buddha-nature (*tathagatagrarbha*), the ultimate, transcendent Reality.

Mahayana teaches that there are three Buddha-bodies, all relating to each other. The *Dharmakaya* is the ultimate reality, the transcendent truth. It is emptiness and Nirvana itself; it is Suchness, Oneness, the Dharma nature. It exists not as an abstract or principle, but Absolute Buddha-nature. The *Sambhogakaya*, or body of bliss, is the transcendent existence that all these innumerable Buddhas know and experience. The *Nirmanakaya* body is the transformed body, one that can manifest itself in whatever way would best meet the needs of those under their care. A given *Nirmanakaya* is an instantiation of *Dharmakaya*.[9]

---

[7] Ibid., 129.

[8] Sao. Pannyanada, "Saddha (Faith) Is the Fundamental Step to Become a Buddha," http://www.myanmarnet.net/nibbana/article1.htm.

[9] Hisao Inagaki, *The Three Pure Land Sutras: A Study and Translation from Chinese*, revised (Kyoto: Nagata Bunshodo, 1995), 24–25.

What we see from all this is that the Buddhist traditions cannot be easily disassociated from faith, from grace, and from the Absolute working in and through them. In no way can these traditions be termed *atheistic* as this word is typically used, nor their respective paths distinct from the Absolute existing on their behalf to bring about their liberation and radical flourishing in an Ultimate Existence. This is a religious set of traditions premised, sometimes quite clearly and sometimes less so, on grace. The devotion to Buddhas and bodhisattvas is less like a devotion to lesser gods or mediators as it is devotion to the compassionate expression of Buddha-nature being itself.

Pure Land Buddhism

Faith, grace, and reliance on the compassionate ministry of Buddhas are most clear in Pure Land Buddhism. It is a form of Buddhism that relies on three principal sutras: The Sutra on the Buddha of Infinite Life (Larger *Sukavativyuha*), The Sutra on Contemplation of Amitayus, and The Sutra on the Buddha Amitayus (Smaller *Sukavativyuha*). The Larger Sutra, composed around 100 CE, depicts a conversation between the Buddha and his disciple Ananda about a king who renounced his throne and became a monk under the guidance of the Buddha Lokeshvararaja. The king-turned-monk took the man Dharmakara and showed him innumerable Buddha-lands and the Buddhas that dwelled there. Inspired, Dharmakara made forty-eight vows in the presence of Buddha Lokeshvararaja to become a Buddha and create his own Buddha-land, one that would be accessible to all sentient beings for their enlightenment. Through five kalpas he worked to fully achieve these vows, becoming the Buddha Amitayus, meaning "Infinite Life." Buddha Gautama then told Ananda to worship Amitayus, who manifested to Ananda both himself and his Buddha-land, the Pure Land.

In the Sutra on Contemplation we find the story of Queen Vaidehi, whose husband was wrongly imprisoned. Vaidehi felt abandoned by all. In order to assist her, the Buddha showed her many Buddha-lands and promised he would help her to enter one of them. She chose the Pure Land of Amitayus. Through the Buddha's power and detailed instruction, provided by the sutra, she learned how to meditate on and visualize the Pure Land.

In the Smaller Sutra, we find the Buddha teaching disciples that there was a Buddha-land called "Utmost Bliss" where Amitayus presides. All beings, he declared, who entered that Pure Land would dwell in the stage of nonretrogression—that is, assurance of attaining enlightenment with no more rebirths. In order to be born there, one had to concentrate on Amitayus. Holding fast to the name for even as short as a single day assured believers of this rebirth.[10]

Early in Buddhism, contemplation on the Buddha was a recommended practice, though principally one aimed at controlling passions and inspiring aspirants. In Mahayana, the object of mindfulness was no longer limited to the historical Buddha, but included all Buddhas throughout the universe. Later in China and consequently in Japan, "mindfulness of the Buddha" fell exclusively to Amitayus/Amitabha, often accompanied by visualizations of his Pure Land.[11]

Jodo Shinshu or Pure Land is, by far, the most popular form of Buddhism in Japan. Its earliest importance began at the temple monastery on Mount Hiei, when the abbot Ennin (794–864), upon returning from China, established the practice of *jogyo-zammai*, the perpetual chanting of the name Amida. It worked like a practice of *samadhi*. Other temples followed Mount Hiei's example. Pure Land was significantly advanced a century later by Mount Hiei's abbot Genshin (942–1017), who advocated meditating on Amida and the Pure Land as a means of attaining rebirth there.[12] The school known as Jodo Shinshu or Pure Land was founded by the monk and later abbot Honen (1133–1212). Honen believed that his era represented a significant decay in the power of the Dharma, one where the possibilities of enlightenment were virtually nonexistent. This general belief of the day, coupled with Honen's own frustration at his lack of spiritual progress, led him to believe in the necessity of relying on the power of Amida's vow.

Honen writes, "How pitiful! What should I do? . . . . Does there exist, besides the three disciplines [precepts, concentration, wisdom], a path suited for me, a discipline practical by one of my character? I paid visits to numerous scholars, yet there was none to teach me, no friend to show me the way."[13] Honen then read a passage from Shan-tao's (613–638) commentary on the Contemplation Sutra: "Whether walking or standing, sitting or lying, only repeat the name of Amida with all our heart. Never cease the practice of it even for a moment. This is the very work which unfailingly issues in salvation, for it is in accordance with the Original Vow of that Buddha."[14] The "Original Vow" was the eighteenth of Dharmakara's forty-eight:

---

[10] Ibid., 4–12.

[11] Ibid., 17.

[12] Tamaru Noriyoshi, "Early Pure Land Leaders," in Takeuchi Yoshinori, ed., *Buddhist Spirituality II: Later China, Korea, Japan, and the Modern World* (New York: Crossroad, 1999), 201–02.

[13] Ibid., 205.

[14] Ibid.

> If, when I attain Buddhahood, sentient beings in the lands of the ten directions who sincerely and joyfully entrust themselves to me, desire to be born in my land, and call my Name even ten times, should not be born there, may I not attain perfect Enlightenment. Excluded, however, are those who commit the five grave offenses and abuse the right Dharma.[15]

What Honen discovered was his own inability to significantly advance as well as the saving power of (now) Amida's vow and grace. Jodo Shinshu will distinguish between "self-power" (*jiriki*) and "other-power" (*tariki*). Ultimately, one is brought to the Pure Land—one is *saved*—through Amida's power.

Is this other-power, the grace of Amida, a corruption of Buddhism? It need not be at all. Carter notes that while the term "other-power" is technically foreign to the Theravada tradition, its implications are not. Even in Theravada there is a necessary transcendental element at work, something supramundane (*lokuttara*).[16] Suzuki also defends other-power as a necessary correlative to self-power:

> The teaching of the "other-power" school does not mean to annihilate the karma phase of human life in order to make it absolutely transcend itself. What the other-power tries to do is to live at the same time a life of transcendence, a life of spiritual freedom, a life not tied down to the chain of causation. Without the idea of Suchness the human consciousness cannot go any farther than that; without Suchness there is no bridge or background where karma and akarma [outside the dynamics of karma] could be linked. . . . [The] Buddhist idea of Emptiness is one that unites both fullness and nothingness, both karma and akarma, both determination and freedom, both immanence and transcendence, both *jiriki* (self-power) and *tariki* (other-power).[17]

Honen's practice was dominated by the recitation of the name, a practice called *nembutsu*. The recitation is *namu-amida-butsu* (Homage to Amida Buddha). His practice was daunting, regularly reciting the *nembutsu* as many as sixty thousand times a day. From this kind of devotion and meditative concentration, he records in his journal, the *Senchakushu*, that he was

---

[15] Inagaki, *Three Pure Land Sutras*, 243.

[16] Carter, *In the Company of Friends*, 126.

[17] D. T. Suzuki, *On Indian Mahayana Buddhism*, ed. Edward Conze (New York: Harper Torchbook, 1968), 135–37.

able to see the Pure Land distinctly. The practice filled him with assurance and even impatient anticipation. Late in his journal, he writes,

> I rejoice in the years piling up and ready to topple over, since I see it as the Pure Land finally having come near. . . . I look forward to that moment, for then I shall go to the Pure Land and sit on the lotus throne of Kannon Bodhisattva [Avalokiteshvara] come to welcome me. . . . How I love Paradise! May this life end quickly![18]

Fujimoto Kiyohiko consolidates Honen's doctrine: (1) the goal of faith is rebirth in the Pure Land, (2) the object of faith is Amida Buddha as a result of the fulfillment of Dharmakara's vows, and (3) the means of faith is the *nembutsu*. The *nembutsu* takes all priority as Amida's holy name embraces all inward and outward powers and virtues of Amida Buddha.[19]

One of Honen's chief disciples was Shinran (1173–1262), who studied under his master for six years. Like Honen, Shinran found little more than frustration through his diligent Buddhist practice. Shinran believed that any self-striving (self-power) was ultimately a fool's errand, as it necessarily got tangled up in the interests of the ego. Thus, it was impossible to purify oneself. Any deliverance, therefore, could only come from Amida Buddha's other-power, and one's true practice was that of faith, of single-minded trust, itself endowed by Amida.[20]

For Shinran, Amida was not simply an "ordinary" Buddha. In the Larger Sutra we find that it took Dharmakara five kalpas to become Amida Buddha, and this was ten kalpas ago. Thus, Shinran concluded that Amida was fundamentally timeless or eternal. Amida symbolized Buddha-nature itself, that which pervades the entire cosmos and is evident in the aspiration for enlightenment in all sentient beings. As Amitayus, he is *literally* "eternal/infinite life," and as Amitabha, he is *literally* "infinite light." He is the primordial *Dharmakaya*, the utter expression of *Sambhogakaya* existence, and *Nirmanakaya* as Dharmakara. Thus, for Shinran, deliverance is only possible through Amida's vow, and faith becomes not only trust in Amida but also *by that trust* the realization of Buddha-nature in oneself.

For Shinran, self-power and other-power become one. Leo Lefebure observes, "Any dualism between self-power and Other-power is overcome in the realization that Amida Buddha is realizing his vow in our actions. . . .

---

[18] Cited in Fujimoto Kiyohiko, "Honen's Spiritual Legacy," in *Buddhist Spirituality II*, 215.

[19] Ibid., 216–18.

[20] Alfred Bloom, "Shinran's Way," in *Buddhist Spirituality II*, 229.

We realize that Other-power is not simply other than ourselves; self-power is one with Other-power."[21] So, returning to the eighteenth vow, Shinran saw that authentic practice of *nembutsu* was really an expression of Buddha-mind, a realization of Buddha-nature. Through the *nembutsu* one became a compassionate Buddha, instantiating *Dharmakaya-as-Suchness* and *Dharmakaya-as-compassion*. This did not simply mean, for Shinran, that one would attain a final rebirth in the Pure Land; it meant that one attained Nirvana itself—this, for all sentient beings. In assessing Jodo Shinshu, Carter writes,

> Those among us who are Jodo Shinshu or Shin Buddhists have also affirmed that there is that which transcends conceptuality, namely that to which we refer when we use the Japanese term *hosshin* (*dharmakaya*). We have found that within this oneness there are integral, inseparable dimensions, spoken of by representative translators as "dharmakaya-as-suchness" (*hossho hosshin*) and "dharmakaya-as-compassionate-means" (*hoben hosshin*). We have found that his fundamental principle of Salvific Truth, dharmakaya, enters our awareness as an activity of compassion rooted in and forming an inseparable part of this Salvific Truth, as Amida, who has acted on our behalf and continues to act on our behalf. . . . Moreover, Amida, in the form of the Bodhisattva Dharmakara, uttered the Primal Vow, made the Vow, gave the Vow. This primal Vow is not merely a statement; it is, when understood more fully, an act, an event. It is not an isolated act, but an act that permeates all dimensions of human understanding and yet also transcends those dimensions.[22]

Recitation of the Holy Name: Buddhist and Christian

As we saw above, the *nembutsu* or repeated recitation of *namu-amida-butsu* (Homage to Amida Buddha) dominated Pure Land spirituality since the time of Honen. What are we to make of this practice? Initially, it was believed to create *samadhi*, or deep concentration, perhaps much like we saw in earlier forms of Buddhism going back to the Theravada tradition. In that tradition, meditation on the Buddha or his qualities represented an extremely fruitful practice. Buddhaghosa writes,

---

[21] Leo Lefebure, *The Buddha and The Christ: Explorations in Buddhist and Christian Dialogue* (Maryknoll, NY: Orbis, 1993), 107.

[22] Carter, *In the Company of Friends*, 66–67.

> When a bhikkhu is devoted to this recollection of the Buddha, he is respectful and deferential towards the Master. He attains fullness of faith, mindfulness, understanding and merit. He has much happiness and gladness. He conquers fear and dread. He is able to endure pain. He comes to feel as if he were living in the Master's presence.[23]

Buddhaghosa also notes that such a practice does not lead to a deep concentration, perhaps because of the *conceptualizing* quality of it. "The jhana [level of absorption] is only access and does not reach [full] absorption."[24]

For Honen and the Pure Land tradition, the *nembutsu* is far deeper, something that allows not only a high level of *samadhi* but also provides the condition of possibility for actually experiencing Amida and/or his Pure Land. This is to say, the *nembutsu* allows for direct contact with the Absolute. According to Honen's journal, the *Senchakushu*, he experienced this vividly in 1198:

> On the seventh day of the first month I started my *nembutsu* practice as usual. During that day I had some clear visions of the Pure Land. It was all so natural and clear. . . . On the seventh day of my *nembutsu* practice, I had a view of the lapis lazuli section of the visualization of the ground. On the morning of the fourth day of the second month the lapis lazuli ground appeared to me in detail. Six days later at night I had a vision of the jeweled pavilions. These appeared to me again on the morning of the seventh day. From the first day of the first month to the seventh day of the second month, for thirty-seven days, I recited the *nembutsu* constantly, seventy thousand times a day. On the strength of this I obtained the five visualizations of the water, the ground, the jeweled trees, the jeweled ponds, and the jeweled pavilions. . . . On the morning of the twenty-second day of the ninth month, the ground appeared to me clearly and distinctly. Around it the ground was terraced in about seven or eight levels. Afterwards, in the late night and morning of the twenty-third day, I had again this clear and distinct vision.[25]

The Christian tradition has a long-standing practice of its own version of *nembutsu*. The great patristic spiritual master John Climacus writes,

---

[23] *Visuddhimagga* VII.67.

[24] *Visuddhimagga* VII.66.

[25] Cited in Kiyohiko, 'Honen's Spiritual Legacy," 214.

"Let the remembrance of Jesus be present with your every breath."[26] A more modern expression comes to us from the nineteenth-century Russian bishop, spiritual director, and eventual hermit, Theophan the Recluse:

> When he who prays is wholly concentrated within his heart and mentally contemplates God, present to him and within him . . . he experiences the feelings corresponding to such a state—fear of God and worshipful admiration of Him in all his greatness; faith and hope; love and surrender to his will; contrition and readiness for every sacrifice. He who prays thus for a long time and in the proper way will enjoy such a state more and more frequently until it may finally become permanent: then it can be called walking before God, and constitutes unceasing prayer.[27]

The Jesus Prayer

One of the most popular expressions of unceasing prayer, particularly in the Orthodox tradition, is the Jesus Prayer.[28] By the thirteenth century, it had become a standard method of contemplation for monastics. If I might consolidate the tradition, the prayer technique is the following: One sits with head and shoulders bowed, with the gaze of the eyes toward the heart. Ancient Greek Christians called this "descending of the mind into the heart," where intellect, emotions, and soul unite. In praying, one slows down the speed of breathing and coordinates the Jesus Prayer to one's inhalation and exhalation. The inhalation of the breath is imagined as a physical exercise of having the mind descend into the heart. Early on in the practice, one uses words, but as the prayer intensifies and one integrates, it becomes a silent prayer coming from one's heart-center. The typical words on the inhalation are "Lord Jesus Christ" and on the exhalation, "have mercy on me."

The Jesus Prayer has four elements: the invocation of the name of Jesus, itself considered spiritually powerful; the appeal to God's mercy, accompanied by a spirit of *penthos*, or compunction; the repetition of the words with each

---

26 John Climacus, *The Ladder of Spiritual Ascent*, trans. Colm Luibheid and Norman Russell (New York: Paulist Press, 1982), 270.

27 Cited in Igumen Chariton and Timothy Ware, eds., *The Art of Prayer: An Orthodox Anthology*, trans. E. Kadloubovsky and E. M. Palmer (London: Faber & Faber, 1997), 85.

28 I first addressed the Jesus Prayer in *Christian Spirituality: Lived Experience in the Life of the Church* (Winona, MN: Anselm Academic, 2015), 130–32, and am relying on my work there.

breath repeatedly (perhaps for hours); and the eventual movement to nondiscursive, nonconceptual prayer. Eventually, one ought to *become* the prayer.

The most famous modern expression of the Jesus Prayer comes from *The Way of the Pilgrim*, which tells the story of a Russian peasant who desires to become a truly prayerful person.[29] He goes to a spiritual elder who teaches him the prayer. Initially, the master advises him to repeat the prayer three thousand times a day. For several days the Pilgrim attempts this, though it is extremely difficult for him to sustain that high number. As he gets used to the prayer, however, he finds his mind and heart increasingly centered and his love for God dramatically deepened. On his next month's visit, the master increases the task to six thousand times a day. He soon learns to achieve this. On his third visit, his master now instructs him to pray it twelve thousand times a day. He exhorts the Pilgrim to rise earlier and retire to bed later, and it turns out that the prayer itself is so centering and energizing that he needs less sleep. Finally, it is as though his heart is praying this prayer constantly. "I stopped vocalizing the prayer and began to listen attentively as the heart spoke," he says.[30] According to the Pilgrim, the Jesus Prayer bore great spiritual fruits:

> In the spirit one can experience the sweetness of the love of God, inner peace, purity of thought, awareness of God's presence, and ecstasy. In the emotions a pleasant warmth of the heart, a feeling of delight throughout one's being, joyful bubbling of the heart, lightness and courage, joy of life, indifference to sickness and sorrow. And in revelation, one receives the enlightenment of one's mind, understanding of Holy Scripture, knowledge of speech of all creatures, renunciation of vanities, awareness of the sweetness of the interior life, and confidence in the nearness of God and his love for us.[31]

In both Pure Land and Christian traditions, a *nembutsu* practice has the possibility of real transformation. Honen sees and to a degree experiences the Pure Land. Something of the presence and blessings of Amida himself is encountered, bringing the aspirant deeper faith and spiritual assurance. This is not merely a *samadhi* exercise, it is an experience of the Pure Land—something that, according to Shinran, was there among and within us all the time but needed to be realized. The Pilgrim also experiences the "nearness

---

[29] Helen Bacovcin, trans., *The Way of the Pilgrim and The Pilgrim Continues His Way* (New York: Image Books, 1992).

[30] Ibid., 26.

[31] Ibid., 41.

of God and his love" in his own version of *nembutsu*. Surely, God was never absent from the Pilgrim, and we could confidently say that his very desire to become a person of prayer was inspired by God's grace and supported by God's presence. But it took the Jesus Prayer for him to realize the God who was already there. The Jesus Prayer reconstitutes his mind, bringing him all the joys of such a spiritual transformation.

These practices surely have a different nuance in each tradition. For the Pure Land tradition, at least in Shinran's mind, the aspirant already has Buddha-nature, is already one with eternity, and *has* something of eternity indwelling as a substantial part of oneself. Realizing Amida or the Pure Land is realizing one's own Buddha-nature. For the Pilgrim and for Christians in general, the divine life is something supernatural, something they cannot claim as their own. But as far as the actual practice and experience, I find little to no difference. For a Pure Land aspirant, *nembutsu* is a concentrated form of worship. Amida is *Dharmakaya*, Amida is *Sambhogakaya*, Amida is *Nirmanakaya*. As Shinran writes, "We know that taking refuge manifests itself as worship."[32]

Christian Love and Buddhist Compassion

Throughout this book, we have come to see compassion (*karuna*) as a central Buddhist value. In the Theravada tradition, it typically goes with lovingkindness (*metta*), sympathetic joy (*mundita*), and equanimity (*upekkha*). They are the *brahma-vihara* meditations that provide the most skillful way to engage the world and purify the mind. Regarding compassion, Buddhaghosa writes, "When there is suffering in others it causes good people's hearts to be moved. . . . Compassion is characterized as promoting the aspect of allaying suffering."[33] Within the Theravada tradition, compassion does not take much of a pride of place, even if it is important.

In Mahayana, however, compassion dominates. It is the raison d'être for taking on the bodhisattva vow, and in Pure Land it became the very expression of *Dharmakaya* (*hoben hosshin*). It seems most fruitful that if we were to compare Mahayana and Christianity in terms of essential qualities, it would not be Christian love (*agape*) and Buddhist lovingkindness (*metta*) or Christian compassion (*splangnizomai*/*eleos*) and Buddhist compassion (*karuna*); a better comparison is Christian love and Buddhist compassion.

---

[32] Cited in Carter, *In the Company of Friends*, 91.

[33] *Visuddhimagga* IX.92, 94.

Both act as agents of transformation and both define something essential about Ultimate Reality.

The Septuagint uses the noun and verb forms of *agape* as translations for the Hebrew verb forms *ahav'*, *ahe-v',* and *ahavah'*, representing God's love for us, and our love for God and others. In the New Testament, *agape* dominates as the expression of God's salvific activity and the very quality that unites God with us and us with one another. We might consider a few classic texts from the Gospel of John: "For God so loved the world that he gave his only Son, so that everyone who believes in him may not perish but may have eternal life" (Jn 3:16); "As the Father has loved me, so I have loved you; abide in my love. . . . This is my commandment, that you love one another as I have loved you" (Jn 15:9, 12). It is in this love "that they may all be one. As you, Father, are in me and I am in you, may they also be in us" (Jn 17:21).

Love appears in the New Testament over two hundred times, and faith appears almost three hundred times. But these are not isolated concepts or virtues; they necessarily include mercy and compassion, these appearing around sixty times. One simply cannot read the first citation above, "For God so loved the world," without recognizing that this love is God's expression of mercy and compassion. Or consider the classic verses from the letter of James: "What good is it, my brothers and sisters, if you say that you have faith but do not have works? Can faith save you? If a brother or sister is naked and lacks daily food, and one of you says to them, 'Go in peace; keep warm and eat your fill,' and yet you do not supply their bodily needs, what is the good of that?" (Jas 2:14–16). This is the very point that Jesus makes in his haunting parable in Matthew's Gospel when the Son of Man comes in his glory and separates the sheep from the goats. Those welcomed in to inherit the kingdom were those who fed, welcomed, clothed, cared for, and visited those most in need. When they did that, they were doing this for Christ himself. And those condemned had failed to act compassionately (Mt 25:31–46).

Buddhist compassion is not exactly the same as Christian love. Its correlative is *prajna*, salvific wisdom or insight. One key commentarial passage—from the Theravada tradition no less—sums up the connection nicely: "Here, the Teacher's being endowed with vision indicates the greatness of wisdom [*prajna*], being endowed with [right] conduct, the greatness of compassion."[34] Carter notes, "*Panna* [*prajna*] indicates how one is to

---

[34] *Paramatthamanjusa of Bhandantacariya Dhammapala Thera: or The Commentary of the Visuddhimagga*, ed. Morontuduwē Dhammnānda Thera (Columbo: Mahabodhi Press, 1928), 192–93, as cited in Carter, *In the Company of Friends*, 103.

understand reality; *karuna* indicates how one is to live it."[35] The wisdom in Buddhism, the kind of insight necessary for liberation, is one of nonduality, of a subtle but real interpenetration of all sentient beings, of recognizing universal Buddha-nature.

None of these corresponds well conceptually to traditional Christian framings. On the ground, however, in deep Christian experience, is there not a remarkable unity? Christian love is a love that is premised on God's universal love and presence, a love that acts like compassion and mercy and demands from truly liberated believers the same universal love, compassion, and mercy. A truly integrated and transformed Christian does not differentiate her own love with God's love; they are one love. A truly integrated and transformed Christian does not differentiate her own identity with that of God's, as God is recognized as the foundation for all that she is and does. St. Paul saw this: "It is no longer I who live, but it is Christ who lives in me" (Gal 2:20); "But you are not in the flesh; you are in the Spirit, since the Spirit of God dwells in you" (Rom 8:9). We already saw this in chapter 3 with John of the Cross, where the flame of the soul's love and God's love become a single flame, indistinguishable from each other.[36]

Considering Shinran's path of utter faith and trust in Amida, his committed belief that Amida as *Dharmakaya* is the same Buddha-nature that represents one's very self, how different is this from what we have learned from our own Christian spiritual masters? I'd like to remind us of Thomas Merton's inspiring and challenging experience:

> The secret of my full identity is hidden in God. . . . To say that I am made in the image of God is to say that love is the reason for my existence, for God is love. Love is my true identity. Selflessness is my true self. Love is my true character, Love is my name. . . . [One] lives in emptiness and freedom, as if one had no longer a limited and exclusive *self* that distinguished oneself from God and other people. . . . What happens is that the separate identity that is *you* apparently disappears and nothing seems to be left but a pure freedom indistinguishable from infinite Freedom, love identified with Love. . . . God is the *I* who acts there. God is the one Who loves and knows and rejoices.[37]

---

[35] Carter, *In the Company of Friends*, 103.

[36] *Living Flame* 3:10.

[37] Thomas Merton, *New Seeds of Contemplation* (New York: New Direction, 1961), 33, 60, 210, 283, 286–87 (with exclusive language adjusted).

What we see here and numerous times throughout this book is that Christianity has a *both/and* understanding of union with God. On the one hand, we find a personal God who is a divine *Thou*. Here love requires a relationship between two. And on the other hand we find a blurring of identities in the divine. Likewise, for Shinran, there really is Amida who acts for the benefit of the believer, and that Amida is also not other than Buddha-nature—one's very selfhood.

Chapter 10

A Christian Commentary on the Heart Sutra

The Heart Sutra

The Heart Sutra is perhaps the best known and revered sutra in the Mahayana canon. It may have been created relatively early in Mahayana *Prajnaparamita* literature with the earliest version in Chinese possibly dating to the third century CE,[1] though we do not have extant Chinese translations until the fifth, or its specific title as it is now known until the seventh.[2] The Heart Sutra represents the Heart or Essence of the Perfection of Wisdom, the distillation of Mahayana teaching on emptiness.

Longer Version Preamble

> The Blessed One was staying in Rajgriha at Vulture Peak along with a great community of monks and a great community of bodhisattvas, and at that time, the Blessed One entered into the meditative absorption on the varieties of phenomena called the *appearance of the profound.* At that time as well, the noble Avalokiteshvara, the bodhisattva, the great being, clearly beheld the practice of the profound perfection of wisdom itself and saw that even the five aggregates are empty of intrinsic existence.

[1] Red Pine, trans. and commentary, *The Heart Sutra: The Womb of Buddhas* (Berkeley, CA: Counterpoint, 2004), 18.

[2] Kazuaki Tanahashi, *The Heart Sutra: A Comprehensive Guide to the Classic of Mahayana Buddhism* (Boston: Shambhala, 2014), 61.

Thereupon, through the Buddha's inspiration, the venerable Shariputra spoke to the noble Avalokiteshvara, the bodhisattva, the great being, and said, "How should any noble son or noble daughter who wishes to engage in the practice of the profound perfection of wisdom train?"

When this had been said, the holy Avalokiteshvara, the bodhisattva, the great being, spoke to the venerable Shariputra and said, "Shariputra, any noble son or noble daughter who so wishes to engage in the practice of this profound perfection of wisdom should clearly see this way: they should see perfectly that even the five aggregates are empty of intrinsic existence."[3]

The Original Sutra

Here, Shariputra, form does not differ from emptiness, emptiness does not differ from form. Form is emptiness, emptiness is form. The same is true of sensations, perceptions, impulses, consciousness. Here, Shariputra, all dharmas [realities] are empty; they do not appear or disappear, are not tainted or pure, do not increase or decrease.

Therefore in emptiness, no form, no sensations, no perceptions, no impulses, no consciousness. No eyes, no ears, no nose, no tongue, no body, no mind; no form, no sound, no smell, no taste, no touch, no object of mind; no realm of eye, ear, nose, tongue, body, or mind consciousness.

No ignorance, nor extinction of ignorance, no old age and death, nor extinction of them. No suffering, no cause of suffering, no cessation of suffering, no path, no wisdom, no attainment with nothing to attain.

The Bodhisattva relies on prajnaparamita, therefore the mind has no hindrance; without any hindrance, no fears exist, free from delusion, one dwells in Nirvana. All buddhas of the past, present, and future rely on prajnaparamita and attain supreme enlightenment.

Therefore know that the prajnaparamita is the great mantra, is the great enlightening mantra, which is able to eliminate all

---

[3] This prologue is taken from Tenzin Gyatso (Fourteenth Dalai Lama), *Essence of the Heart Sutra*, trans. Geshe Thupten Jinpa (Boston: Wisdom Publications, 2002), 59–60. It is provided in what is sometimes known as the "longer version" of the sutra.

suffering. This is true, not false. So proclaim the Prajnaparamita mantra, which says: gate gate paragate parasamgate bodhi svaha.[4]

The Longer Version Ending

"Shariputra, the bodhisattvas, the great beings, should train in the perfection of wisdom in this way." Thereupon, the Blessed One arose from that meditative absorption and commended the holy Avalokiteshvara, the bodhisattva, the great being, saying this is excellent. "Excellent! Excellent! O noble child, it is just so; it should be just so. One must practice the profound perfection of wisdom just as you have revealed. For then even the *tathagatas* will rejoice." As the Blessed One uttered these words, the venerable Shariputra, the holy Avalokiteshvara, the bodhisattva, the great being, along with the entire assembly, including the worlds of gods, humans, asuras, and gandharvas, all rejoiced and hailed what the Blessed One had said.[5]

Some Introductory Comments

The longer version is almost certainly a later addition, and used to associate the Heart Sutra as part of the Buddha's own teaching and weighted with his authority. The bodhisattva who offers the teaching is Avalokiteshvara, the bodhisattva of compassion. Given that this sutra is a distillation of the perfection of wisdom, one might expect the teacher to be Manjushri, the bodhisattva of wisdom or even the Buddha himself. It seems to me that in using Avalokiteshvara as the prime teacher we ought to understand the teaching under the auspices of compassion. Avalokiteshvara hears the suffering of all sentient beings and desires nothing other than to assuage their pain. Showing the complete end of suffering as entering the fullness of *prajnaparamita* represents the ultimate act of compassion. It is as though compassion itself declares: This is how suffering fully ends.[6]

---

[4] This is Dosung Yoo's translation based on both Sanskrit and Chinese recensions. See Dosung Yoo, *Thunderous Silence: A Formula for Ending Suffering: A Practical Guide to the Heart Sutra* (Boston: Wisdom Publications, 2013), 5–6.

[5] Gyatso, *Essence of the Heart Sutra*, 61.

[6] Joseph O'Leary, "Knowing the Heart Sutra by Heart," *Religion and the Arts* 12 (2008): 356, 361.

Shariputra is another interesting choice. According to pan-Buddhist tradition, Shariputra was the son of a brahmin priest, who intended to follow his father's footsteps. With his lifelong friend, Maudgalyayana, he went to Rajgir, the nearby capital of the kingdom of Magadha, to attend an important festival. Both friends decided that their lives were wasted on transient pleasures and became determined to pursue deeper spiritual training. On their way to visit one of their old teachers, Sanjaya, they encountered a Buddhist monk, Ashvajit, who taught them what he had learned from the Buddha. What he shared with them became something of a widely quoted summary: "Of what arises from causes, the Buddha shows how it begins, and also how it ceases; thus does the Great Recluse instruct." Immediately, upon hearing this teaching Shariputra became a *stream enterer*.[7] On their first visit to see the Buddha personally, he points them out to his disciples and announces that they will become his two chief disciples. Within a week of their ordination Maudgalyayana became an arhat. By the next week Shariputra did as well, and faithfully followed the Buddha for the next forty years.[8] In both Theravada and Mahayana canons we regularly find Shariputra as a premier disciple. Thus, he acts as the perfect candidate to hear the full message, the perfection of wisdom.

To fully get our bearings on the Heart Sutra we must remind ourselves of Nagarjuna and the early development of Mahayana. Recall that both Theravada and Mahayana traditions believed that everything was impermanent and conditioned. Where they differed was whether the momentary arisings of phenomenal reality (*dharmas*) had an inherent existence, a *svabhava*, or not. For the Theravada tradition, they certainly did, which is why they could be analyzed and assessed. But Nagarjuna and the *prajnaparamita* tradition challenged this: *dharmas* are empty (*svabhavashuna*), and in this sense are nonexistent, or without their own being. Without distinctive properties, they are not separate from other *dharmas*, they have never been produced, never come into existence (as self-entities), and never leave original emptiness. Having never been produced, they cannot act as a contrast to Nirvana, which itself is empty.[9]

---

[7] Recall from chapter 3 that a stream-enterer is one virtually enlightened.

[8] Pine, *Heart Sutra*, 71–74.

[9] Edward Conze, *Buddhist Thought in India: Three Phases of Buddhist Philosophy* (Ann Arbor: University of Michigan Press, 1967), 220–22.

Making Sense of the Heart Sutra

The Heart Sutra can be approached in several ways. Heng Sure describes it as a "discourse taught primarily to meditators. When advanced meditators begin to experience changes in body and mind from their practice of deep mental absorption, they need instruction in navigating the states that arise."[10] Indeed, the Heart Sutra will include every aspect the meditator might encounter, including the five skandhas (form, sensations, perceptions, impulses, consciousness), the six modes of change (arising, perishing, staining, purifying, increasing, decreasing), the six sense organs (eyes, ears, nose, tongue, body, mind), objects of the sense organs (form, sound, smell, taste, object of the mind). It will even deconstruct the chain of causation (dependent origination) and the Four Noble Truths.

Everything seems to be negated in a dizzying collection of claims. D. T. Suzuki observes, "What superficially strikes us most while pursuing the text is that it is almost nothing but a series of negations, and what is known as Emptiness is pure negativism, which ultimately reduces all things into nothingness."[11] If the skandhas are not real in terms of having their own self-existence and if what they perceive is equally unreal, then there can be no ignorance nor extinction of ignorance, at least on an ultimate level. Nor is there a self that ages and dies, nor then the extinction of the same. Seemingly oddly, the way to eliminate suffering is to realize that there is no substantial thing as suffering or a substantial thing that suffers. All mental constructs are simply that, *constructs*, so if one were to fully realize this, then there is no (substantial) path and there is neither anything to attain nor anything that could attain. What we end up with is a pathless path located in sheer *shunyata*.

In Mahayana, *prajna* or wisdom can be understood in three levels. The first kind of wisdom is an ordinary sense of seeing the world as substantial. This is the wisdom of skillfully negotiating the day-to-day operation of life. The second kind is a metaphysical wisdom that sees all things as impermanent. What appears to be pure is recognized as impure, and what appears to be self is really nonself. Mahayana tends to charge Theravada with imagining this second level as the final absolute truth. Their third level of wisdom (*prajnaparamita*) recognizes that all *dharmas* are neither permanent nor

[10] Heng Sure and Peter Feldmeier, "Buddhism: Texts and Commentary," in *World Religions in Dialogue: A Comparative Theological Approach*, ed. Pim Valenberg (Winona, MN: Anselm Academic, 2013), 230.

[11] D. T. Suzuki, *Essays in Zen Buddhism* (London: Rider & Co., 1973), 27, as cited in Tanahashi, *Heart Sutra*, 5.

impermanent, neither pure nor impure, neither having a self nor not having a self.[12] This is Mahayana's understanding of the *middle way* between eternalism and nihilism.

Such a perspective might help us negotiate the last paragraph, which otherwise would seem to be nothing other than contradiction. Once the adept sees clearly that *form is emptiness, emptiness is form*; sees clearly that *in emptiness,* there is *no form, no sensations, no perceptions, no impulses, no consciousness*; sees clearly that in emptiness there is *no ignorance, nor extinction of ignorance, no suffering*, and thus ultimately *no path, no wisdom, no attainment*; only then can one also see that one does in fact *attain supreme enlightenment*, which *eliminates all suffering*. The Heart Sutra places everything "in emptiness," that is, in the context of the perspective of *shunyata*.

One must remember that *shunyata* does not mean "nothingness" or "nonexistence," nor does it merely mean the absence of self-being. *Shunyata* itself is empty of emptiness. It carries the weight of Suchness (*tathata*) that lies outside of delusion, of the *Unconditioned, Nirvana, Buddhahood*. *Shunyata* takes us into another way of being. As Pine observes, "Emptiness is what makes everything real."[13] One of the essential qualities of the Mahayana spirit is that of nonduality, a way of existing that transcends conceptuality. Pine again: "When we establish a *dharma* that either exists or does not exist, we create a separation in time, in space, and in our minds. *Dharmas* as self-existent or non-existent are fictions. *Dharmas* as emptiness are real. . . . They are not outside emptiness nor inside emptiness. They *are* emptiness."[14]

The Heart Sutra challenges us to work through our intellect in order to transcend that intellect into another realm of realization. Edward Conze writes,

> Everything that is at all worth knowing is contained in the Hridaya [Heart Sutra]. But it can be found there only if spiritual insight is married to intellectual ability, and coupled with a delight in the use of the intellect. This Sutra, it is true, points to something that lies far beyond the intellect. But the way to get to that is to follow the intellect as far as it will take you. And the dialectical logic of this Sutra enables the intellect, working through language, to carry the understanding a stage further than the conceptual thinking based on ordinary logic can do.[15]

---

12 Pine, *Heart Sutra*, 30.

13 Ibid., 97.

14 Ibid., 97–98 (emphasis added).

15 Edward Conze, *Buddhist Wisdom Books: The Diamond Sutra and The Heart Sutra* (London: George Allen & Unwin, 1958), 99.

In the end, the full fruition of the bodhisattva path is to realize that the compassionate liberation of all beings has everything to do with being liberated from the *concept* of being itself, where neither attainment nor nonattainment is pursued, where the categories of time and space disappear. Master Chen-k'o summarizes the great completion:

> Once the Five Skandhas are seen as empty, the light of the mind shines alone. When all the clouds are gone, the full moon fills the sky. Thus, birth and destruction, purity and defilement, completeness and deficiency are all snowflakes on a red-hot stove. Once you realize true emptiness, how could the Five Skandhas alone be empty? The Twelve Abodes of Sensation, the Eighteen Elements of Perception, the Twelve Links of Dependent Origination, and the Four Noble Truths are all tortoise fur and rabbit horn. Ice doesn't melt by itself. It disappears when the sun comes out. Dharmas such as the Five Skandhas and Eighteen Elements of Perception and Twelve Links of Dependent Origination are like ice, and the illumination of prajna is like the sun.[16]

The Concluding Mantra

If the Heart Sutra summarizes and condenses the whole of the *prajnaparamita* path, its ending, the "great enlightening mantra, which is able to eliminate all suffering," provides the final conclusion: *gate gate paragate parasamgate bodhi svaha*. What is this mantra that eliminates all suffering and is guaranteed to be "true, not false"?

The Mahayana commentarial tradition has been fascinated by this mantra. Typically, in both Hindu and Buddhist traditions, mantras are esoteric utterances taught by masters to qualified students for a variety of purposes. They were recited to ward off negative powers, to reformulate the mind, to attain particular powers (usually supramundane), or to create a kind of magical thwarting of one's enemies. This mantra is outside of and goes beyond such interests. The eleventh-century commentator Vajrapani writes, "This mantra of the perfection of wisdom is the heart of the meaning of all secret mantras. . . . The mantra of the perfection of wisdom is not a mantra for pacification, increase, power, or wrath. What is it? By merely understanding the meaning of this mantra, the mind is freed."[17]

---

[16] Cited in Yoo, *Thunderous Silence*, 138.

[17] Donald Lopez, "Inscribing the Bodhisattva's Speech: On the 'Heart Sutra's' Mantra," *History of Religions* 29, no. 4 (1990): 353.

The mantra is imagined as having its own kind of power. The great Buddhist scholar Donald Lopez calls it a "performance utterance."[18] It is amazing that the whole of the sutra is happily translated into Tibetan, Chinese, Japanese, and so on. But never has this mantra been translated. All the texts merely transliterate the Sanskrit so as to preserve the words as they are supposed to be spoken. Lopez writes, "For those who recite the transliterated sound, the mantra offers this promise of the symbol, representative of the strangely atemporal priority of sacred speech and of origin."[19]

Gate is the locative absolute of *gata* (gone) meaning "when one is gone," or simply "now gone." Following this, *paragate* means "when one is gone beyond" or "now gone beyond," and *parasamgate* is "when one is gone completely beyond" or "now gone completely beyond." *Bodhi* simply means enlightenment, and *svaha* is kind of an exclamation, often used at the end of Vedic rituals.[20] It means something like, "at last," "amen," "alleluia." Let us translate the whole of the mantra as this: *now gone, now gone, now gone beyond, now gone thoroughly beyond. Enlightenment, Yes!* The great eleventh-century master Atisha claims that the teaching in the Heart Sutra was for bodhisattvas with "dull faculties," who needed the text; those bodhisattvas with "sharp faculties" only needed to recite the mantra for its truth to be realized.[21] Others, such as Kamalashila (740–795) and Shrimahajana (c. 1050) imagined that the words represented stages along the bodhisattva path. Each of the five words represent the "five paths" of *Accumulation*, *Preparation*, *Vision*, *Meditation*, and *No Further Learning*.

Modern commentator Tenzin Gyatso, the Fourteenth Dalai Lama, sees these stages as represented in the main body of the text. According to Gyatso, the stages work like this: *Accumulation* refers to realizing emptiness as an intellectual exercise. *Preparation* represents actually experiencing emptiness, but not directly. Here one progressively sees emptiness while concepts gradually recede. The path of *Vision* is attained when dualistic perceptions of subject and object are removed, and where emptiness becomes unmediated and direct. During the stage of *Meditation*, one progresses through subtle "imprints" of mental afflictions, eventually eradicating them. This finally leads to full Buddhahood, or the stage of *No More Learning*.[22]

---

18 Ibid., 364.

19 Ibid., 368.

20 Pine, *Heart Sutra*, 158.

21 Lopez, "Inscribing the Bodhisattva's Speech," 356.

22 Gyatso, *Essence of the Heart Sutra*, 132–33.

It is difficult to see from the text that it has any of this in mind. Nor is it obvious at all that even the words of the mantra refer to these *five paths of the bodhisattva*. As we might recall from chapter 7, the logic of stages of the bodhisattva path—be they five, seven, ten, or twelve—all seemed a bit haphazard and even logically problematic as a clear progression. What I would recommend to the reader is simply to allow the mantra to be its own "performance utterance."

One can meditate on the Heart Sutra, as it is indeed a meditation manual. Again and again, one enters deeply the mysteries of *form is emptiness, emptiness is form . . . no ignorance, nor extinction from ignorance, no old age and death, nor extinction of them, no suffering, no cause of suffering, no cessation of suffering, no path, no wisdom, no attainment with nothing to attain . . . free from delusion, one dwells in nirvana*. One finds, ultimately, "the light is not *outside* the knower enabling the knower to 'see,' but is generated by the knower. The knower is the source of light. Perception, or rather, awareness itself, is the light."[23] The conclusion of deeply, fully engaging in reality through these truths, through the perspective of emptiness, is: *now gone, now gone, now gone beyond, now gone thoroughly beyond. Enlightenment, Yes!*

A Christian Commentary

A Dogmatic Prelude

In what way could the Heart Sutra say anything relevant to the Christian Spirit? Respecting the principle of noncontradiction, we may imagine finding only frustration. Christianity has a Divine Absolute, Being itself, and Christians believe that people have eternal souls—that is, something truly essential and substantive about us, something that is saved and enjoys divine communion even now, while anticipating eternal communion in the afterlife. None of this sounds remotely like emptiness. Perhaps we might begin with some humility about what we actually believe and why.

In Pope John Paul II's brilliant encyclical *Fides et Ratio* he reminds us of several principles that I think are helpful. The first is that the Church needs philosophical help in understanding its faith, but that the essence of faith always transcends such help; it "remains charged in mystery."[24] John

---

[23] Louis Wei-lun Lu and Wen-yu Chiang, "Emptiness We Live By: Metaphors and Paradoxes in Buddhism's Heart Sutra," *Metaphor and Symbol* 22, no. 4 (2007): 338.

[24] John Paul II, *Fides et Ratio*, in *The Encyclicals of John Paul II*, ed. Michael Miller

Paul also reminds us, "The Church has no philosophy of her own nor does she canonize any one particular philosophy in preference to others."[25] And finally, he reminds us that not all philosophical discourse is valuable or even good. He writes, "It is the Church's duty to indicate the elements in a philosophical system that are incompatible to her own faith."[26] The question as to whether Madhymika philosophy or Mahayana in general can undergird authentic Christian truth can remain open for now. What concerns me here is whether the philosophical underpinnings of our dogmas are worth clinging to. Are they not, in fact, subject to critique?

The Neoplatonic influence of the church fathers is well known. They used Platonic *essentialist* categories to conclude that Jesus Christ had to have the same *ousia* (substance) as the Father. He also had the same *ousia* as humans. He represents the hypostatic union of the two. How could there be two *substances* in one being and that being retain the integrity of both? The fathers of Chalcedon did not think that divinity was a "thing" conjoined to another "thing" (human), nor was the divine fused into his humanity. They remain unmixed and unconfused, and each *ousia* retained its singular integrity. This raises questions: If they were truly unmixed, unconfused, how could Jesus's instantiation of both human and divine work? Further, how was his preaching a revelation that went beyond any other human revelatory expression? When he spoke, was it as God with divine guarantees or as a human with all the limitations that go with being one? It had to be the latter, if the divine and human *ousias* were to remain unmixed.

Trinitarian debates also reflect complications. Chalcedon's conclusions about the Trinity contrast with three competitors. Dynamic monarchianism saw the Son and Holy Spirit as simply not being God proper, thus retaining monotheism. Modalistic monarchianism saw each member of the Trinity as merely a persona of God, an expression of the singular God as we experience God, but not God qua God, thus retaining monotheism. Imagining each *person* of the Trinity as having its own individual existence amounted to tritheism—three Gods having the same substance but being different from each other. This could hardly be acceptable. Following the leadership of the Cappadocian fathers, particularly Gregory of Nazianzus, Chalcedon concluded that the Trinity references the inner life of God, and this one God consists of a community of *relations*—a relationally dynamic monad. Thus, the Father, the Son, and the Holy Spirit are persons only insofar as they can be distinguished by divine inner relations. The Father has a kind of priority in

(Huntington, IN: Our Sunday Visitor, 1996), nos. 5, 13.

[25] Ibid., no. 49.

[26] Ibid., no. 50.

that the Father *begets* the Son and the Holy Spirit *proceed* from the Father. This begetting and procession were eternal, intrinsic to the nature of the Divine.

And Jesus's relationship to this triune God? The fathers of the Council of Chalcedon came to assert that the second person of the Trinity (with the Trinity representing the infinite, transcendental, supernatural ground and horizon of all reality) became intrinsically one with and personally identified with the human person of Jesus of Nazareth from the moment of his conception—all this without ever undermining the dynamic triune nature of the original monad of the Trinity.[27] Let me ask: Is this intellectually compelling? I have tried to explain the Trinity to friends who are analytic philosophers, and they all keep coming back to the problem: How can there be relations in a singularity? How is it possibly meaningful to say that a referent (Father) can have another referent (Son or Holy Spirit) that is not distinguishable from itself, save solely by being referential?

Let us add complications to Christian dogmatics. Christianity holds that Jesus of Nazareth was conceived by a virgin birth. But why would this be necessary? If the dual natures of Jesus Christ are not mixed or confused with each other, why wouldn't it be more reasonable that the human nature of Jesus be created by the regular exchange of DNA between two humans, all the while uniting this human to that of the relation of the Divine Son? It is not as though Jesus had Mary's DNA (the X chromosomes) while receiving God's DNA (the Father's Y chromosomes). This would make Jesus something like Heracles (Roman Hercules) whose father was the god Zeus and mother was the human Alcmene. The Council of Ephesus gives Mary the title of *theotokos* (God-bearer) to ensure that, from his very conception, the Incarnation took place. Such a title ensures against an adoptionist position, whereby Jesus is raised to some form of divine status after his conception. But we must wonder what this could really mean. In Jesus, did God become man? Did the Son-relation ever leave the Trinity? Taking church dogmatics seriously actually contends against such descriptors. God did not *become* anything, except to intrinsically identify the Son relation of the Trinity with the human Jesus of Nazareth.

Are Christian claims intellectually compelling? Do they make sense? My answer is that they do make sense, and I am happy to sign off on them. But they *only* make sense insofar as they provide us with some guideposts to proceed or, maybe better, with a fence that allows for creativity and theological discourse with some consistency. And they *only* make sense with the proviso insisted upon by the Cappadocian fathers themselves that all

[27] See Peter Feldmeier, *The Christian Tradition: A Historical and Theological Introduction* (Oxford: Oxford University Press, 2017), 99–100.

language about God is analogical and not literal-descriptive. And, indeed, we already saw in Gregory of Nyssa that any conceptualizations about God end up being idolatrous if we imagine they reference God *as* God. God *as* God remains an absolute mystery to the conceptualizing mind. When pushed, we have to realize that both the New Testament and Christian doctrine are filled with competing theologies, claims, and positions that stretch or even undermine the above-noted dogmas. Christian theology is just as problematic, as it regularly imagines Jesus speaking with divine authority, as though his dual natures were in fact mixed and confused. Christian theology also typically references each relation of the Trinity as if in some way independent. If Christians stepped back to take a look at what they write, much of it is philosophically problematic.

This takes us back to Pope John Paul II. If there is no Christian philosophy per se, and if a variety of philosophies might be employed to understand something of the divine mystery, then could it be that the Madhymika philosophy of Mahayana might be useful in understanding the divine in a different way, one that respects the continuity of tradition and our already-stated guideposts, but one that also could reap insights that continue to make Christian theology relevant? As John and Linda Keenan note, "To cling to thought structures of bygone ages preserves a certain elegance, but it is the elegance of an antique shop."[28] In an earlier work, John Keenan writes,

> In the history of Christian doctrine some philosophical models have been adopted and adapted. The fathers employed Neoplatonic ideas freely and the medieval scholastics found a welcome model in Aristotle. More recently, some theologians have adopted the existential philosophy of Martin Heidegger, while others employ Marxist categories in explicating a theology of liberation.[29]

We have already seen abundantly throughout this book that *shunyata* or emptiness is a complicated term. As an ontological category, it gets conflated with Suchness, Nirvana, and so on. But it isn't primarily that. Essentially, emptiness represents a procedure of deconstruction, even allowing itself to be deconstructed where "emptiness is empty of emptiness." As Streng argues

---

[28] John Keenan and Linda Keenan, *I Am / No Self: A Christian Commentary on the Heart Sutra* (Leuven: Peeters, 2011), 76.

[29] John Keenan, *The Meaning of Christ: A Mahayana Theology* (Maryknoll, NY: Orbis Books, 1989), 187.

regarding Nagarjuna's take, it is a "*means* for ultimate transformation."[30] Once one rarifies either a *view* or any other kind of referent, be it emptiness or Nirvana or anything else, Mahayana challenges it. Streng again: "Statements about *nirvana* or any metaphysical statements are not meant to be unassailable semantic pillars on which to construct a system of necessary propositions; rather they were mental prods to induce an apprehension which was validated by its success in putting an end to suffering."[31] One can, if one wishes, approach Christ's message and his very being under the auspices of *shunyata*, and fruitfully so.

Shunyata and the Kingdom of God

The master symbol for Jesus's preaching is the kingdom of God. In Matthew's Gospel alone, Jesus addresses this theme fifty-six times. The kingdom of God represents God's active lordship and saving power, and it is available to anyone. Jesus's fellowship with sinners expresses the kingdom's radical inclusivity (Mk 2:16–19). While the kingdom often referred to a future reality (Mt 6:10), it also represented God's truth and life here and now (Rom 14:17). Jesus proclaimed that the kingdom was near (Mt 10:7; Lk 10:9–10), that it was among his listeners (Lk 17:21), and even that it was upon them (Mt 12:28; Lk 11:20). It was a transcendent mystery that could be known but not observed (Lk 17:20). So Jesus used metaphors and similes that might provoke his hearers' imaginations to engage the kingdom, but the kingdom could not be accessed directly.

How was the kingdom to be engaged or realized? The biblical witness is challenging, offering various versions. Jesus, in his apocalyptic-prophet role, announced a kind of ultimate deconstruction based on God's initiatives: "But in those days, after that suffering, the sun will be darkened, and the moon will not give its light, and the stars will be falling from heaven, and the powers in the heavens will be shaken. Then they will see the Son of Man coming in the clouds with great power and glory. Then he will send out the angels and gather his elect from the four winds, from the ends of the earth to the ends of heaven" (Mk 13:24–27). Peter imagines that "the heavens will pass away with a loud noise, and the elements will be dissolved with fire, and the earth and everything that is done on it will be disclosed. . . . [W]e wait for new heavens and a new earth, where righteousness is at home"

[30] Frederick Streng, *Emptiness: A Study of Religious Meaning* (Nashville: Abingdon Press, 1967), 156.

[31] Ibid., 157.

(2 Pet 3:10–13). Paul imagines a spiritualized transformation of this world: "For the creation waits with eager longing for the revealing of the children of God; for the creation was subjected to futility, not of its own will but by the will of the one who subjected it, in hope that the creation itself will be set free from its bondage to decay and will obtain the freedom of the glory of God" (Rom 8:19–21). Finally, the book of Revelation imagines "a new heaven and a new earth" where God would radically dwell among us:

> See, the home of God is among mortals. He will dwell with them; they will be his people, and God himself will be with them. . . . I saw no temple in the city, for its temple is the Lord God the Almighty and the Lamb. And the city has no need of sun or moon to shine on it, for the glory of God is its light, and its lamp is the Lamb. . . . [T]he river of life, bright as crystal, flowing from the throne of God and of the Lamb through the middle of the street of the city. On either side of the river is the tree of life with its twelve kinds of fruit. (21:1–22:6)

Surely, no one knows exactly what the kingdom of God is or will be, except that it references something truly realizable now and unimaginably realizable in its fullness. There will be no want, no hatred, no fear, no greed, no (dare I say it) attachment. It will be a Nirvanic life.

The cost of realizing the kingdom is nothing less than everything. If the kingdom of God is the master symbol of Jesus's preaching, death to self is key to opening the kingdom's door. Lynn de Silva writes that "'self' is at the heart of man's problem, the 'self' must be conquered if the goal is to be realised. The egocentric life of craving and self-interest must be put to an end by the deliberate denying of the self."[32] Consider the following: "Whoever does not take up the cross and follow me is not worthy of me. Those who find their life will lose it, and those who lose their life for my sake will find it" (Mt 10:39; cf. Mt 16:24–25; Mk 8:34–35; Lk 9:23–25; 14:27; Jn 12:25); "We are . . . always carrying in the body the death of Jesus, so that the life of Jesus may also be made visible in our bodies" (2 Cor 4:10); "Do you not know that all of us who have been baptized into Christ Jesus were baptized into his death?" (Rom 6:3); "I die every day" (1 Cor 15:31); "For you have died, and your life is hidden with Christ in God. When Christ who is your life is revealed, then you also will be revealed with him in glory. Put to death, therefore, whatever in you is earthly. . . . Anger, wrath, malice, slander, and

[32] Lynn A. de Silva, *The Problem of the Self in Buddhism and Christianity* (London: Macmillan Press, 1979), 125.

abusive language . . . seeing that you have stripped off the old self with its practices and have clothed yourselves with the new self" (Col 3:3–10); "If we have died with him, we will also live with him" (2 Tim 2:11).

Our hagiographical and mystical traditions assure us that real sainthood, real union with God, is not merely reforming ourselves or becoming somewhat more virtuous or more prayerful. Rather, it really does demand an existential experience of death to the old self. We have seen this in the examples of this book. John of the Cross insists that union is following the path of "nothing," and even at the summit of union, self remains "nothing." Meister Eckhart joins the chorus that you really have to denude yourself of everything that is yourself so that God can become your absolute value, your absolute reality. Eckhart writes,

> Supposing someone asks me, what then is the poor man who wills nothing? I should answer this: As long as it can be said of a man that it is in his will to do the will of God, that man has not the poverty I am speaking of, because he has the will to satisfy the will of God, which is not as it should be. If he is genuinely poor, a man is free from his created will as he was when he was not. I tell you by the eternal truth, as long as you possess the will to do the will of God, and have the least desire for eternity and for God, you are not really poor. The poor man wills nothing, knows nothing, wants nothing.[33]

Henry Suso, Eckhart's spiritual disciple, adds, "When the good and faithful servant enters into the joy of his Lord, he is inebriated by the riches of the house of God. . . . He forgets himself, is no longer conscious of his selfhood; he disappears and loses himself in God, and becomes one spirit with him."[34]

Obviously, this kind of *death* is a death to the egoic self. It is the kind of self that clings, that craves, that identifies itself as its own center of the universe instead of relocating itself—and thereby losing itself—in the mystery of the Divine. It is the kind of self that suffers. Death to *that* self is really a new life, an unimaginable life in the Spirit. Consider the following medley as a corollary to the above set of verses: "I came that they may have life and have it abundantly" (Jn 10:10); "I am the resurrection and the life. Those who believe in me, even though they die, will live, and everyone who lives and believes in me will never die" (Jn 11:25–26); "I am the way, and the truth and the life" (Jn 14:6); "But you are not in the flesh; you are in the Spirit, since the Spirit of God dwells in you" (Rom 8:9); "to set your mind

[33] Cited in ibid., 126.

[34] Cited in ibid., 127.

on the flesh is death, but to set the mind on the Spirit is life and peace" (Rom 8:6); "for the letter kills, but the Spirit gives life" (2 Cor 3:6). We become living temples of God: "Do you not know that you are God's temple and that God's Spirit dwells in you?" (1 Cor 3:16; cf. 1 Cor 6:19); "in him [Christ] the whole structure is joined together and grows into a holy temple in the Lord; in whom you are also built together spiritually into a dwelling place for God" (Eph 2:21); "I will make you a pillar in the temple of my God; you will never go out of it" (Rev 3:12). This new life is a change of identities from oneself to Christ himself: "For to me living is Christ" (Phil 1:21); "I have been crucified with Christ; and it is no longer I who live, but it is Christ who lives in me" (Gal 2:20).

Jesus's preaching about the kingdom and its daunting demands include, of course, justice, taking the interest of those most in need, authentic worship of God, and so on. Above all, it can be represented as a kind of new community of love. Love shows up over 250 times in the New Testament. To live in the kingdom is to "love the Lord your God with all your heart, and with all your soul, and with all your mind. . . . [and] love your neighbor as yourself" (Mt 22:37–39) and "love your enemies" (Mt 5:44); "the one who loves another has fulfilled the law" (Rom 13:8); "the only thing that counts is faith working through love" (Gal 5:6); "whoever does not love does not know God, for God is love. . . . God is love and those who abide in love abide in God, and God abides in them" (1 Jn 4:8, 16).

It is love that both creates communion and signifies communion. Jesus commands his disciples, "As the Father has loved me, so I have loved you; abide in my love" (Jn 15:9). And thus, he prays for his disciples to the Father, "that they may all be one. As you, Father, are in me and I am in you, may they also be in us, so that the world may believe that you have sent me. The glory that you have given me I have given them, so that they may be one, as we are one, I in them and you in me, that they may become completely one" (Jn 17:21–23). Lynn de Silva writes, "The all-embracing and crowning idea in the New Testament is that of the Kingdom of God, or in other words the Community of Love, for 'Kingdom' implies Community, and God is Love."[35] Such a kingdom or community involves all dimensions of the human being, and its universality is expressed in the day-to-day, the mundane. It shows no partiality (Jas 2:9), but acts as a light in every dark corner (1 Jn 2:10), and discovers that service and love of God are exactly service and love of those most suffering (Mt 25:31–46). De Silva notes, "Thus, the Kingdom of God has a double quality of embracing the particular and the universal in such a way that the individual is transcended in

[35] Ibid., 129.

a social reality and the historical in a trans-historical reality without any aspect being denied, but rather fulfilled."[36]

Who Is Christ?

Just as the kingdom of God is something we can't pin down—can't codify in a political, social, or moral manifesto—so, too, Jesus is doggedly difficult to pin down. The Synoptic Gospels have Jesus frequently rejecting any identity. The so-called messianic secret is not reserved to Mark alone, but we find Jesus resisting titles in all three. And even when he does self-identify with such terms as *messiah*, he only does so privately to his disciples and he never aligns with what they themselves might have understood by that term.

In order to understand Jesus's identity, Paul principally draws on two streams of Jewish thought. The first is Wisdom, a preexistent creative power of God through which the universe was created. Paul writes, "There is one God, the Father, from whom are all things and for whom we exist, and one Lord, Jesus Christ, through whom are all things and through whom we exist" (1 Cor 8:6). To Paul, Jesus "is the image of the invisible God, the firstborn of all creation; for in him all things in heaven and on earth were created. . . . [A]ll things have been created through him and for him" (Col 1:15–16). While he is not the Father (God), still "in him the wholeness of deity dwells bodily" (Col 2:9).

Paul's second stream of Jewish thought is that of an anticipated preexistent messiah who will come to redeem God's chosen ones: "But when the fullness of time had come, God sent his Son, born of a woman, born under the law, in order to redeem those who were under the law" (Gal 4:4–5). God sent Christ as redeemer "to gather up all things in him, things in heaven and on earth" (Eph 1:10). Paul's vision of Christ is utterly cosmic: "when all things are subjected to him, then the Son himself will also be subjected to the one who put all things in subjection under him, so that God may be all in all" (1 Cor 15:28). It seems that the "Father," whom Paul also simply calls God, has the ultimate priority, while Christ works to carry out God's cosmic plan of salvation. Christ is not, however, merely a human worker; he is an expression of God, or at least of God's presence.

Central to Paul's message and understanding of the ministry and person of Christ is the activity of the Holy Spirit. Paul distinguishes the Holy Spirit from the Father and the Son, but also blurs their distinctions. Sometimes he

---

[36] Ibid., 130.

even seems to identify Christ himself with the Holy Spirit: "Now the Lord is the Spirit" (2 Cor 3:17). Consider this fascinating and frustrating passage:

> But you are not in the flesh; you are in the Spirit, since the Spirit of God dwells in you. Anyone who does not have the Spirit of Christ does not belong to him. But if Christ is in you, though the body is dead because of sin, the Spirit is life because of righteousness. If the Spirit of him who raised Jesus from the dead dwells in you, he who raised Christ from the dead will give life to your mortal bodies also through his Spirit that dwells in you. (Rom 8:9–11)

Here we see a complete blurring of Father, Son, and Holy Spirit. Initially the Spirit is the Spirit of God (Father). In the next sentence the Spirit is identified with Christ. Then this same Spirit is identified either with the Father who raised Jesus or as separate from the Father who apparently raised Jesus. This same Spirit is finally said to reside in believers, and again is identified as Christ within.

John, like Paul, aligns the Spirit with Wisdom, the deuterocanonical "kindly spirit" (Wis 1:6) who is "radiant and unfading," bringing "perfect understanding," assuring "immortality" (6:12, 15, 18). Wisdom is "intelligent, holy, unique, manifold, subtle, mobile, clear, unpolluted . . . free from anxiety, all-powerful, overseeing all, and penetrating through all spirits . . . She pervades and penetrates all things. For she is a breath of the power of God, and a pure emanation of the glory of the Almighty . . . a reflection of eternal light, a spotless mirror of the working of God and an image of his goodness" (Wis 7:22–26). This is the wisdom or *Logos* that is "with God" and "was God," through whom "all things came into being," who then "became flesh and lived among us," the "glory of a father's only son, full of grace and truth" (Jn 1:1, 3, 14).

Like Paul, John has his own blurring. Jesus is utterly subordinate to the Father: "The Son can do nothing on his own, but only what he sees the Father doing" (Jn 5:19); "for I have not spoken on my own, but the Father who sent me has himself given me a commandment about what to say and what to speak" (12:49). On the other hand, Jesus assumes the divine name of Yahweh for himself: "before Abraham was, I am" (8:58); "The Father and I are one" (10:30). To see Jesus is to see God: "Whoever has seen me has seen the Father. . . . I am in the Father and the Father is in me" (14:9, 11). Most crucial to Johannine theology is the recognition that Jesus's self-offering on the cross is his place of glory and exaltation (17:5, 22, 24), a moment when he "will draw all people to myself" (12:32). His own emptying of himself on the cross becomes an icon of God and God's love for the world (3:16; 15:13).

Who is Jesus Christ? Is he an instantiation of eternal Wisdom, the principal emanation of the Divine? A cosmic apocalyptic figure? Both God and not God at the same time? An icon of God? The face of God? God enfleshed, who is both divine and human in an oddly framed monotheistic cosmology? All of these? None of these? All of these, but also beyond all of these to that which cannot be signified by concepts or known by the normal way the mind works? Paul writes, "Let the same mind be in you that was in Christ Jesus, who, though he was in the form of God, did not regard equality with God something to be exploited, but emptied himself, taking the form of a slave, being born in human likeness" (Phil 2:5–7). Is he the icon and presence of that ultimate *tathata*, the Compassionate Suchness of the universe, Buddha-nature expressing itself in *shunyata*? Is he the self-emptying God that necessarily expresses divinity in the context of a dependently originated world? Is he *Dharmakaya* (universal Absolute) expressed as *Nirmanakaya* (instantiation body)? Should these categories be seen as out of bounds for us?

I suggest that Jesus Christ is, in fact, the *Dharmakaya*. His salvation is conditioned upon the principle that the *Dharmakaya* has to be known in and through a dependently originated, interdependent universe. Humans live in history, and if God is to save us from our condition, in our condition, then God will have to provide that salvation in real-time human history. God's historical presence is his *Nirmanakaya*, that is, Jesus of Nazareth. But Jesus of Nazareth is not merely an appearance of God, like some kind of gnostic poser who really isn't human at all. No, God's salvific drama can only work in the real world of dependent origination, subject to the laws of cause and effect. God saves as one who radically participates in the interdependent, constantly changing world. Jesus has to be both an expression of dependent origination and *Dharmakaya*, this without confusing those categories as if he did not really participate in the world of samsara. This is the message of the synoptics: our messiah is really one of us, one fully bound in a world of samsara and dependent origination. The message of John is that he is also *Dharmakaya* as expressed in time as *Nirmanakaya*. As *Nirmanakaya*, he expresses the Absolute *tathata*, the Suchness or Buddha-nature by his very life in *shunyata*, self-emptiness. And he demands of us the very same. If we want to realize the fullness of *tathata*, we must follow his way of *shunyata*.

A Christian Heart Sutra

The following is my own version of a Heart Sutra allowing the philosophical presuppositions we have seen in the *prajnaparamita* of Mahayana Buddhism to ground the mystery of Christ. I consider it a creative act of poetics as much as any actual set of claims about Christ. And yet I also intend it to really express something of the mystery of Christ through *prajnaparamita* lenses. The prologue is fundamentally taken from Mark 8:27–9:8, though mostly with my own words. The final mantra is taken from Revelation 19:6: "Hallelujah! For the Lord God the Almighty reigns."

The Prologue

As they were walking through the villages of Caesarea Philippi Jesus asked his disciples, "Who do people think I am?" They replied that some thought he was John the Baptist, others Elijah or a returned prophet. "And who do you think I am?" Peter said, "You are the Christ." He ordered them to keep this quiet. Then he told them that they had to go to Jerusalem where he would be rejected and killed, and after this rise again. Peter rebuked him, for this was senseless. Jesus replied, "Get behind me, Satan! For your mind is set on human truths and not divine truths." Then he said, "Whoever wants to follow me must take up their cross with me. Those who save their lives will lose them. But those who lose their lives for my sake will save them."

Six days later, Jesus took Peter, James, and John and led them to the top of a high mountain. He was transfigured before them, and his clothes became dazzling. Suddenly, Moses and Elijah appeared. Then a cloud overshadowed them, and from the cloud came a voice, "This is my beloved Son; listen to him!"

The Heart Sutra

Jesus, anointing them with the divine eye of wisdom, then spoke thus: *Here, disciples, I am the all and I am nothing. My nothingness reveals the all and is the all. To know the all and to be the all, you must be nothing yourself. What you take to be real is not real, it is false, for I am the real and I am not of this world. What you take to be yourself is not yourself, it is your false self. Seek for your true self and you will not find your true self; refrain from seeking for your true self and you will find your true self. For your self is selfless and your truth is outside of truth. If you seek your God, then renounce your god. Find the God that is no god; the God who is no-thing. When you find your God that is no god, when you find your true self that is no self, then you will see: there is no evil and there is no virtue, there is no transcendence and there is no profanity.*

This is the Kingdom of God. Elijah and Moses know this and rely on this. All saints know this and rely on this. They know it without encumbrance, they know it without delusion, they know it without fear; they dwell in the Kingdom. All saints of the past, present, and future rely on this truth outside of truth—the supreme truth. Therefore, they all proclaim the great mantra of life, the mantra that eliminates all suffering, all fear, all greed, all separation: alleluia hoti ebasileusen kurios ho theos ho pantokrator.

Bibliography

Abe, Maseo. *Zen and Western Thought*. Honolulu: University of Hawaii Press, 1985.

Addis, Stephen, et al. *Zen Sourcebook: Traditional Documents from China, Korea, and Japan*. Indianapolis: Hackett Publishing, 2008.

Adikarem, E. W. *The Early History of Buddhism in Ceylon*. Dehiwala, Sri Lanka: Buddhist Cultural Centre, 1946.

Augustine. *Augustine of Hippo: Selected Writings*. Translated by Mary Clark. Mahwah, NJ: Paulist Press, 1984.

———. *Confessions*. Translated by Henry Chadwick. Oxford: Oxford University Press, 1986.

Bacovcin, Helen, trans. *Way of the Pilgrim and The Pilgrim Continues His Way*. New York: Image Books, 1978.

Barnett, L. D. *The Path of Light: Rendered from the Bhodhi-charyavatara of Santi-Deva—A Manual of Mahayana Buddhism*. 2nd edition. London: John Murray, 1947.

Batchelor, Martine. "The Ten Oxherding Pictures." *Tricycle: The Buddhist Review* 9 no. 3 (2000): 31–41.

Bodhi, Bhikkhu, trans. *The Connected Discourses of the Buddha: A Translation of the Samyutta Nikaya*. Boston: Wisdom Publications, 2000.

———. *The Numbered Discourses of the Buddha: A Translation of the Anguttara Nikaya*. Boston: Wisdom Publications, 2012.

Bonaventure. *Bonaventure: The Soul's Journey into God; Tree of Life; The Life of St. Francis*. Translated by Ewert Cousins. Mahwah, NJ: Paulist Press, 1978.

Boucher, Daniel. *Bodhisattvas of the Forest and the Formation of the Mahayana: A Study and Translation of the Rastrapalapariprccha Sutra*. Honolulu: University of Hawaii Press, 2008.

Brassard, Francis. *The Concept of Bodhicitta in Satideva's Bodhicaryavatara*. Delhi: Vasu, 2013.

Brenan, Gerald. *St. John of the Cross: His Life and Poetry*. London: Cambridge University Press, 1993.

Buddhadasa. *Under the Bodhi Tree: Buddha's Original Vision of Dependent Co-Arising*. Edited and translated by Santikaro. Boston: Wisdom Publications, 2017.

Buddhaghosa, Bhadantacariya. *The Path of Purification* [*Visuddhimagga*]. 5th edition. Translated by Nanamoli. Kandy, Sri Lanka: Buddhist Publication Society, 1991.

Burrows, Ruth. *Ascent to Love: The Spiritual Teaching of St. John of the Cross*. Denville, NJ: Dimension Books, 1987.

Burton, David. *Emptiness Appraised: A Critical Study of Nagarjuna's Philosophy*. London: Curzon, 1999.

Burtt, E. A., ed. *The Teachings of the Compassionate Buddha*. New York: New American Library, 2000.

Buswell, Robert, and Dongal Lopez, eds. *Princeton Dictionary of Buddhism*. Princeton, NJ: Princeton University Press, 2013.

Byamtso, Khenpo Tsultrim. *The Sun of Wisdom: Teachings on the Noble Nagarjuna's Fundamental Wisdom of the Middle Way*. Boston: Shambhala, 2003.

Carter, John Ross. *In the Company of Friends: Exploring Faith and Understanding with Buddhists and Christians*. Albany: State University of New York Press, 2012.

——. *On Understanding Buddhists: Essays on the Theravada Tradition in Sri Lanka*. Syracuse: State University of New York Press, 1993.

Cassian, John. *The Conferences*. Translated by Boniface Ramsey. New York: Paulist Press, 1997.

Catechism of the Catholic Church. St. Paul, MN: Wanderer Press, 1994.

Cheriton, Igumen, and Timothy Ware, eds. *The Art of Prayer: An Orthodox Anthology*. Translated by E. Kadloubovsky and E. M. Palmer. London: Faber & Faber, 1997.

Chetwynd, Tom. *Zen and the Kingdom of Heaven*. Boston: Wisdom Publications, 2001.

Chien, Cheng, trans. *Manifestation of the Tathagata: Buddhahood according to the Avatamsaka Sutra*. Boston: Wisdom Publications, 1993.

Climacus, John. *The Ladder of Spiritual Ascent*. Translated by Colm Luibheid and Norman Russell. New York: Paulist Press, 1982.

Clooney, Francis X. *Comparative Theology: Deep Learning across Religious Borders* Chichester: Wiley-Blackwell, 2010.

——. *Hindu Wisdom for All God's Children*. Maryknoll, NY: Orbis Books, 1998.

——. *The Truth, The Way, The Life: Christian Commentary on the Three Holy Mantras of the Srivaisnavas*. Leuven: Peeters, 2008.

Clooney, Francis X., ed. *The New Comparative Theology: Interreligious Insights from the Next Generation*. New York: T & T Clark, 2010.

Cobb, John, and Christopher Ives, eds. *The Emptying God: A Buddhist -Jewish-Christian Conversation*. Maryknoll, NY: Orbis Books, 1990.
Collins, Ross. *John of the Cross*. Collegeville, MN: Michael Blazier, 1990.
Collins, Steven. *Selfless Persons: Imagery and Thought in Theravada Buddhism*. Cambridge: Cambridge University Press, 1982.
Conze, Edward, ed. and trans. *Buddhist Scriptures*. New York: Penguin, 1959.
———. *Buddhist Thought in India: Three Phases of Buddhist Philosophy*. Ann Arbor: University of Michigan Press, 1967.
———. *Buddhist Wisdom Books: The Diamond Sutra and the Heart Sutra*. London: George Allen & Unwin, 1958.
———. *The Perfection of Wisdom in Eight Thousand Lines and Its Verse Summary*. Bolinas, CA: Four Seasons Foundation, 1973.
Cooper, David. "Emptiness: Interpretation and Metaphor." *Contemporary Buddhism* 3, no. 1 (2002): 7–20.
Cornille, Catherine. *The Im-Possibility of Interreligious Dialogue*. New York: Herder & Herder, 2008.
Cornille, Catherine, ed. *Many Mansions? Multiple Religious Belonging and Christian Identity*. Maryknoll, NY: Orbis Books, 2002.
Cornille, Catherine, and Christopher Conway, eds. *Interreligious Hermeneutics*. Eugene, OR: Cascade, 2010.
Cugno, Alain. *St. John of the Cross: Reflections on Mystical Experiences*. Translated by Barbara Wall. New York: Seabury, 1982.
D'Costa, Gavin. *Theology and Religious Pluralism*. Malden, MA: Blackwell, 1986.
de Silva, Lily. "Cetovimutti, Pannavimutti, and Ubhatobhagavimutti." *Pali Buddhist Review* 3 (1978): 142–43.
———. "Nibbana as Living Experience / The Buddha and the Arahant: Two Studies from the Pali Canon," *Access to Insight* (BCBS Edition), https://accesstoinsight.org/lib/authors/desilva/wheel407.html.
de Silva, Lynn A. *The Problem of the Self in Buddhism and Christianity*. London: Macmillan Press, 1979.
Dhavamony, Mariasausai, ed. *Méditation dans le Chrisianisme et les autres religions*. Rome: Gregorian University Press, 1976.
Dogen. *Zen Master Dogen: An Introduction with Selected Writings*. Translated and edited by Yuho Yokoi and Daizen Victoria. New York: Weatherhill, 1990.
Drew, Rose. *Buddhist and Christian? An Exploration of Dual Belonging*. Routledge: Abingdon, 2011.

Driscoll, Jeremy. *Spiritual Progress: Studies in the Spirituality of Late Antiquity and Early Monasticism*. Rome: Studia Anselmiana, 1994.

Dryer, Elizabeth, and Mark Burrows, eds. *Minding the Spirit: The Study of Christian Spirituality*. Baltimore, MD: Johns Hopkins University Press, 2005.

Dubay, Thomas. *Fire Within: St. Teresa of Avila, John of the Cross, and the Gospel—On Prayer*. San Francisco: Ignatius Press, 1989.

Dumoulin, Heinrich. *Zen Buddhism: A History: India and China*. Translated by James Heisig and Paul Knitter. New York: Macmillan, 1999.

Dupuis, Jacques. *Christianity and the Religions: From Confrontation to Dialogue*. Translated by Philip Berryman. Maryknoll, NY: Orbis Books, 2003.

———. *Toward a Theology of Religious Pluralism*. Maryknoll, NY: Orbis Books, 2001.

Eckhart, Meister. *Meister Eckhart: The Essential Sermons, Commentaries, Treatises, and Defense*. Translated by Edmund Colledge and Bernard McGinn. New York: Paulist Press, 1981.

———. *Meister Eckhart: A Modern Translation*. Translated by Raymond Blackney. New York: Harper Torchbook, 1957.

Egan, Harvey. *Ignatius Loyola: The Mystic*. Wilmington, DE: Michael Glazier, 1987.

———. *The Spiritual Exercises and the Ignatian Mystical Horizon*. St. Louis: Institute of Jesuit Resources, 1976.

Egan, Keith, ed. *Carmelite Prayer: A Tradition for the 21st Century*. New York: Paulist Press, 2003.

Eliot, T. S. *The Four Quartets*. New York: Harcourt Brace Javanovich, 1971.

Enomiya-Lassalle, Hugo. *Zen Meditation for Christians*. Translated by John Maraldo. LaSalle, IL: Open Court, 1974.

Eppert, Claudia. "Heart-Mind Literacy: Compassionate Imagining and the Four Brahmaviharas." *Paideuis* 19, no. 1 (2010): 17–28.

Feldmeier, Peter. *Christianity Looks East: Comparing the Spiritualities of John of the Cross and Buddhaghosa*. New York: Paulist Press, 2006.

———. *Christian Spirituality: Lived Experience in the Life of the Church*. Winona, MN: Anselm Academic, 2015.

———. *The Christian Tradition: A Historical and Theological Introduction*. Oxford: Oxford University Press, 2017.

———. "Christian Transformation and the Encounter with the World's Holy Canons." *Horizons* 40, no. 2 (2013): 178–98.

———. *Encounters in Faith: Christianity in Interreligious Dialogue*. Winona, MN: Anselm Academic, 2011.

———. "Perils and Possibilities of Mutual Religious Belonging: Test Case in Roman Catholicism." *Open Theology* 3 (2017): 73–89.

———. "Is the Theology of Religions an Exhausted Project?" *Horizons* 35 no. 2 (2008): 253–70.

Fisher, Eugene, and Leon Klenicki, eds. *Spiritual Pilgrimage: Pope John Paul II—Texts on Jews and Judaism, 1979–1995*. New York: Crossroad, 1995.

Flannery, Austin, ed. *Vatican Council II.* Volume I revised. Northport: NY: Costelo, 1975.

Fredericks, James. *Buddhists and Christians: Through Comparative Theology to Solidarity*. Maryknoll, NY: Orbis Books, 2004.

———. *Faith among Faiths: Christian Theology and Non-Christian Religions.* New York: Paulist, 1999.

Gadamer, Hans-Georg. *Truth and Method.* Translated by Garret Barden and John Cumming. New York: Seabury, 1975.

Glass, Newman Robert. *Working Emptiness: Toward a Third Reading of Emptiness in Buddhism and Postmodern Thought*. Atlanta: Scholars Press, 1985

Gombrich, Richard. *Theravada Buddhism: A Social History from Ancient Benares to Modern Columbo*. London: Routledge, 1988.

Gregory of Nyssa. *Life of Moses*. Translated by Abraham Malherbe and Everett Ferguson. New York: Paulist Press, 1978.

Gunaratana, Henepola. *Bhavana Vandana: Book of Devotion*. Taipei: Bhavana Society, 1990.

———. *Mindfulness in Plain English*. Boston: Wisdom Publications, 1994.

Gyatso, Tenzin (Fourteenth Dalai Lama). *Essence of the Heart Sutra*. Translated and Edited by Geshe Thupten Jinpa. Boston: Wisdom Publications, 2002.

———. *A Flash of Lightning in the Dark of Night: A Guide to the Bodhisattva's Way of Life*. Translated by the Padmakara Translation Group. Boston: Shambhala, 1994.

———. *Practicing Wisdom: The Perfection of Shanideva's Bodhisattva Way*. Translated and edited by Geshe Thupten Jinpa. Boston, MA: Wisdom Publications, 2005.

———. *Transcendent Wisdom: A Teaching on the Wisdom Section of Shantideva's Guide to the Bodhisattva Way of Life*. Translated and edited by Alan Wallace. Ithica, NY: Snow Lion, 1988.

Habito, Ruben. *Healing Breath: Zen for Christians and Buddhists in a Wounded World.* Boston: Wisdom Publications, 2004.

Haight, Roger. *Jesus the Symbol of God.* Maryknoll, NY: Orbis Books, 1999.

Hanh, Thich Nhat. *The Heart of the Buddha's Teaching.* New York: Harmony, 1998.

Harper, Katherine Anne, and Robert Brown, eds. *The Roots of Tantra.* Albany: State University of New York Press, 2002.

Hart, Patrick, ed. *Thomas Merton, Monk: A Monastic Tribute.* New York: Sheed & Ward, 1974.

Hausser, Irenee. *Penthos: The Doctrine of Compunction in the Christian East.* Translated by Anselm Hufstader. Kalamazoo, MI: Cistercian Publications, 1992.

Heft, James, ed. *Catholicism and Interreligious Dialogue.* Oxford: Oxford University Press, 2012.

Heim, S. Mark. *The Depth of Riches: A Trinitarian Theology of Religious Ends.* Grand Rapids, MI: Eerdmans, 2001.

——. *Salvations: Truth and Difference in Religion.* Maryknoll, NY: Orbis Books, 1995.

Heine, Steve. *Zen Skin, Zen Marrow: Will the Real Zen Buddhism Please Stand Up?* Oxford: Oxford University Press, 2008.

Hick, John. *The Fifth Dimension: An Exploration of the Spiritual Realm.* London: Oneworld, 1999.

——. *An Interpretation of Religion: Human Responses to the Transcendent.* 2nd edition. New Haven, CT: Yale University Press, 2004.

Hoffman, Frank, and Deegalle Mahinda, eds. *Pali Buddhism.* London: Curzon Press, 1996.

Hua (Hsuan Tsang). *The Heart of the Prajna Paramita Sutra.* Translated by the Buddhist Text Translation Society. San Francisco: Sino-American Buddhist Association, 1980.

Ignatius of Loyola. *Ignatius of Loyola: The Spiritual Exercises and Selected Works.* Edited by George Ganss. New York: Paulist Press, 1991.

——. *Ignatius of Loyola: The Spiritual Exercises of St. Ignatius.* Translated by Louis Puhl: Chicago: University of Loyola Press, 1951.

——. *A Pilgrim's Journey: The Autobiography of Ignatius of Loyola.* Translated and Commentary by Joseph Tylenda. Collegeville, MN: Michael Glazier, 1991.

Inagaki, Hisao. *The Three Pure Land Sutras: A Study and Translation from Chinese.* 2nd edition. Kyoto: Nagata Bunshodo, 1995.

Ireland, John, trans. *The Udana and the Itivuttaka: Two Classics from the Pali Canon.* Kandy, Sri Lanka: Buddhist Publication Society, 1997.

Jang, Scarlett Ju-Yu. "Oxherding Painting in the Sung Dynasty." *Artibus Asiae* 51 no. 2 (1992): 54–93.

Johannson, Rune. *The Psychology of Nirvana*. London: Allen Unwin, 1969.

John of the Cross [San Juan de la Cruz]. *The Collected Works of St. John of the Cross*. Translated by Kieren Kavanaugh and Otilio Rodriguez. Washington D.C.: Institute of Carmelite Studies, 1991.

———. *Obras Completas: Edicion Critica.* 14th edition. Edited by Lucinio Ruano de la Iglesia. Madrid: Bibioteca de Autores Chrisianos, 1994.

John Paul II. *Crossing the Threshold of Hope*. Translated by Jenny McPhee and Martha McPhee. New York: Knopf, 1994.

———. *The Encyclicals of John Paul II*. Edited and commentary by Michael Miller. Huntington, IN: Our Sunday Visitor, 1996.

Johnston, William. *Christian Zen: A Way of Mindfulness*. San Francisco: Harper & Row, 1971.

Joshu. *The Recorded Sayings of Zen Master Joshu*. Translated by James Green. Walnut Creek, CA: AltaMira Press, 1998.

Kalupahana, David. *The History of Buddhist Philosophy: Continuities and Discontinuities*. Honolulu: University of Hawaii Press, 1992.

Kane, Thomas. *Gentleness in John of the Cross*. Oxford: SLG Press, 1985.

Kaplan, Steven. *Different Paths, Different Summits: A Model for Religious Pluralism*. New York: Rowman and Littlefield, 2002.

Kapleau, Philip. *The Three Pillars of Zen*. Revised. Garden City, NY: Anchor Books, 1980.

Kasulis, Thomas, ed. *Self as Body in Asian Theory and Practice*. Albany: State University of New York, 1993.

Kazmierczak, Zbigniew. "A Trial of Interpretation of Meister Eckhart's Thought on God and Man through the Analysis of its Paradoxes." *Annals of Philosophy* 65, no. 1 (2017): 5–22.

Keel, Hee-Sung. *Meister Eckhart: An Asian Perspective*. Louvain: Peeters Press, 2007.

Keenan, John, and Linda Keenan. *I Am / No Self: A Christian Commentary on the Heart Sutra*. Leuven: Peeters, 2011.

———. *The Meaning of Christ: A Mahayana Theology*. Maryknoll, NY: Orbis Books, 1989.

Keizan. *The Record of Transmitting the Light: Zen Master Keizan's Denkoroku*. Translated by Francis Cook. Los Angeles: Center Publications, 1991.

Kennedy, John. *Zen Gifts to Christians*. New York: Continuum, 2004.

———. *Zen Spirit, Christian Spirit: The Place of Zen in Christian Life*. New York: Continuum, 1995.

Kieckherfer, Richard, and George Bond, eds. *Sainthood: Its Manifestations in World Religions*. Berkeley: University of California Press, 1988.

Knitter, Paul, ed. *The Myth of Religious Superiority*. Maryknoll, NY: Orbis Books, 2005.

———. *Without the Buddha I Could Not Be a Christian*. Oxford: Oneworld, 2009.

Krishan, Y. "Buddhism and Belief in *atma*." *Journal of the International Association of Buddhist Studies* 7, no. 2 (1984): 117–35.

Kuo'an. *The Oxherder: A Zen Parable Illustrated*. Introduction by Stephanie Wada. Translated by Gen Sakamoto. New York: George Braziller, 2002.

Lakeland, Paul. *Postmodernity*. Minneapolis: Augsburg Fortress, 1997.

Law, Bimala Charan. *The Life and Work of Buddhaghosa*. Dehli: Nag Publishers, 1976.

Lefebure, Leo. *The Buddha and The Christ: Explorations in Buddhist and Christian Dialogue*. Maryknoll, NY: Orbis Books, 1993.

Leroy, Olivier. "Quelques traits de Saint Jean de la Croix comme mairtre spirituelle." *Carmelus* 11 (1964): 3–43.

Linbeck, George. *The Nature of Doctrine: Religion and Theology in a Postliberal Age*. Philadelphia: Westminster, 1984.

Loori, John Daido. *Riding the Ox Home: Stages on the Path to Enlightenment*. Boston: Shambhala, 2002.

Lopez, Donald. "Inscribing the Bodhisattva's Speech: On the 'Heart Sutra's Mantra." *History of Religions* 29, no. 4 (1990): 351–72.

Lopez, Donald, ed. *Religions of Tibet in Practice*. Princeton, NJ: Princeton University Press, 1997.

Lu, Louis Wei-lun, and Wen-yu Chiang. "Emptiness We Live By: Metaphors and Paradoxes in Buddhism's Heart Sutra." *Metaphor and Symbol* 22, no. 4 (2007): 331–55.

Mahathera, Paravahera Vajiranana. *Buddhist Meditation in Theory and Practice*. Kuala Lumpur, Malaysia: Buddhist Missionary Society, 1975.

Mann, William E. *The Blackwell Guide to Philosophy of Religion*. Malden, MA: Blackwell, 2005.

McCagney, Nancy. *Nagarjuna and the Philosophy of Openness*. Lanham, MD: Rowman & Littlefield, 1997.

McGinn, Bernard. *The Foundations of Mysticism: Origins to the Fifth Century*. New York: Crossroad, 1992.

———. *The Harvest of Mysticism in Medieval Germany*. New York: Crossroad, 2005.

——. *The Mystical Thought of Meister Eckhart: The Man from Whom God Hid Nothing.* New York: Crossroad, 2001.

Merton, Thomas. *The Intimate Merton: His Life from His Journals.* Edited by Patrick Hart and Jonathan Montaldo. New York: HarperSanFrancisco, 1999.

——. *New Seeds of Contemplation.* New York: New Direction, 1961.

——. *Spiritual Direction and Meditation.* Collegeville, MN: Liturgical Press, 1960.

Mojsisch, Burkhard. *Meister Eckhart: Analogy, Univocity, and Unity.* Translated by Orin Summerell. Amsterdam: B. R. Gruner, 2001.

Mommaers, Paul, and Jan van Gragt. *Mysticism: Buddhist and Christian: Encounters with Jan van Ruusbroec.* New York: Continuum, 1995.

Moyaert, Marianne, and Joris Geldhof, eds. *Ritual Participation and Interreligious Dialogue: Boundaries, Transgressions, and Innovations.* London: Bloomsbury, 2015.

Mumon, Yamada, *Lectures on the Ten Oxherding Pictures.* Translated by Victor Sugen Hori. Honolulu: University of Hawaii Press, 2004.

Nanamoli, Bhikkhu, and Bhikkhu Bodhi, trans. *The Middle Length Discourses of the Buddha: A New Translation of the Majjhima Nikaya.* Boston: Wisdom Publications, 1995.

Neuner, J., and J. Dupuis, eds. *The Christian Faith in Doctrinal Documents of the Catholic Church.* Revised. New York: Alba House, 1981.

Nyanaponika. *The Heart of Buddhist Meditation.* York Beach, ME: Samuel Weiser, 1965.

——. *The Vision of Dhamma: The Buddhist Writings of Nyanaponika Thera.* York Beach, ME: Samuel Weiser, 1986.

Odin, Steve. "The Middle Way of Emptiness in Modern Japanese Philosophy and the Zen Oxherding Pictures." *Eastern Buddhist* 23, no. 1 (1990): 26–44.

O'Leary, Joseph. "Knowing the Heart Sutra by Heart." *Religion and the Arts* 12 (2008): 356–70.

Olson, Karl. *The Different Paths of Buddhism: A Narrative-Historical Introduction.* New Brunswick, NJ: Rutgers University Press, 2005.

Otsu, D. R. *The Ox and His Herdsman.* Translated by M. H. Trevor. Tokyo: Hokuseido Press, 1969.

Palmer, G., et al., trans. and ed. *Philokalia.* London: Faber & Faber, 1979 (vol. 1); 1981 (vol. 2); 1984 (vol. 3); 1995 (vol. 4).

Panikkar, Raimon. *The Intra-Religious Dialogue.* New York: Paulist Press, 1978.

Payne, Steven, ed. *John of the Cross*. Washington, DC: ICS Publications, 1992.

Pelden, Kunzang. *The Nectar of Manjushri's Speech: A Detailed Commentary of Shanitdeva's Way of the Bodhisattva*. Translated by Padmakara Translation Group. Boston: Shambhala, 2007.

Phan, Peter. *Being Religious Interreligiously: Asian Perspectives on Interfaith Dialogue*. Maryknoll, NY: Orbis Books, 2004.

Pine, Red, trans. *The Heart Sutra: The Womb of Buddhas*. Berkeley, CA: Counterpoint, 2004.

——. *The Lankavatara Sutra*. Berkeley, CA: Counterpoint, 2012.

Po, Huang. *The Zen Teaching of Huang Po: On the Transmission of Mind*. Translated by John Blofeld. New York: Grove Weidenfeld, 1958.

Pond, Kathleen. *The Life of St. John of the Cross*. London: Longmans, 1958.

Pope, Stephen, and Charles Hefling, eds. *Sic et Non: Encountering Dominus Iesus*. Maryknoll, NY: Orbis Books, 2002.

Pseudo-Dionysius. *Pseudo-Dionysius: The Complete Works*. Translated by Colm Luibheid. New York: Paulist Press, 1987.

Quest, Christopher, ed. *Engaged Buddhism in the West*. Boston: Wisdom Publications, 2000.

Radler, Charlotte. "'In Love I am more God': The Centrality of Love in Meister Eckhart's Mysticism." *Journal of Religion* 90, no. 2 (2010): 171–98.

——. "Losing the Self: Detachment in Meister Eckhart and Its Significance for Buddhist-Christian Dialogue." *Buddhist-Christian Studies* 26 (2006): 111–17.

Rahner, Karl. *Ignatius of Loyola Speaks.* Translated by Annemarie Kidder. South Bend, IN: St. Augustine's Press, 2013.

Rahula, Walpola. *What the Buddha Taught*. Revised. New York: Grove Press, 1974.

——. *Zen and the Taming of the Bull: Towards the Definition of Buddhist Thought*. London: Gordon Fraser, 1978.

Ratzinger, Joseph. *Truth and Tolerance: Christian Belief and World Religions*. Translated by Henry Taylor. San Francisco: Ignatius Press, 2004.

Ricoeur, Paul. *Hermeneutics and the Human Sciences: Essays on Language, Action, and Interpretation*. Translated and edited by John B. Thompson. Cambridge: Cambridge University Press, 1981.

——. *Interpretation Theory: Discourse and the Surplus of Meaning*. Fort Worth: Texas Christian University Press, 1976.

Rinchen, Geshe Sonam. *The Heart Sutra*. Translated and edited by Ruth Sonam. Ithaca, NY: Snow Lion, 2003.

Robinson, Richard. *Early Madhyamika in India and China*. Madison: University of Wisconsin Press, 1967

Robinson, Richard, Willard L. Johnson, and Thanissaro Bhikkhu (Geoffrey DeGraff). *Buddhist Religions: A Historical Introduction*. 5th edition. Belmont, CA: Wadsworth. 2005.

Roy, Louis. "Meister Eckhart's Construal of Mysticism." *The Way* 56, no. 1 (2017): 77–88.

Ruffing, Janet. *Spiritual Direction: Beyond the Beginnings*. New York: Paulist Press, 2000.

Ruiz, Frederico, ed. *Experiencia y pensamiento en San Juan de la Cruz*. Madrid: Editorial de Espiritualidad, 1990.

Ruiz, Frederico, and Crisógono de Jesús Sacramento, eds. *God Speaks in the Night: The Life, Times, and Teachings of St. John of the Cross*. Washington, DC: ICS Publications, 1991.

Sacks, Sheldon, ed. *On Metaphor*. Chicago: University of Chicago Press, 1979.

Sacramento, Crisógono de Jesús. *San Juan de la Cruz, vida y obras*. Madrid: Biblioteca de Autores Cristianos, 1995.

Sayadaw, Mahasi. *The Progress of Insight*. Kandy, Sri Lanka: Buddhist Publication Society, 1985.

Sayadaw, U Pandita. *In This Very Life: The Liberation Teachings of the Buddha*. 2nd edition. Translated by Ven. U Aggacitta. Edited by Kate Wheeler. Boston: Wisdom Publications, 1993.

Schebera, Richard. "Comparative Theology: A New Method in Interreligious Dialogue." *Dialogue and Alliance* 17 (2003): 7–18.

Schillebeeckx, Edward. *The Understanding of Faith: Interpretation and Criticism*. Translated by N. D. Smith. New York: Seabury, 1974.

Shantideva, *Santideva's Bodhicaryavatara*, 2 vols. [with Original Sanskrit text and English translation]. Translated by Parmananda Sharma. New Delhi: Aditya Prakashan, 1990.

———. *The Bodhicaryavatara*. Translated by Kate Crosby and Andrew Skilton. Oxford: Oxford University Press, 1995.

———. *The Way of the Bodhisattva*. Translated by the Padmakara Translation Group. Boston: Shambhala, 2003.

Sheng-yen. *There Is No Suffering: A Commentary on the Heart Sutra*. Berkeley, CA: North Atlantic Books, 2001.

Sheng-Yen, with Dan Stevenson. *Hoofprint of the Ox: Principles of the Chan Buddhist Path as Taught by a Modern Chinese Master*. Oxford: Oxford University Press, 2002.

Siderits, Mark. *Buddhism as Philosophy: An Introduction*. Indianapolis: Hackett Publishing, 2007.

Smith, Wilfred Cantwell. *Towards a World Theology: Faith and Comparative History of Religion*. Philadelphia: Westminster Press, 1981.

Soeng, Mu, *The Diamond Sutra: Transforming the Way We Perceive the World*. Boston: Wisdom Publications, 2000.

Stcvherbatsky, Fedor. *The Conception of Buddhist Nirvana*. London: Mouton & Co., 1965.

Steggink, Otger, ed. *Juan de la Cruz, espiritu de llama: estudios con occasion del cuarto centenario de su muerte (1591–1991)*. Kampen: The Netherlands: Kok Paros Publishing House, 1991.

Streng, Frederick. *Emptiness: A Study of Religious Meaning*. Nashville: Abingdon Press, 1967.

Strong, John. *The Buddha*. Oxford: Oneworld, 2009.

Suzuki, D. T. *Essays in Zen Buddhism: First Series*. New York: Grove Press, 1949.

———. *The Essentials of Zen Buddhism*. Edited by Bernard Phillips. Westport, CT: Greenwood Press, 1962.

———. *On Indian Mahayana Buddhism*. Edited and Introduction by Edward Conze. New York: Harper Torchbooks, 1968.

Tamura, Yoshiro. *Introduction to the Lotus Sutra*. Translated and edited by Gene Reeves and Michio Shinozaki. Boston: Wisdom Publications, 2014.

Tanahashi Kazuaki. *The Heart Sutra: A Comprehensive Guide to the Classic of Mahayana Buddhism*. Boston: Shambhala, 2014.

Teresa of Ávila. *The Collected Works of St. Teresa of Ávila*. 3 vols. Translated by Kieran Kavanaugh and Otilio Rodgiguez. Washington, DC: ICS Publications: 1987 (revised; vol. 1); 1980 (vol. 2); 1985 (vol. 3).

Tobden, Geshe Yeshe. *Shantideva's Guide to Awakening: A Commentary on the Bodhicaryavatara*. Edited by Fiorella Rizzi. Translated by Manu Bazzano and Sarita Doveton. Boston: Wisdom Publications, 2017.

Tracy, David. "Comparative Theology." In *Encyclopedia of Religion*, Volume 13. Edited by Lindsay Jones, 9125–34. Detroit: Macmillan Reference USA, 2005.

———. *Plurality and Ambiguity: Hermeneutics, Religion, Hope*. Chicago: University of Chicago Press, 1987.

Vajiranana, Paravahera. *Buddhist Meditation in Theory and Practice: A General Exposition According to the Pali Canon of the Theravada School*. 2nd edition. Kuala Lumpur, Malaysia: Buddhist Missionary Society, 1975.

Valkenberg, Pim, ed. *World Religions in Dialogue: A Comparative Theological Approach*. Winona, MN: Anselm Academic, 2013.

Victoria, Brian. *Zen at War*. New York: Rowman & Littlefield, 2005.

———. *Zen War Stories*. London: Routledge/Curzon, 2003.

Walsh, Maurice, trans. *The Long Discourses of the Buddha: A Translation of the Digha Nikaya*. Boston: Wisdom Publications, 1995.

Watson, Burton, trans. *The Lotus Sutra*. New York: Columbia University Press, 1993.

Welch, John. *The Carmelite Way: An Ancient Path for Today's Pilgrim*. New York: Paulist Press, 1996.

Williams, Paul. *Mahayana Buddhism: The Doctrinal Foundations*. 2nd edition. London: Routledge, 2009.

———. *Studies in the Philosophy of the Bodhicaryavatara: Altruism and Reality*. Delhi: Montilal Banarsidass, 2000.

Wood, Thomas. *Nagarjunian Disputations: A Philosophical Journey through an Indian Looking Glass*. Honolulu: University of Hawaii Press, 1994.

Woods, Richard. *Meister Eckhart: Master of Mystic*. New York: Continuum, 2011.

Wright, Dale. *What Is Buddhist Enlightenment?* Oxford: Oxford University Press, 2016.

Wu, John. *The Golden Age of Zen*. New York: Image Books, 1996.

Xisahn. *A Paragon of Zen House*. Translated and commentary by O'hyun Park. New York: Peter Lang, 2004.

Yampolsky, Philip, trans. *The Platform Sutra of the Sixth Patriarch*. New York: Columbia University Press, 1967.

Yoo, Dosung. *Thunderous Silence: A Formula for Ending Suffering: A Practical Guide to the Heart Sutra*. Boston: Wisdom Publications, 2013.

Yoshinori, Takeuchi. *The Heart of Buddhism: In Search of the Timeless Spirit of Primitive Buddhism*. Translated and edited by James Heisig. New York: Crossroad, 1983.

Yoshinori, Takeuchi, ed. *Buddhist Spirituality I: Indian, Southeast Asian, Tibetan, Early Chinese*. New York: Crossroad, 1995.

———. *Buddhist Spirituality II: Later China, Korea, Japan, and the Modern World*. New York: Crossroad, 1999.

Zimmerman, Michael. *The Buddha Within: The Tahagatagarbha Sutra—The Earliest Exposition of the Buddha-Nature Teaching in India*. Tokyo: International Research Institute for Advanced Buddhology, 2002.

Index